Molly

Molly

The
TRUE STORY
of
the Amazing Dog
Who Rescues Cats

Colin Butcher

CELADON
BOOKS

NEW YORK

For David

They are called sleuth-hounds by the people. These dogs have such a marvellous cleverness that they seek for thieves, and follow them only by the scent of the goods that are taken away.

—*THE HISTORY AND CRONIKLIS OF SCOTLAND* (1536) BY JOHN BELLENDEN (SCOTS TRANSLATION OF HECTOR BOECE'S *HISTORIA GENTIS SCOTORUM*)

Molly

1

Molly's First Test

At 9 a.m. on Friday, 3 February 2017, just as my assistant, Sam, had settled at her desk, booted up her computer and taken her first sip of espresso, the telephone rang. I was outside on the Bramble Hill Farm driveway, preparing to exercise Molly in the early-morning sun. My cocker spaniel had woken up in a particularly frisky mood—so much so that she'd knocked over my girlfriend Sarah's favorite Lladró vase in the hallway—and she needed to run off some excess energy.

"UK Pet Detectives," said Sam, picking up the phone. "Can we help?"

"I really hope so," replied a glum male voice. "Our cat, Rusty, has gone missing. We've looked everywhere, but there's no sign of her. We've hit a brick wall, really, so we thought we'd give you guys a call."

Tim was a graphic designer who lived in the Hertfordshire city of St. Albans with his physiotherapist girlfriend, Jasmine. They were saving hard for a deposit for a two-bedroomed house, but in the meantime were renting a modest first-floor apartment in a quiet cul-de-sac. The couple shared a love of cats and had gladly welcomed little Rusty into their lives, a black, white and copper rescue moggy with almond-shaped eyes and a long, fluffy tail. Since the flat was pretty cramped—many of their personal belongings were still boxed up—they often let their cat outdoors; there, she'd mooch around the crescent, lazing on driveways and sitting on doorsteps, neither straying too far nor staying out late.

The previous Friday, however, Rusty had failed to turn up for her weekly treat of steamed haddock—she adored her fresh fish—and her owners were totally flummoxed.

"It's just so out of character," Tim told Sam. "We've spent the whole weekend searching in streets and gardens—we've even printed out leaflets and posters—but she's nowhere to be found. We're at a total loss."

"I'm so sorry to hear that," said Sam, who—being a cat owner herself—genuinely felt their pain. "Leave it with me. I'll have a word with my boss and I'll get back to you."

She promptly bounded over to the large sash window and yanked it up.

"*COLIN!*" she yelled, causing Molly and me to stop dead in our tracks as we strode toward the meadow. "Make sure you pop in after your training session. Think I might have found Molly's first proper job . . ."

Fast-forward half an hour and I was sitting in the office discussing Rusty's disappearance with Sam while a bushwhacked Molly enjoyed a snooze. I felt my pulse quicken as my colleague reiterated her conversation with Tim and outlined the missing pet's circumstances. If our inaugural cat-seeking assignment was to be a success, the search conditions had to be as favorable as possible and this seemed to tick all the boxes. Firstly, Rusty came from a single-cat household, thus enabling me to obtain a decent hair sample and giving Molly the best chance of isolating the scent and matching it to the lost cat. Secondly, the puss had been missing for less than a week, which increased the likelihood of finding it alive. Also working in our favor was the fact that the weather was calm and settled, unseasonably so, in fact, for early February. Any excessive winds or any form of precipitation (rain, snow or mist, for example) would dilute the cat scent and would interfere with my dog's ultra-sensitive nose.

Luckily, as a former serviceman, I was well versed in all things meteorological and geographical. Prior to my long career in the police force I'd spent over a decade in the Royal Navy, which had prompted a serious interest in weather, climate and coastal navigation. I had studied all subjects voraciously in my cabin on HMS *Illustrious*, expanding my scientific knowledge of air masses, frontal systems and cartography, for instance, and had become something of an expert. Little did I know then how useful this knowledge would become in the world of pet detection.

In December 2016 Molly had completed an intensive period of scent-recognition training at a Milton Keynes–based charity— Medical Detection Dogs—and since then she and I had staged countless practice scenarios at my Bramble Hill Farm HQ, honing our skills in preparation for our first real-life search for a missing cat. I had been quietly confident that Molly and I had attained the required level of competence, but it was only when I'd sent some video footage of our training to the experts at MDD that we'd finally been given the green light.

"From what we've seen, we think you're both ready for your first proper search," they'd said, causing a tingle to shoot up my spine. "Your interaction and teamwork are excellent and, as far as we're concerned, you're good to go."

Now, following Sam's phone conversation, I finally faced the prospect of solving a live search with Molly by my side. I felt a mixture of exhilaration and trepidation. I had spent so much time and energy developing my innovative cat-detection-dog idea—it had been five years in the making—and, having eventually found my perfect sidekick, I was desperate for that conclusive "proof of concept" to make all our hard work worthwhile.

"This could be it," I said to Sam. "This could be Molly's first test."

"Oh my goodness, how exciting!" grinned my colleague.

That evening I spent an hour or so on the phone to Tim, obtaining as much background information as possible. I asked him whether there'd been any triggers that might have caused

Rusty to flee (upheaval in the household, for example, or a marauding feline foe), but Tim was adamant that, as far as he was concerned, nothing had changed.

"The elderly lady who lives in the opposite flat died last week, which was quite upsetting," he said, "but other than that, things have been pretty humdrum around here."

As for sightings, they'd drawn a blank in their own neighborhood, but that morning had received calls from two separate witnesses in a village located a few miles away who claimed to have seen a cat answering Rusty's description in their respective gardens.

"I doubt it's our cat, because she's never, ever roamed that far," admitted Tim, "but we'd still like you to investigate, if you don't mind."

"I'm more than happy to help," I replied, before casually mentioning that I'd be accompanied by a canine colleague.

"My cocker spaniel, Molly, will be coming, too," I said. "She's got a decent sense of smell and she doesn't yap at cats so she might be quite useful. Hope that's okay with you."

I was purposely downplaying things, so as not to heap any pressure upon Molly, or myself.

"No problem," said Tim. "Anything that might help us find Rusty is fine with me."

I burned the midnight oil that evening, poring over digital maps, plans and photos of the St. Albans area as Sarah slept beside me. It was important that I found out as much as possible about the area so as to give Molly and me the best chance of locating the missing cat. When I felt myself beginning to nod off, I shut down my laptop and went to check on Molly, as I did every night. She sensed me peering through the gap in the door, raised her head and drowsily opened one eye.

"We've got a big day ahead, young lady," I whispered, "so I'll see you bright and early in the morning."

Yeah, I know, Dad, Molly seemed to say, *so how's about letting me get some sleep?*

She held my gaze for a couple of seconds before curling up tight and continuing her slumbers.

We both left the house at 5 a.m. The weather forecast had correctly predicted a cool and cloudy day with a slight underlying breeze: the perfect conditions for our big search, I hoped. Sarah had awoken early to wave us off, fully aware of the magnitude of the next few hours. She had watched me build up to this moment for a long time and knew exactly how much it meant to me.

"Hope it all goes well, darling." She'd smiled, and I almost did a double-take when she gently, yet gingerly, patted my spaniel's glossy black head before wishing her good luck. Sarah hadn't quite acclimatized to Molly's presence in the household—she was no dog-lover, put it that way—and this was indeed a rare display of affection.

My dog quite literally lapped it up, giving my girlfriend's palm a big, sloppy lick in return for her kind words. I smiled to myself, imagining Sarah darting straight to the antiseptic handwash as soon as she returned indoors.

Following a two-hour drive from West Sussex to Hertfordshire, I was greeted by Tim and Jasmine outside their modern four-story apartment block. They were young, fair-haired and athletic-looking—I guessed they were in their mid-twenties—but both wore a kind of glazed expression that I recognized only too well. Like many of my clients before them, their precious pet had gone AWOL, and they were sick to their stomachs with worry.

My eye was drawn to a huge poster in their front window. PLEASE HELP, I'M LOST, it declared. CAN YOU HELP ME FIND MY HOME?

Staring out from behind the printed text was a beautiful photograph of the missing moggy. Rusty was a pretty cat with a friendly face; her white bib and legs, topped with two black splodges above her eyes, made her look like a feline caped crusader.

"I wish all my clients could produce something so professional-looking," I said.

"Being a graphic designer comes in handy sometimes . . ." replied Tim with a wan smile.

". . . and our Rusty is a dream to photograph," added Jasmine wistfully.

I followed the couple indoors, leaving Molly safe and secure in the car (and, as always, in my line of vision) with her favorite toys for company. I knew that she'd experience serious sensory overload if she entered an unfamiliar flat, and I needed her to remain as calm as possible. Not only that, it was imperative that she was able to focus solely on Rusty's scent, if I was going to be lucky enough to obtain a decent sample.

The three of us then discussed a plan of action. Jasmine had to attend work that morning—her Monday clinic was always busy with sporting injuries—so Tim would be accompanying Molly and me on the search. Our first port of call would be the nearby village in which the two cat sightings had occurred, but before we set off I posed a question.

"I know this may sound a little odd, Tim, but would you mind if I took a sample of Rusty's cat hair?" I asked cautiously. "Molly's a trained sniffer dog and—you never know—she might detect some scent."

I was soft-pedaling, of course, keeping things nicely understated. I needed to manage his expectations, rather than having him believe that the deployment of a search dog would guarantee Rusty's recovery.

"Yeah, sure, help yourself," he replied. "She moults a lot. Her cat bed's full of it."

Out came my sterilized jam jar, and in went a wad of whitish hair; more than enough for Molly to get her amazing nose into.

The hamlet of Broomfield comprised a smattering of small cottages surrounded by acres of ancient woodland. The grass verges lining the lane were swathed in daffodils and narcissi, their petals and trumpets ranging in color from vanilla white to egg-yolk yellow. Nest-building blackbirds flitted from hedge to shrub, straw and twigs clamped firmly in their beaks. We parked up in a pub car park, where I strapped on Molly's special harness and zipped up my UKPD fleece. She and I had often practiced the transition from pet mode to work mode at Bramble Hill Farm and donning our respective "uniforms" had always been a vital part of this routine. I was buzzing with excitement but did my utmost to adopt a professional demeanor. Molly picked up on my nervous energy, however, and started whining and spinning around in her crate.

As Tim and I surveyed our surroundings a brisk wind began to whip up, with enough vigor to ruffle our hair. *This wasn't forecast*, I thought to myself. I looked to the horizon and saw the telltale signs of a warm front heading our way. I knew this would bring steady winds for the rest of the day, followed by rain. I did a quick calculation of the wind speed; I figured that we had about six hours before the first band of rain reached us.

"We really need to get started, Tim," I said, looking at my watch.

"Okay," he said. "Let's go for it."

Tim and I swiftly identified the two gardens that Rusty had reportedly been sighted in—they were on opposite sides of the road—and, fortunately, both householders allowed us access. Then, with a deep breath, and with my heart racing, I introduced Rusty's cat-hair sample to Molly for the first time. I could see Tim's eyes widen with a mixture of surprise and fascination as I unscrewed the jam jar and, following my customary command of *Toma*—the Spanish translation of "take"—I offered it up to Molly's snout. This distinctive word had been carefully selected by Molly's trainers at MDD, since she'd never hear it spoken around the house or within any other context.

She inhaled the scent, awaited my usual exhortation to "Seek, seek," and careered off into the first garden, her tail wagging furiously.

"Oh, wow . . ." said my client, slowly twigging on to the fact that Molly was not your average dog. "Has she . . . has she been trained to do this?"

"She has." I smiled. "But, Tim, you need to know that this is her first live search and it would be unfair on you—and Molly—if I was to promise anything. But she'll do her very best to find Rusty, I can assure you of that."

Molly searched everywhere for the odor—beneath a holly bush, inside the greenhouse, behind the compost heap—but to no avail. All the while, she increased her eye contact with me, which, as I knew from our many training searches, meant that she had finished sweeping the area.

There's no cat here, Dad . . . let's go . . . was how I deciphered her body language.

It was a similar story in the second garden. Molly failed to locate any scent trails and—such was my faith in her ability—I could only surmise that Rusty had never ventured there. However, as I recalled my dog with a command of "Molly, come," I suddenly noticed a black, gray and tan cat tiptoeing across the lawn. I squinted as it came closer.

Oh my goodness, I thought. *Is that Rusty walking toward me? Is Molly having an "off" day?*

"THAT'S HER!" squawked the homeowner from her kitchen window. "That's the cat I saw!"

Tim nearly jumped out of his skin, but his reaction when he caught sight of the animal was telling. Molly had remained unmoved, too, which should have told me all I needed to know.

"That's not her," said my client, shaking his head sadly. "Same coloring, but different markings. Rusty's got this really weird half-pink, half-black nose. I'd recognize her anywhere."

Crestfallen after this case of mistaken identity, we trudged over to the pub for a coffee, while Molly slurped noisily from a large bowl of water. She needed plenty of breaks and drinks when she was on a search, and I took great care to ensure that she was never overworked. I didn't want her to suffer from scenting fatigue (also known as "nose blindness"), whereby she'd lose the ability to isolate a particular odor.

Tim also took the opportunity to update his girlfriend.

No joy yet, Jaz, he texted. *Will keep u posted xxx*

In an attempt to glean more clues about Rusty's disappearance, I probed a little deeper, quizzing Tim about his local neighborhood. The subject of the deceased old lady in the apartment block cropped up again so I pressed him for more information. According to Tim, she'd died of natural causes and, within hours, her body had been taken away in an ambulance. This nugget of information got me wondering.

"Do you happen to remember which day your neighbor passed away?" I said.

"Erm, let me think," he replied, counting back with his fingers. "Friday. Yeah, it must have been last Friday."

"The same day that Rusty went missing?"

Tim paused for a moment, furrowing his brow.

"Yes . . . I suppose it would have been. I know what you're thinking, Colin, but Rusty had a fear of cars. She associated them with being taken to the vet's."

"Private ambulances tend not to be cars, though," I explained. As a police officer, I'd dealt with many sudden deaths and seen dozens of such vehicles, and most of them were large, roomy minibuses with blacked-out windows and easy-access ramps. "Right," I said, as my sleuthing instincts kicked in. "Can you give me a couple of minutes? I need to make a few phone calls."

"Yeah, of course," replied Tim, "I'll go outside for a cigarette. I gave up last year, but I've had a relapse since Rusty went."

I rang the local GP, who informed me that, since the woman had been in her nineties—and had been under his long-term care—her death was deemed "expected" and he'd been able to certify it on the scene, without any police involvement. The lady's body had then been transported by a private ambulance to the funeral directors' chapel of rest in Stonebridge—about a mile away from my clients' home—and, according to their staff, the vehicle—a large, dark blue minibus—had been parked up outside their offices for the remainder of the day. Slowly but surely, the jigsaw pieces began to slot together.

I headed out to the car park (with a fully refreshed Molly in tow), where we found Tim perched against the car's hood, deftly aiming his extinguished cigarette butt into a nearby bin.

"Right," I said briskly. "I'm starting to think this may be a case of accidental transportation."

I told him that there was a very real possibility that Rusty had snuck into the undertaker's ambulance outside the apartment block—perhaps tiptoeing along its ramp—and been driven off as a consequence. The timeline of events definitely tallied, and it would explain the sudden nature of her disappearance.

"Next stop, Stonebridge," I said, gesturing for Tim to get back into the car.

While the funeral directors' receptionist confirmed the ambulance's route on the day in question, she'd received no reports of a cat being found inside. She did admit, however, that the vehicle's rear doors would have been opened and closed on numerous occasions, firstly, to transport the deceased woman and, secondly, to facilitate the weekly valet.

"Sorry I can't be more helpful," she said, "but you might want to speak to the ladies at the post office next door. If there's any news or gossip flying around, they'll know about it. But beware," she grinned. "They'll talk your hind legs off if you let them."

She wasn't wrong. The ladies behind the counter took a real shine to Molly—as well as the handsome six-footer who'd lost his poor little cat—and, after they'd heard our story, agreed to display one of Tim's posters on the noticeboard. As I securely affixed it with some drawing pins, an elderly gentleman walked in, took one look at Rusty's photo and gasped.

"That cat was sat on our fence this morning, I'm sure of it," he declared. "Beautiful creature, lovely bushy tail. Remember my wife saying that she'd never seen it before. Oh, and it had this really strange-looking nose . . ."

Tim grabbed my arm in excitement. Perhaps my ambulance theory was bang on the money.

"Can you possibly take us to your garden now?" I asked.

"Let me collect my pension first, old chum." He smiled. "But by all means, follow me over."

Ten minutes later I was crouching outside old Mr. Renshaw's red-brick semi, grasping a jam jar, going through the scent-sniffing routine with Molly for the second time that day. With Rusty's odor coursing through her nostrils, she sprinted into the back garden and within seconds—wham-*bam*—did her so-called "down" in the center of the lawn. Molly's trademark success signal, this rapid response had been drilled into her at Medical Detection Dogs in order to alert her handler without alarming any cats. The "down" involved her lying flat, still and silent, with her front paws outstretched, her back legs tucked under her body, her head upright and her eyes locked. Her body would quiver with excitement at the thrill of the "victory" and the expectation of a reward for her achievement. My heart began to pound like a drum. We had practiced this drill so often at Bramble Hill Farm, but this was the first time that I'd seen her do it for a real-life client.

"What does that mean?" whispered Tim as he watched Molly trembling before us.

"She's signaling that she's detected a high concentration of Rusty's scent," I replied, "so you can be pretty certain that your cat has been here fairly recently. We just need to work out where she is now."

While a pepped-up Tim texted Jasmine, I rewarded Molly for doing her job; she'd made a scent match, when all was said and done, despite the cat herself not being present. Her favorite black-pudding treats were munched in a millisecond.

Using my meteorological know-how, I tried to figure out why Molly had "downed" in the dead center of the garden and why the scent had accumulated at that specific point. I stood at the precise spot where Molly had lain and turned to face the wind. The breeze was coming directly across the fence and I knew that this would have forced the air upward, causing it to roll across the lawn like a wave, washing the scent to the exact place where Molly had indicated.

What a good girl, Molly, I thought to myself. *She's absolutely spot-on.*

With Rusty very likely to be in the immediate area, it was now vital that I invested all my faith in Molly and employed a strategic and methodical approach. First and foremost, we had to narrow down the search area as best we could. There were about thirty houses on Mr. Renshaw's side of the road, and beyond their long, sixty-foot gardens lay a huge stretch of arable farmland. We needed to pinpoint the properties that seemed most promising—we'd already lost half a day looking in the wrong village—so I decided to run Molly along a gravel footpath that divided the residents' gardens from the farmers' fields. As we passed a couple of adjoining semis, I noticed her becoming very focused and performing a number of 180-degree turns. I felt a sudden rush of blood to the head, since this was often a sure sign that she'd detected something significant.

"Tim, could you do me a favor and knock on the owners' front doors?" I asked. "Molly's desperate to get in and we'll need their say-so."

The first house—number 36—was occupied by two octogenarian sisters who, despite being somewhat bewildered by the hullabaloo—were more than happy for us to search their grounds.

These poor old dears might live to regret this, I thought, as Molly shot through the back gate like an arrow from a bow and darted into one of the most pristine gardens I'd ever seen.

"My god, it looks like a Chelsea Flower Show exhibit," whispered Tim.

"It won't by the time Molly's finished with it," I replied.

My keyed-up dog slalomed around ornamental birdbaths and Japanese plant pots, churning up the manicured lawn as she went. She then scrambled up an alpine rockery, her swishing tail scything the heads off the paper-thin cyclamen.

"I'm really sorry about this," I told the sisters. "I can put her on a lead, if you prefer."

"Absolutely not!" one replied. "This is *fascinating . . .*"

Molly then slammed on her brakes and executed another 180-degree turn, before veering off toward their freshly painted garden fence, scraping her sharp claws down the dark green panels. Her intensity levels were increasing, and I just needed to know why.

What are you trying to tell me, Molls? I wondered, feeling a bit like Sherlock Holmes quizzing Dr. Watson.

I wanna go next door, I wanna go next door, she seemed to be saying, her eyes searching mine for some guidance. *Let. Me. Go. Next. Door.*

Bear with me, Molly, I whispered.

I peered over the fence. A middle-aged woman and a teenage boy—mother and son, I presumed—were standing on their patio and craning their necks, clearly alarmed by all the noise and commotion coming from the sisters' house. Their garden wasn't as ornate as their neighbor's, I noted, although it boasted an impressive, glass-fronted summer house and a large area of wooden decking.

"Can we come over, please?" I yelled, giving them a potted version of events, then dashing to their front gate with Molly and Tim in tow. Meanwhile, a small group of people, including one of the post-office ladies, had congregated on the pavement outside; news of the Missing Cat and the Detection Dog had clearly traveled.

I gave my dog the signal to proceed. With Tim and I trailing behind her, an all-guns-blazing Molly charged across number 38's lawn, her stride unbroken as she gobbled up some bacon rind that had been left for the birds. She sprang up on to the decking, whirled around to face me, locked her eyes with mine, and—a slither of bacon rind drooping from her mouth—gave me the most emphatic "down" I'd ever seen.

"Oh my god, she's doing that trembly thing again," whispered Tim, his voice shaking. "Has she found her?"

"One moment . . ." I said, before creeping stealthily toward the summer house and peering through the slightly ajar glass door. Sitting in a dark corner, atop a blue cushion, was a cat. A white, black and copper cat. An almond-eyed, bushy-tailed cat. A pink-and-black-nosed cat.

"RUSTY!" cried Tim, unable to control his emotions. "My cat!!! Molly's found my cat!!!"

"A *cat*? No *waaaay* . . ." drawled the teenage son, clearly unaware that they'd had a feline lodger in their summer house.

"That's what happens when your dad doesn't lock the door properly," tutted his mother. "Poor little thing."

Within seconds, however, calamity had struck. Perhaps spooked by her owner's hooting and hollering, Rusty suddenly shot out of the summer house, then bombed up the driveway and scampered through a succession of front gardens. Tim sprinted after her, clearing the privet hedges like an Olympic hurdler and eventually scooping her up from beneath a hazel bush. I hurried over, with Molly on a lead, to find him standing on the pavement, cradling his cat in his arms, tears of joy streaming down his cheeks.

"I don't know what to say," he sobbed. "I just can't believe you've found her. Thank you, Colin. Thank you, Molly. Thank you *so, so* much."

A spontaneous ripple of applause rang out from the assembled neighbors.

"Most exciting thing that's happened in the village for years," said one, laughing.

"Better than *Mission Impossible*, that," chuckled another.

The sisters at number 36 kindly allowed Tim to take Rusty indoors for a while, where she glugged a bowlful of water and devoured a pouch of cat food that had been donated by a neighbor. As he sat at the kitchen table, Tim relayed the happy news to Jasmine (she'd received the call on the train home and had dissolved into tears), then gave her a low-down of the day's events.

He told her how Rusty had almost certainly taken a ride to Stonebridge in the undertakers' ambulance and crept out at some stage. Then, in search of shelter, warmth, food and water—every cat's basic needs—she'd roamed around the village then migrated to number 38. It had been a very smart decision on her part. The summer house had acted as a sanctuary, and the protein-rich bacon rind (as well as the water in next-door's birdbaths) had given her vital sustenance.

"She's a smart little cookie, according to Colin," said Tim, half laughing, half crying.

After Tim finished his call I stood up and said my goodbyes, then headed off to the green fields beyond the back gardens. The sky was now dark, with heavy clouds all around us but, in my head and my heart, it felt like a beautiful summer's day. As I let everything sink in, my eyes began to mist over. Four years previously I'd first set out to find and train a cat-detection dog, and had figured that it would take me just six months. I'd spent hundreds of hours researching canine cognition, traveled thousands of miles to meet the country's top experts in this field and overcome a great deal of resistance and hostility. So many people had told me that it couldn't be done and had implied that I was foolish and delusional.

Now, however, in this tiny corner of Hertfordshire, I finally had my proof of concept and, by using our Holmes and Watson–type sleuthing skills, Molly and I had solved the case and reunited a pet with its owner. I had adopted the strategic and analytical role, drawing upon my raft of detecting experience to assess the probabilities and possibilities regarding Rusty's whereabouts and to establish the credibility and reliability of witnesses. My partner, Molly, had turned out to be my perfect foil—energetic, determined and blessed with an amazing natural talent—and, by working as a team, we'd done our job proficiently and professionally.

I knelt down and gently brushed my hand against the side of Molly's face, knowing how much she liked to bond with me through touch.

"Can you believe it, Molly?" I smiled as she gently nibbled the inside of my palm. "We've only gone and found our first missing cat!"

Stealing a quick look over my shoulder to make sure we were alone, I jumped into the air and yelled *"YES!"* as loudly as I possibly could. Molly was taken by surprise at first, but then she, too, leaped up high and started to bark her very own *"YES!"* response. We both cavorted around the field like a pair of mad March hares, totally oblivious to the heavy rain that had just begun to fall.

2

Scenting Success

My pet-detecting skills can probably be traced back to the summer of 1989, when I first joined Surrey Police as a constable. In my early days as a beat officer I'd become accustomed to dealing with all manner of crime. From assault to arson, and from poaching to pick-pocketing, I'd faced plenty of menacing situations and unsavory characters. Being a rookie, however, meant that I was also assigned to some of the more commonplace incidents.

"You like your pets, PC Butcher, so this one will be right down your street," said my patrol sergeant, grinning, as he handed over the report slip one autumn morning.

"An old dear with a missing cat in Farnham. Nutty as a fruit cake. Thinks her neighbor's half-inched it."

He was right, I did love animals—since childhood I'd kept a succession of dogs, cats, birds and rodents—but, even so, I found myself questioning whether this case was a priority for the resource-starved, time-stretched "C" Watch.

"Isn't this a bit, er, trivial?" I asked.

"On the contrary," replied my superior. "It's important that we're visible in the community, whether it's a lost cat or a runaway dog. Gets the locals on side. Off you trot, then."

I didn't realize it at the time, but dealing with these apparently trifling issues would help me enormously further down the line. Getting to know the neighborhood—and securing the confidence of residents—was often vital when investigating a serious crime.

Irene, a gray-haired lady in her late seventies, answered her front door wearing a friendly smile on her face and a frilly apron over her dress. As I followed her into the lounge, I couldn't help but notice all the plastic and ceramic ornaments, predominantly cat-shaped, that were crammed on to every shelf, mantelpiece and window ledge. The cushions on the sofas sported embroidered kitties and above her fireplace was a photo-gallery featuring felines of varying breeds and vintages, presumably those that she had owned through the years. Herein lived a devoted cat-lover, that was for sure.

"These have come straight out of the oven," she said, placing a tin of banana muffins on the coffee table. "Do help yourself, dear."

In between mouthfuls of cake, I questioned Irene about her missing moggy, who, I gathered, had been absent for over two days. I gleaned that she'd had regular bust-ups with her next-door neighbor, Cliff, a fellow pensioner and a champion gardener who'd taken exception to little Polly using his vegetable patch as drop-and-go cat litter. He would regularly hurl abuse—and the offending matter, as it happened—over the fence, and relations between the two had become decidedly tetchy.

"That filthy cat of yours has dug up my onions AGAIN!" he'd hollered one morning, brandishing his spade in anger.

"She's only doing what comes naturally, you old goat," she'd retorted. "Isn't it supposed to be good for your soil, anyway?"

When her darling Polly had gone unexpectedly AWOL, Irene had immediately assumed foul play, pointed the finger of blame in Cliff's direction and reignited their feud.

"D'you want to see what Polly looks like?" asked Irene, sliding a small, silver picture frame across her coffee table. Staring out from the photo was a well-fed, round-faced ginger and black cat with fierce lime-green eyes.

"Gosh, that looks like a cat who can take care of herself," I said.

"Yes, she gives as good as she gets," grinned Irene, "but she's got a soft nature, too, and is ever so friendly. She often sits on my front wall, meowing at the kids as they walk to school."

As she pictured Polly in her mind, the lady's smile faded and she stared blankly at the floor. I noted how frail and vulnerable she looked and felt a pang of guilt as I recalled my earlier conversation with my desk sergeant. To Irene, this was no trivial matter.

"I'm ever so concerned about her, Officer," she said, looking up at me forlornly.

"Don't worry," I replied. "I'm sure you'll find her. But I need you to tell me why you think your neighbor might be responsible."

This question perked her up a bit and she recounted an incident that had taken place earlier that week. She and Cliff had embarked upon another cross-fence ding-dong. She'd objected to his liberal dosage of slug pellets—"You're trying to poison my Polly," she'd complained—and the situation had become so volatile that she'd called the police.

I polished off my second banana muffin—some days I'd go a whole eight-hour shift without a break, so snacks were always welcome—before agreeing to pay her nemesis a visit. I needed to obtain his side of the story.

Cliff clearly hadn't expected to find a police officer on his doorstep. His face turned a deep shade of puce when I explained the reason for my call and he pulled out a handkerchief to dab the globules of sweat off his forehead.

Indoors, he chronicled a conflicting story, claiming that Irene was "over-bloody-reacting" and that, while he was far from impressed with Polly's toilet habits, he'd threatened neither pet nor owner.

"The woman is obsessed with her bloomin' cat, Officer," he said. "Only the other day she accused me of trying to poison it, but all I was doing was sprinkling a few slug pellets."

Then, with some gentle cajoling, he allowed me to search his back garden, more than half of which was taken up with his cherished vegetable patch. I took the opportunity to thoroughly explore Cliff's garage, greenhouse and potting shed, while Farnham's answer to Alan Titchmarsh raved about his prize-winning artichokes. Disappointingly, the only living things I encountered were beetles, spiders and woodlice.

His cheeks reddened again, however, when I requested access to his basement, the door to which backed directly on to the garden.

"Have you got a legal right to search?" he blustered.

"No, I haven't," I replied, "but if I arrested you on suspicion of cat theft, I'd have the power to search anywhere I wanted. So can I have a quick look, please?"

"Very well," he sighed, realizing that this rookie PC wasn't going to be deterred. "Be my guest."

I unbolted the cellar door and—*hey presto!*—out of the darkness padded an angry-looking, dirt-encrusted tortoiseshell cat. It sprang over a tray of cat litter, shot out of the door and scaled the fence before, no doubt, jumping into the arms of its ecstatic owner.

I stared at the crafty cat-napper, who scratched his head and shuffled from one foot to the other.

"Care to explain, Cliff?"

"It piddled on my parsnips, Officer," he said. "It was the final straw, and that cat needed to be taught a lesson."

The old man went on to explain that he'd only intended to keep Polly in the basement for a couple of days and was at pains to tell me that he'd provided her with ample food and water.

"I'm not going to get into any trouble, am I?" he asked anxiously.

"On this occasion, probably not," I replied, "but I do think you could have handled that better, Cliff. I'll do my best to smooth things over with Irene, but if the station receives one more call from her—just one—I'll be knocking on your door again, mark my words."

"I understand," he mumbled. "There'll be no repeat, I promise."

I unlatched the garden gate and bade him farewell. Within moments, I heard a voice bellowing down the drive after me.

"Just wondering, Officer . . . would you and your colleagues like a box of King Edwards?" shouted Cliff. "Fresh from the ground this morning."

"Thanks for the offer," I said, "but perhaps your neighbor might appreciate them instead. Call it a peace offering . . ."

Within just three years I'd climbed to the rank of sergeant and, as my responsibilities increased, I was able to assign my own staff to specific cases and incidents. This, I was pleased to discover, involved close liaison with the force's police-dog section. Much of the time, I enlisted the help of German shepherds, probably the most traditional and recognizable of all police dogs. These versatile and resilient "general purpose" canines were trained to operate under a variety of conditions, whether it was tracking and confining suspects (their intimidating bark often did the trick), controlling large crowds or searching for missing persons. Some of the smaller, more agile German shepherds would be deployed in other specialist roles, too: cadaver search dogs were trained to detect the odor of decomposing bodies, for example, and firearms dogs were trained to find hidden guns and ammunition.

One of my favorite police canines was a long-haired hulk of a dog nicknamed Wolf who'd built up an excellent reputation during his five years' service. Incredibly strong and ridiculously powerful, he exuded an air of menace that could terrify the toughest of reprobates.

"Never get in between Wolf and his quarry," a fellow sergeant had once warned me, "because he'll gladly take a chunk out of your backside. His bite's worse than his bark, and that's saying something."

One Friday night in 1992 he'd helped me to apprehend a group of paratroopers who'd made the short trip from Aldershot to Farnham for a stag night. Following a beery pub crawl, they'd had an altercation with a fast-food-van owner—a dispute about the quality of his burgers, apparently—which had resulted in the tanked-up squaddies upending the vehicle with the poor guy still inside. They had then fled into the darkness, hooting with laughter at this rather cruel and cowardly deed. A witness to the incident had called 999, and I'd arrived first on the scene, along with Wolf and his handler, Barry.

The van owner—a small, squat Greek Cypriot—had somehow managed to crawl out of the hatch. He emerged, dazed and confused, his curly hair matted with boiled onions and his white coat covered in Jackson Pollock–style sauce splats. A convoy of soft-drinks cans rolled down the high street, most of which were gleefully scooped up and cracked open by passers-by.

Some onlookers might well have found this whole sight a tad comical, but I was in no mood for laughing. To me, this was an extremely serious matter. Had this chap failed to dodge an airborne chip pan, he could well have suffered horrific, life-changing burns to his body. His thuggish tormentors needed to be caught, and quickly.

"They try to kill me," he murmured, clearly shocked and shaken, as I radioed for an ambulance. "Those soldiers, they try to *kill* me."

"Which direction did they go in, sir?" I asked, prompting him to wearily point toward nearby West Street. Wolf, Barry and I went in hot pursuit, arriving just in time to see half a dozen males, all with similar lean physiques and short buzz cuts, athletically scrambling over a twelve-foot-high brick wall. No doubt they'd practiced this on the army's assault course but, unfortunately for them, this time they found themselves landing in an enclosed courtyard. It was a case of nowhere to run and nowhere to hide.

"POLICE!" I yelled as we approached the wall. "You lot are in serious trouble. Do yourselves a favor and give yourselves up."

I heard some feverish whispering from the other side, coupled with a few drunken snorts and sniggers.

"Right," I said. "You need to get back over this wall and hand yourselves in immediately, otherwise I'll be putting a police dog over."

Wolf reared up and growled at the mere mention of "dog," causing Barry to tug hard on his leash in order to restrain this giant canine.

Suddenly, one of the squaddies hurled a brick over the wall, which whizzed within inches of my left ear before thudding on to the pavement. It was high time to play my trump card. I gave Barry a solemn nod and, as I so often did on these occasions, stood back and studied the interaction between dog and handler. Wolf's leash was loosened and he was given a specific signal which prompted him to bark madly.

"Jump up," came the next command and, as Wolf nimbly scrabbled up the wall, Barry gave his rear end a shove so that he could drop down into the courtyard.

What followed was a blood-curdling, wince-inducing cacophony of human shrieks and canine snarls as Wolf terrorized the suspects in his own inimitable fashion. One by one, the petrified soldiers—most sporting ripped clothing and bite marks—tumbled over the wall and straight into the handcuffs of the back-up officers who'd arrived on scene. Their stag night had come to an abrupt and sobering end, thankfully, and a stay in police custody beckoned. More pertinently, the hapless van owner was likely to see some form of justice down the line. All in a night's work, as the saying goes.

As the police vehicle sped off, Barry instructed Wolf to jump back over the wall to rejoin us, which he did with his customary compliance. His reward was a ten-minute play session in a car park with a thick rubber Frisbee, and I couldn't help but smile as I watched him effortlessly switch from a slavering, teeth-baring brute to a playful, doe-eyed pooch.

Once he'd finished his well-earned run-around, I gave this incredible dog a hefty pat on his rump. This highly trained animal had done his job and had helped us to collar and confine these idiots.

"No way could we have done that without you, buddy," I said, smiling. "No way."

Working with the peerless Wolf was both an honor and a privilege. In my eyes, he wasn't just a police dog; he was an invaluable, integral member of staff who worked *with* the force, not for us.

My recruitment to Surrey Police CID in May 1993 was an incredibly proud moment for me. For years I'd dreamed of becoming a detective—I'd always been fascinated by the investigative side of policing—and I was delighted when I received the green light to hang up my uniform and replace it with a smart blue suit.

I was tasked with spearheading the Guildford Crime Unit, which dealt primarily with drug enforcement. The mid-1990s had brought a huge upsurge in narcotics use, with many towns and villages in Surrey being swamped with Class-A substances like heroin, cocaine and ecstasy. Worryingly, the county had also seen a sharp rise in hard drugs being diluted—or "cut"—in order to maximize dealers' profits. My colleagues and I would regularly seize narcotics that had been bulked up with cheaper agents, ranging from washing powder and baking soda to brick dust and corn starch. This highly dangerous, deeply unpleasant practice was putting hundreds of lives at risk, and it became my personal crusade to rid the streets of these reckless dealers.

Every new member of my team was required to attend a one-week attachment to our local drugs-rehabilitation unit. I needed them to witness first hand just how much damage drug abuse caused to people's lives and how other agencies were working hard to reduce the demand for them. I also wanted my officers to understand just how important their role was within the drugs-enforcement unit.

"It's not just about catching the culprits and locking them up," I'd stress during my regular motivational rally cries. "It's about working with the local community and making a real, tangible difference."

I was very fortunate to have a magnificent team of detectives at my disposal. Just as crucial, however, were the force's specially trained drugs-detection dogs. The vast majority were working cocker spaniels whose natural-born traits and attributes lent themselves perfectly to this unique role. Other than their innate intelligence, obedience and agility, what set these amazing dogs apart from other breeds was their phenomenal work rate and search stamina. This is backed up with a sense of smell which is 10,000 to 100,000 times more acute than a human's, which enabled them to follow a scent trail or decipher a specific odor that was undetectable to the nose of an average man or woman.

Not only that, their skill in searching was so economical, and their desire to hunt so effective, that they were able to cover large or hard-to-reach areas much more quickly than a police officer. I came to realize that a cocker spaniel's hyper-sensitive nose was one of the finest tools in our crime unit, if not one of the most valuable assets in modern-day policing.

The drugs-detection canines—and their designated handlers—underwent extensive training at Surrey Police HQ for four months in order to receive their fit-for-practice certification. The dog would go through an intensive scent-recognition program and be trained to identify the unique odor of narcotics. With each successful find, they were rewarded with play sessions involving their favorite toys.

I liked to share a break-time cuppa with the handlers, most of whom would gladly regale me with tales about their dogs' exploits and adventures. They clearly adored their canine companions and often formed close and loving bonds with them, despite the fact that the animals, technically, belonged to the force. Indeed, it was a well-known fact that most dog handlers would spend their entire careers on the dog section.

I had always had a great affection for cocker spaniels—I loved their spirit, loyalty and exuberance—so it was a delight to work with them in the crime unit. I would regularly deploy them on drugs raids and would gaze in awe as they deftly located an of-fending substance, often squeezing into the tiniest, most inaccessible space in order to retrieve it. Unlike "general purpose" canines, these sniffer dogs were not trained to show aggression or menace but their innate energy and enthusiasm made them perfect for this vital role.

Some dogs were more adept than others, I realized, and I'd often request a specific handler if I knew that he'd be accompanied by a particular sniffer. A case in point was Rainbow, an exceptionally talented liver-colored cocker spaniel with yellow-amber eyes who habitually greeted everyone with a comical bum-shuffle. She was Surrey Police's finest detection dog, with the best success rate, and she worked in tandem with a brilliant handler called John. I remember once watching, open-mouthed, as this hugely impressive dog found a stash of amphetamines that had been wrapped in layers of tinfoil and hidden under a mattress, which—as an added distraction—had been doused in chilli powder. The offender had assumed he was a step ahead of us, but he'd clearly underestimated Rainbow's skill and intellect.

John and Rainbow had a fabulous rapport and an almost tele-pathic connection. Whenever I had an important drugs raid to coordinate, I always requested the assistance of this expert duo and I would find it immensely frustrating if, for whatever reason, they were unavailable.

"Sorry, Detective Sergeant Butcher, but they've been ear-marked for another case that day," an inspector would say, and my heart would sink.

This indeed happened to be the case in August 1994, when I received a tip-off that a serial offender, a local low-life called Darren, was dealing in Class-A narcotics. He had not long left prison—he'd been released on license—but this clearly hadn't deterred him. We suspected he'd been adulterating his supplies, too, since there always seemed to be more drugs-related over-doses and emergencies in the area whenever he was peddling his wares.

"He's got more effing visitors than a bookies' on Derby Day," commented one of my surveillance team, who, over the previous fortnight, had witnessed a conveyor belt of comings and goings at his flat and had recognized dozens of small-time villains.

We were dealing with a one-man crime wave, it seemed, and I was determined to get Darren off the streets and back into a cell. The fact that he remained on parole meant that any repeat offense would send him straight to jail, no questions asked.

Meticulous plans were drawn up for an early-morning raid of his flat—he lived in a run-down estate—and I naturally requested the assistance of John and Rainbow. Just prior to my 4 a.m. briefing to the search team, however, I was informed that John was needed elsewhere. He worked with a firearms sniffer dog, too—a springer spaniel called Sparky—and they'd been recruited to a Special Branch operation in Woking. To say that I was deflated was an understatement. I still proceeded with the raid as planned but had to draft in a replacement dog and handler, who, in my opinion, couldn't hold a candle to John and Rainbow.

"*POLICE . . . STAY WHERE YOU ARE!*" my entry team yelled as they broke into Darren's flat that morning. As the suspect made his bleary-eyed appearance, I noted that he hadn't changed much since the last time I'd seen him, standing in the dock of Guildford Crown Court. Skinny and gangly, with pale, pitted skin and limp, mousy hair, he was wearing his usual twenty-four-hour uniform of white T-shirt and gray jogging pants.

"Good morning, Darren," I said, as he eyed me with contempt. "Lovely to see you again. We'd like a look around, if you don't mind."

I dropped a search warrant in his sweaty hand and gave the order for the search to commence. The flat was damp and dingy, with peeling wallpaper, threadbare carpets and a severe lack of furniture. If its occupant was raking in drug money, as we suspected, he certainly wasn't spending it at Ikea.

Despite turning the place upside-down—and despite the best efforts of the substitute sniffer dog—by mid-morning we'd still not hit upon the all-important Class As. All we'd unearthed was a small sachet of marijuana (for personal use, Darren claimed), as well as the usual paraphernalia of scales, foil and Rizla papers. All this amounted to a minor offense, which wasn't the result I wanted, but at least it allowed me to arrest our suspect on a so-called holding charge, which afforded me a little more time to investigate his flat and find his drugs stash.

Darren remained nonchalant.

"I keep telling you, Mr. Butcher, there's nothing hidden here," he drawled, raking his hand through his stringy hair. "I'm on the straight and narrow these days. I'm even going to get a proper job. You're all wasting your time."

As the clock ticked into the afternoon, my frustration levels rose. Search operations were so costly in terms of time, staffing and resources and, as it stood, there'd be serious questions asked by my uncompromising chief superintendent. Based on all the intelligence I'd received, however, I remained convinced that there were hard drugs on the premises; it was merely a case of locating them.

As I reluctantly began to wind down the operation—I'd dismissed most of the search team, including the sniffer dog and his handler—my radio sputtered into life: someone wanted to meet me in the car park.

To my utter delight, when I got there I found John leaning on the hood of his patrol car, Rainbow sitting obediently at his feet.

"The job with Sparky finished ahead of schedule, Sarge, so we just dropped in on the off chance that you'd still be searching," he said. "Will you be needing our help?"

"Damn right I will," I grinned, beckoning them to follow me upstairs.

I have to say, I'd seen nicer kitchens than Darren's. Every surface in this long and narrow space was grime-encrusted, from floor to ceiling, and the place was littered with unemptied bins and unwashed pans. A dehydrated spider plant overhung the window ledge and, above it, a trio of bluebottles hurled themselves against the filthy, cracked glass in what looked like a bid for fresh air and freedom.

My gut instinct told me to recommence the search in the kitchen, so I duly ushered in John and Rainbow, the latter eagerly straining at her leash, fully aware that she had a job to do. Following them into the room was a handcuffed Darren, alongside an arresting officer; it was standard procedure for a suspect to witness a search.

"Right, let's start at ground level," I told John, who eyeballed his dog and gave the search command of "Rainbow, find it!" His Glaswegian lilt made "Rainbow" sound like "Rambo," which I thought was pretty apt for this tough and fearless little spaniel.

As John systematically opened each cupboard door and cubby hole, Rainbow shot in like a firework, using her shiny black nose to sniff every corner while her tail wagged furiously behind her. Such was her ability and intelligence, she didn't need commands barked at her every second; John simply observed and monitored her, scrutinizing and interpreting any tell-tale signs or revealing body language. I watched closely as she occasionally spun around in mild excitement—as if she was getting the occasional whiff of something interesting—but it was clear that she had not yet hit the jackpot.

Witnessing this diligent little spaniel doing her job seemed to greatly unnerve Darren, who became increasingly antsy and agitated.

"I bloody hate dogs," he muttered, glaring at Rainbow as she snuffled under the fridge-freezer and around his scruffy trainers. "And I'm allergic to 'em. Look, I'm coming out in hives."

Ignoring our suspect as he theatrically hitched up his trouser leg—his distraction techniques weren't cutting any ice with me—I signaled for John to change tack slightly and to move our sniffer dog up a level.

She reacted to her handler's command by athletically springing on to the melamine worktop. Negotiating her way around the clutter of dirty dishes proved to be tricky—it was like a crockery obstacle course—and I noticed that Darren didn't take his eyes off her. I caught him smirking as Rainbow's paws slipped and slid across the grimy surface, but his smile soon faded when she suddenly became drawn to the cooker.

Rearing up on her back legs, she let out a shrill yelp and pawed frantically at the stainless-steel extractor hood above the hob. She then deliberately touched it with her snout before making direct eye contact with John, who in turn threw me a knowing glance. This was Rainbow's positive signal, instilled during her training, that indicated we should search more exhaustively.

John loosened the extractor hood's screws and carefully wrested the metal away from the wall, revealing a rectangle of dark blue tiles.

"What d'you think you're effing doing?" yelled Darren, who was getting sweatier and swearier by the minute. "You've got no right to tear my effing cooker apart."

"You may not need it for a while, Darren," I replied. "With any luck, it'll be prison food for you again."

With that, Darren lashed out his left leg and booted a waste bin across the floor, hurling a string of expletives in our direction as he was restrained by the arresting officer.

Disappointingly, though, the tiles bore no cracks or holes to suggest that they'd been tampered with. However, as a ray of sunlight filtered through the kitchen window, it illuminated a circular imprint on one of the upper tiles. It looked like the residue from a sticker, perhaps, or a plastic sucker. I scanned the kitchen and caught sight of a fraying tea towel hanging from a round suction hook on the fridge-freezer. I noted how completely out of place it looked in this filthy kitchen with its dozens of unwashed plates and dishes.

"God is in the detail" had been the advice given to me by a seasoned, long-serving detective, a Yorkshireman called Andrew who'd shown me the ropes when I'd first joined CID. "You have to be thorough, lad. It's all the job expects of you, and by being so, you'll help to keep the bad 'uns behind bars, where they be-long."

I prised off the suction hook and, with bated breath, strode across the kitchen and cautiously positioned it against the tile. *Gotcha*.

"A perfect fit!" grinned John. "It's like Prince Charming with Cinderella's slipper!"

With the sucker in place, I gave the suspect tile a gentle tug, which caused it to come away easily. I slipped on a pair of silicone gloves and reached into the dark void behind and, as I groped around the brickwork, I felt something metallic and oblong-shaped. I gently eased it out—it was an old, rusty muni-tions tin—and carefully placed it on the worktop. Darren cursed under his breath and a frisky Rainbow completed a couple of 360-degree turns before sitting down and training her gaze upon John.

Inside the box—*hallelujah!*—were some tightly wound rolls of banknotes, shoehorned next to four plump polythene bags of white powder. I retrieved a spot-test kit from my jacket pocket and removed a tiny amount of the substance before adding it to a small vial. Within seconds, the fluid had turned a dark orange, a clear indication that the powder was heroin. And, if that wasn't a good enough result, beneath the stash of money I found a tiny ring-bound notebook which, as I quickly flicked through it, ap-peared to contain hundreds of handwritten contacts.

Darren was immediately arrested for possession of Class-A narcotics with intent to supply, and by the end of the week he was back in jail. As he was led out of the flat, he laughably at-tempted to take a swing at me, yelling that he'd never effing seen that metal box before and that us effing rozzers had framed him. And as for that effing nosy little dog . . .

"I'm sure you haven't seen the box before, Darren," I said, raising my eyebrows, "but you might need to explain why your fingerprints are all over the notebook."

All things considered, the drugs bust was a fantastic result for us; the neighborhood was now free of a dangerous menace and, as a consequence, we'd probably prevented hundreds of overdoses, maybe even a few fatalities. This particular swoop also highlighted the importance of recruiting a first-class sniffer dog. Drugs-enforcement officers could search a house for hours—days, sometimes—and still fail to find any narcotics, due to clever concealment. But you couldn't hide them from a top dog's nose, and there weren't many better noses than Rainbow's.

With Darren now out of the picture, John took the opportunity to give his dog her well-earned treat, a play session in the stairwell with her favorite toy. I watched, smiling, as he bounced an old, gnarled tennis ball against the wall, prompting Rainbow to leap high, like an acrobat, before catching it in her mouth.

"Attagirl!" He laughed as she scampered up and down the stairs, her paws pitter-pattering as she did so.

Standing there, observing this charming bond between man and dog, induced a sharp pang of sadness. Rainbow, I realized, reminded me very much of Tina, a black and white cross-breed who I'd rescued from Southampton RSPCA a few years previously. She had been neglected and abused prior to being rescued and had been found chained to a rotting tea chest. As a result, she'd developed many behavioral problems. Once I'd showered her with love, care and attention, however, she grew into a fine pet, a sparky playmate and a wonderful companion. During my stint as a uniformed officer Tina would occasionally accompany me on a night shift, sitting quietly on the back seat during a stakeout or plain-clothes operation. I was heartbroken when she passed away—she died of a heart attack in 1990—and, as I watched Rainbow frolicking in the stairwell, all those happy memories came flooding back.

Half an hour later one exhausted cocker spaniel was curled up on the sofa in Darren's lounge, having wedged herself between John and me. While we waited for the police photographer to turn up—a procedural necessity following a drugs raid—we engaged in a pleasant chat about the sniffer dogs that he'd worked with through the years. I loved listening to the handlers' stories; they relished talking about their canine colleagues and often had some interesting tales to tell. I was always keen to absorb their knowledge and expertise, too—the whole concept enthralled me—and they would willingly answer my queries, whether it was "What's the best dog for searches?" or "How many years can a dog work for?"

I had another question for John that day, though.

"I hope you don't mind me asking, but you've been in the force much longer than me. How come you're still a constable? How come you've never applied for promotion?"

His response was to the point, and from the heart.

"It's quite simple," he replied. "Had I gone for promotion and become a sergeant, I'd most likely have been taken off the dog section and would have had to give my dogs back. And I don't think I could have coped with that."

John gazed down at the sleeping dog and I detected a very slight lip-wobble.

"I worship these animals, Sarge, whether it's Rainbow, or Sparky, or all those who've gone before. They're loyal, they're loving, and they're the best workmates you could ask for. Why would anyone in their right mind want to leave them, eh?"

A *few years* later, I was promoted to detective inspector and was transferred to the Major Crimes Unit, which investigated organized crime and homicide. Unfortunately, this role also meant that I had to attend an endless series of strategy meetings, training courses and seminars, which kept me away from operational policing. After much thought, and realizing that my enthusiasm for the job had dimmed, in the spring of 2003 I decided to call it a day. I had been in the Royal Navy for eleven years, and the police force for fourteen (a total of twenty-five years of service to the Queen) and felt that it was high time for a change.

Another reason was my desire to set up my own detective agency. While in the employ of Surrey Police I'd worked alongside large corporations like British Petroleum and British

Airways—I'd advised them how to investigate internal fraud—
and when BP invited me to work for them on a private consul-
tancy basis I was finally motivated to "go it alone" and establish
my own business. By doing so, I'd be pursuing a career path that
really excited me and I'd be devoting much more time to what I
loved most: investigating and solving crimes.

Prior to my departure, however, I was keen to carry out one
final assignment with John and Rainbow. A couple of crooks had
brazenly stolen the floodlights from the grounds of Guildford
Cathedral and, a few weeks later, I'd received a tip-off that the
lights were being used as heat lamps in a nearby cannabis fac-
tory. Naturally, I picked up the phone and called John.

"I've got a great job for you and Rainbow," I said. "I'll meet
you on Ridgemount Road at 6 a.m."

It took our plucky little sniffer dog just thirty minutes to locate this drugs HQ—it had been cunningly hidden in the attic
of a derelict building—and within the hour we'd arranged for
200 cannabis plants to be confiscated and carted over to Guildford police station.

Since it was a bright and sunny morning—and knowing this
might be the last time I saw my favorite dog-and-handler partnership—I suggested a walk to the top of Cathedral Hill. At the
summit, John and I sat on a rickety old bench, gazing across the
roads and rooftops of Guildford while Rainbow haphazardly careered around the grass, snapping at bees and bluebottles.

"I'm really sorry that you're leaving, guv," said John, his eyes
downcast. "Reckon we've done a pretty good job of keeping this
town drug-free."

"Having the best sniffer dog in Surrey certainly helps, John,"
I replied. "I often wonder how many successful finds she's had
and how many lives she's saved."

"Countless," said John, keeping a close eye on Rainbow, "but
if she gets stung by one of those bloomin' bees she's not going to
be much use to me this week, is she?"

He reached into his pocket, pulled out a balding tennis ball and lobbed it down the hill, prompting Rainbow to abandon her bee-baiting and chase her favorite toy instead.

Suddenly, my colleague's radio crackled into life, relaying an urgent request for him to attend an incident in Farnham. A firearm had been used in a hold-up at a local petrol station and, although the suspect had been apprehended, there was no sign of the weapon. John's second sniffer dog, Sparky, was needed on the scene right away.

Having detected the familiar fizzle of radio interference, Rainbow pranced over and perched herself in front of John, panting heavily, her dark eyes dancing at the prospect of their next job.

"Sorry, girl, this one's not for you." He smiled, slotting his radio back in his top pocket before reattaching her leash.

"Well, I suppose I'd better be off then, guv," said John, shaking my hand. "I'll probably see you around, yeah?"

"No doubt you will," I replied, giving his dog's nape a little squeeze. "And keep up the good work, eh?"

I watched him jog down the hill toward his police van, Rainbow tight on his heel. Moments later he tore off along Cathedral Chase Road in a maelstrom of blue lights and screaming sirens.

While I was champing at the bit to kick off my new career as a private sleuth, I knew I'd dearly miss this dynamic duo. I stood on Cathedral Hill, sadly contemplating that prospect, oblivious to the fact that I'd soon have my own canine partner-in-crime.

3

From Private Eye to Pet Detective

By the time I'd launched my own private-investigation business, in autumn 2003, the role of the traditional sleuth had been revolutionized. Thanks to improvements in technology, gone were the days of shadowy men in raincoats peering around street corners and spying through holes in newspapers. Instead, professionals like me were more likely to be found scrutinizing footage from surveillance vehicles or examining someone's online footprint. Old-fashioned police-style detection techniques were still vital, of course—the finest PIs were expert problem-solvers and critical thinkers and had superb legal acumen—but the arrival of the digital age had transformed the industry.

My job was never dull. One week I'd be conducting an internal investigation for a world-famous company, the next I'd be recovering hundreds and thousands of pounds from a fraudulent business transaction. Other times I'd be assigned with verifying the CV of a high-powered interview candidate or secretly filming a sticky-fingered employee. Indeed, such was the demand for my services that I had to train up an assistant, a smart and savvy Slovak called Stefan. He looked after the technical-surveillance side of the business while I concentrated on strategy and keeping clients up to speed with our investigations.

Corporate clients generally dominated my workload, but I'd be hired by private clients, too, who tended to hail from the wealthier side of the tracks. It was commonplace to field calls from suspicious spouses instructing me to track their philandering partners—I'd say ninety-five percent were vindicated—or from frantic parents asking me to locate their errant offspring.

"Toby's somewhere in Thailand and his hire car has been found dumped in a ditch. He's not answering his phone, and he's probably drugged up to the eyeballs," I remember a London-based investment banker informing me one morning. "I haven't got time for all this—I'm closing in on a deal—so could you find out where he is? His mother's hysterical."

Painstaking investigations led me to a hippie commune in Chiang-Rai, where the eighteen-year-old had scarpered following a car crash (he'd been driving illegally while high on ecstasy and had abandoned the vehicle in a ditch). After much trouble-shooting and soft-soaping—the local authorities generally treated boisterous Brits with disdain—I escorted him back to the UK, where he was reunited with his peeved father and his relieved mother. Sometimes I felt more like a "fixer" than a private eye.

As time went by, it wasn't just absent teenagers I was tasked with rescuing. Many of my well-heeled clients happened to own high-value pets and animals—exotic birds, hunting dogs or thoroughbred racehorses—and whenever they went missing, or were subject to an ownership dispute, they'd seek my help and assistance.

I had investigated a handful of animal crimes in the police force, most notably a series of livestock poisonings and the snatching of pedigree puppies from a boarding kennel. In the late 2000s, however, there seemed to be an upsurge in pet-related cases, and Stefan and I found ourselves devoting far more time to investigations concerning premeditated thefts, ownership disputes and dishonest transactions.

For instance, a well-off landowner from Berkshire had got in touch when his vengeful farm manager—who'd just been sacked—stole the top dog from his hunting pack. This dominant foxhound, Cassius, would expertly corral the other dogs and, since he was their main stud, had a sell-on value in the region of £10,000. The landowner wasn't keen to involve the police (I didn't ask why) but he asked me to put my feelers out instead.

Stefan followed the farm manager's girlfriend for a day and discovered she worked as a barmaid in a country pub. The following night I popped into this particular hostelry while my colleague had a snoop around outside; I'd barely had time to take a sip from my pint when in walked our target, looking as if he'd been sleeping in his clothes. Moments later I received a text from Stefan informing me that he had the dog in his possession. It turned out the farm manager had been living in an old caravan at the back of the pub and had tethered Cassius to its rear axle.

I gave this unsavory character a proper dressing-down— "You're bloody lucky your old boss doesn't want to press charges," I said—before heading outside to join Stefan and Cassius. Much to my amusement, the dog spent the whole Berkshire-bound journey chewing my colleague's headrest, which prompted a tirade of Slovakian expletives.

Then there was the case of a wealthy heiress, Lady Jemima, who owned a valuable and venerated racehorse named Gold Runner. Based in stables in North Yorkshire, the two-year-old colt was looked after by a local equine trainer for a sizeable fee. The owner had become suspicious, however, when this very capable horse kept finishing at the back of the field in race after race. Something didn't quite ring true—this was a high-class thoroughbred, not a two-bit also-ran—and Jemima asked me to look into the matter.

What I discovered was a tangled web of deceit. It seemed that Gold Runner was being deliberately undertrained then entered into races against much fitter horses in order to put the others at an advantage. The trainer had accepted huge back-handers from his counterparts for improving their chances of a lucrative first place.

"I don't think my nag will be fit enough to win on Saturday— reckon yours will romp home," this crook had winked, before pocketing a couple of grand for his skulduggery.

Suffice to say, Jemima was horrified when I reported my findings to her and immediately sacked her two-faced, double-dealing trainer. Gold Runner was immediately transferred to a stable of great repute and—following some careful attention and some proper training—went on to win the first of many trophy races.

Having established ourselves—albeit inadvertently—as the go-to detective agency for animal crime, I decided to set up a separate company and a distinct brand to run alongside my PI business. On Monday, 3 October 2005, UK Pet Detectives was born. Launching our business on the eve of the Feast of St. Francis, the patron saint of animals, was wholly intentional on my part.

My first task was to recruit a new member of staff to bolster our team and enhance our new service. Stefan, though an accomplished surveillance operative, wasn't a huge animal-lover and much preferred trailing devious fraudsters to tracing missing Schnauzers.

"Office Manager Needed for New Pet Detection Project in Cranleigh" stated the small advert that I placed in the local newspaper. In the space of a week, I'd received nearly a hundred applications, which I managed to whittle down to half a dozen high-caliber candidates. Sam was the last interviewee on my shortlist and, within minutes of meeting her, I knew she was the right person for the role. A true English rose, with auburn hair and a fresh complexion, she answered all my questions confidently and came across as a highly intelligent, witty and capable woman. Having managed a local RSPCA branch for a decade, she'd amassed a great knowledge and understanding of animal behavior and pet welfare, and her forte was people management. Her warmth and calmness were exactly what I was looking for, and I was thrilled when she accepted my job offer. As far as I was concerned, the RSPCA's loss was UKPD's gain.

We set up our headquarters at Bramble Hill Farm in West Sussex. This beautiful 500-acre estate was owned by an old friend of mine, James, who for over thirty years had farmed hundreds of cows and sheep, in conjunction with running a small shooting estate and some stables. The highly virulent BSE outbreak—commonly known as mad cow disease—had forced him to wind down his livestock business, however, and he'd consequently leased a large part of his land to an alpaca farmer and rented out some of his many outbuildings. When he'd kindly offered me the use of a spacious converted barn for my fledgling business, I'd jumped at the chance.

"I tell you what, Colin," he'd said, as we'd shared a bottle of homemade cider in his farmhouse kitchen, "I'll give you the barn rent-free, if you handle my estate security. Deal?"

"Deal," I'd replied, without hesitation.

It was a crisp autumnal morning when Stefan, Sam and I first drove up to our new HQ, our transit van groaning with desks, computers and office equipment. James took some time to show us around the estate and, as we stood at its highest point, our T-shirts billowing in the stiff breeze, we couldn't help but marvel at the view. Velvety green hills rolled for as far as the eye could see, laced with bluey-gray rivers and streams. Look left, and you saw pear and apple orchards next to fields of swaying ryegrass. Look right, and you saw deciduous forests bordering meadows of grazing alpacas. It was the sort of varied, variegated landscape you could gaze at for hours on end.

Bramble Hill Farm was also a renowned wildlife haven, explained James, who told us to expect to find foxes, rabbits and fallow deer loping past the office. The estate was a veritable paradise for fishermen and birdwatchers, too, its rivers teeming with trout, perch and crayfish, its skies embracing a multitude of raptors, finches and warblers.

"There's an old boar badger that wanders through the yard, too," he said, "but you'd better give him a wide berth because he's a grumpy old codger."

I saw Sam and Stefan exchanging smiles and knew exactly why; this description wasn't too far removed from James himself.

As well as its idyllic setting, our HQ had many practical and logistical advantages. The proximity of stables and paddocks—with robust locks and CCTV—meant that UK Pet Detectives could provide animals with temporary or emergency sanctuary. Situations would inevitably arise whereby we'd have to look after recovered dogs or horses for a couple of days and the farm would offer the necessary safety, shelter and privacy. In most instances, using commercial stables or boarding kennels was just too risky.

Our location—the estate straddled the borders of Surrey, Hampshire and West Sussex—couldn't have been more convenient. We were close to plenty of southeastern towns, villages and hamlets (most of which had large pet populations) and we were also within an hour's drive of London, where many of my existing PI clients lived and worked.

Once we'd settled into our new premises, the first important task I had to address was how I'd allocate my time across the two businesses. After some discussion with Sam and Stefan, it was agreed that we would discontinue some of our private-eye services, such as the vetting of employees, the issuing of court papers and debt recovery below £250,000. I would retain all my current cases until they were concluded and remain as first point of contact for all our long-term clients. Stefan would take on all the new private-eye cases and I'd offer him occasional assistance with the riskier, more complex assignments. All our research work, client liaison and case management would be handled by Sam, who'd also use her network of contacts to spread the word about our new pet-detective agency. I would look after all the pet-detective cases, allocating my time on a 50/50 basis by moving across to each business as and when I was needed.

Sam and I then got straight down to UKPD work, focusing our attention on four distinct areas: dog theft, lost or missing cats, equine-related crimes and bogus rescue centers and animal charities. The latter, sadly, were becoming increasingly prevalent online as a means of swindling money from kind-hearted benefactors. We had received a number of reports from concerned individuals who'd donated to these websites, only to discover that their money had been pocketed by crooks.

Sam dovetailed into the business beautifully. She helped UKPD to expand at an alarming pace, and within nine months the number of pet-related calls to our office had tripled. During our first five years we recovered countless missing dogs: these included Baxter, a springer spaniel who'd become separated from his owner in dense woodland and had been stolen by a passing motorist, and Bertie, a Jack Russell terrier who'd been snatched from a livery yard. The latter was one of our swiftest recoveries; the dog had gone missing just after a delivery from a local animal-feed company and Sam had used her charm to obtain the driver's name from the company. Thirty minutes later we'd recovered Bertie from the soon-to-be-sacked employee's back garden.

"Nice work, Sam," I'd nodded, hugely impressed at the impact she was having on our business.

We also worked on some more outlandish cases, one initiated by a phone call from a lady in Birmingham who'd found our details online.

"My parrot's been stolen," she'd lamented, informing us that, following the disappearance of her beloved African gray after a break-in, she'd received a tip-off that he was at an address in Swindon, over eighty miles away.

"But what you need to know," she'd explained, in a broad Brummie accent, "is that Pongo's a talking parrot. He mimics stuff. I've taught him to say, 'Up the Villa'—I'm a big football fan, you see—and he screeches it all day, every day."

This lady, it seemed, wanted UKPD to drive to the property in question and eavesdrop in order to identify Pongo's hallmark cry and, hopefully, catch his captors red-handed.

"I'll see what I can do," I said, wondering exactly how I was going to break the news of this madcap mission to Stefan.

Our resident technology guru, it's safe to say, wasn't enamored about having to crouch beneath an apartment window in Wiltshire for three hours armed with a high-tech monitoring device, straining to hear Pongo the parrot's football chant. Through the net curtain, he'd been able to make out a gray bird sitting on its perch, but it hadn't emitted a single squawk, let alone an "Up the Villa." It was, in all likelihood, a case of mistaken identity.

Stefan's journey had indeed been a wild-goose chase. That same afternoon, I'd received a call from a farmer in Worcester who, having seen our MISSING PARROT posters, had realized that the "racing pigeon" resting beneath the eaves of his barn, screeching very strange soundbites, was something altogether more exotic. A raggedy-looking Pongo was carefully recaptured, then reunited with his very grateful owner.

Not every case could be solved, though, and often through no fault of our own. One winter we received a call from a hugely flustered advertising executive who'd been staging a flash photo-shoot in a West End studio for a famous design house. Their main prop was Montgomery, a five-foot-long albino ball python, who—to everyone's horror—had somehow escaped from its tank, where it had been left overnight.

"We don't know where the damned thing is and we're absolutely bloody petrified," cried the panicky exec, before pleading for my help.

Stefan and I turned up within the hour, having spoken to a reptile expert during our journey. He told me that ball pythons were so named because of the way they caught their prey; in their natural habitat, they'd curl up in burrows in order to ensnare shrews, gerbils and rabbits as they returned home.

"I'd advise that you look in any kitchens or bathrooms, since it'll probably have headed straight for water," he said, suggesting that I check pipes and wall cavities and telling me to draft in an emergency plumber, which I did.

Stefan, the plumber and I arrived at the studio to find twenty terrified employees shivering outside on the pavement, refusing to return to their workplace until Montgomery had been recaptured. Carrying the snake's empty aquarium, the three of us headed straight to the staff canteen, which seemed an obvious first port of call. We were in the process of rigging up our search equipment and dismantling the sink when a security guard strode in.

"Sorry, gents, but I'm afraid you'll have to leave," he said.

"What do you mean?" I replied. "You do know there's a snake on the loose?"

"Orders from on high, I'm afraid. The client is scared that the news is going to leak out, apparently, and they want to avoid any bad publicity before the ad campaign. So if you could exit the building, please, and just pop us an invoice in the post."

We spent a few minutes arguing our case ("What's worse, the news getting out, or the snake?" I'd asked incredulously), but to no avail.

I never discovered what befell Montgomery the python. I'm hoping he was recovered that day and was quietly found a new home. That would have certainly been the best-case scenario, of course; I didn't dare contemplate the worst.

Whether we were dealing with a trapped python or a lost poodle, UKPD endeavored to treat clients and witnesses respectfully and to take their cases seriously. Indeed, we preferred to describe ourselves as "a private investigation agency that specializes in the investigation of stolen and missing pets."

Not everybody took *us* seriously, however, thanks to a certain Hollywood movie starring Canadian funny-man Jim Carrey. His 1994 performance in *Ace Ventura: Pet Detective* may have been a comedic *tour de force*—the story of a stolen dolphin grossed over $100 million worldwide and shot Carrey to international stardom—but his clownish character and madcap exploits did my business no favors whatsoever. Conducting house-to-house inquiries in relation to a missing pet was commonplace and I lost count of the times that I was greeted with derision on the doorstep.

"What, you're a *pet detective*?" a cynical neighbor would scoff when I introduced myself. "Like Ace Ventura, you mean?"

"Is this some kind of joke?" another would say, suppressing a giggle when they spotted my UKPD uniform. "I didn't know people like you existed in real life."

The hope had always been that our business-like approach and professional branding would help to distance us from the stigma brought to the occupation by the character played by Jim

Carrey and would help others to overcome any preconceptions. Initially, some people found it quite difficult to take UKPD seriously, but as our reputation spread our credibility increased, and any facetious references to Ace Ventura became like water off a duck's back to us. In the police service, we used to have a saying, inspired by the shiny silver buttons on our blue serge jackets. If younger officers were having a rough time, experienced coppers would say, "Just let it bounce off your buttons," that is, ignore the naysayers and don't take things personally. It was great advice that I often heeded.

Throughout 2012, Pet Detectives continued to handle a variety of dog-related incidents, but they were becoming increasingly sinister and unsettling. We were hired by a well-known celebrity to locate his black Labrador, which he feared had been stolen by a vindictive relative. I traveled to his home in the north of England on a fact-finding mission and came to the conclusion that, considering all the evidence I'd gathered, the poor dog had met an untimely, unseemly and possibly painful end. When I broke the bad news to the owner he collapsed into a chair and dissolved into tears, distraught at the prospect of never seeing his pet again.

"Why would she kill my dog? He's my best friend," he sobbed.

It was a truly harrowing experience, and I drove home feeling dreadfully sorry for him.

We also became embroiled in a deeply disturbing case involving a stolen springer spaniel from Tewkesbury, which we traced to an illegal puppy farm in the south of England. During the investigation, we'd put the premises—a run-down old barn— under close surveillance and had been appalled to discover that these dogs were being kept in horrific conditions, with barely any food, light or room to move. And if that wasn't upsetting enough, we'd often hear pained whimpers and pitiful barks that would suddenly cease following the blast of a shotgun. The fact that human beings could wreak such cruelty just broke my heart and left me depressed for days.

Soon our own safety and security became compromised, too.

These monstrous dog traders had a history of violence and intimidation and, once UKPD had taken on this case and passed information to the police, we were deemed prime targets. My car windscreen was smashed in the early hours, Stefan was chased down the street by a gang of thugs and Sam was traumatized by threatening letters she received through the post. For me, the final straw came when I took a call from a withheld number asking me if I'd checked my brakes recently.

"That's it, I've had enough," I sighed, deleting yet another venomous answerphone message. "I don't want anything more to do with criminals like this."

Putting these loathsome dog thieves under scrutiny was taking its toll on my business and my hard-working employees, and I was worried that one of them would get hurt. It was now time, I felt, to change our strategy. From now on, all dog-theft cases would undergo a rigorous threat assessment. We'd continue to work on most cases, but any that we considered to be high risk would be referred to the police. We would assist the authorities but would no longer act alone in tackling the most violent dog thieves. This gave Stefan more time to work on private-eye clients and allowed Sam and me to shift our focus from canines to felines.

While UKPD had always enjoyed incredible success recovering lost or stolen dogs, our ability to find cats had been, in comparison, fairly disappointing. Of all the cases we'd taken on, about thirty percent of the cats were found safe and well; more often than not, however, these pets had been missing for less than forty-eight hours, which often meant that the search area was more confined and manageable.

A particularly memorable investigation, involving a woman called Suzie and a cat named Oscar, ended up having a profound effect upon me, and a pivotal effect upon my business. One morning in April 2012 I'd been feeding the chickens at

Bramble Hill Farm when I felt my mobile phone buzzing in my coat pocket. The woman on the end of the line frantically told me that her nine-month-old cat—a Burmilla cross—had gone missing in their tiny Hampshire village. Having mounted an unsuccessful search, a neighbor had suggested she call my agency. In all my time as a pet detective, I'd rarely heard anyone so desperate for my help.

"Oscar's my world," Suzie had sobbed. "I'm worried sick, Mr. Butcher. I've hardly slept a wink and I need to find out what's happened to him."

Oscar, she explained, was a house cat who'd never before ventured outdoors. It transpired that, ten days previously, her husband had wedged open a kitchen window to rid the room of cooking fumes but had forgotten to shut it before bedtime. The following morning, Oscar had failed to pad upstairs for his usual snuggle and when Suzie had gone to investigate she'd noticed the open window and had gone into panic mode. Despite organizing a thorough search of the village and making numerous house-to-house inquiries, there'd not been a single sighting of him since.

As a general rule, I never took on cases relating to cats that had been missing for ten days or more. The likelihood of recovering them was significantly reduced by that stage, and I wasn't in the business of raising my clients' hopes—or raising invoices—for what was often a lost cause. But there was a certain mournfulness in this woman's voice that compelled me to lend my assistance, and at seven o'clock the next morning I found myself knocking on her front door.

Suzie, a woman in her late thirties with a kind face and a mop of brown curls, lived in the quaint village of East Meon with her husband, Mike. Over a cup of Earl Gray, she answered my questions concerning Oscar. I approached missing-pet investigations meticulously and forensically—just like I'd done earlier in my career, when I'd tackled missing-persons cases for Surrey Police—and gleaned as much as I could about the animal's character, health and routine. This enabled me to compile a detailed behavioral profile and ensured that I didn't waste valuable time searching in the wrong location or at the wrong time of day.

The more Suzie and I chatted, however, the more I understood the true extent of her despair. Speaking in a soft, tremulous voice, she explained that, the previous year, she had experienced two personal tragedies in close succession. The first was the loss of her father who had been killed in a hit-and-run car accident, and the most recent was the loss of her mother who never recovered from the death of her husband, and suffered a fatal heart attack five months later. Not only had she been left utterly devastated, Suzie's mental health had gone into freefall. She worked from home as a graphic designer and would often find herself staring idly at a blank computer screen as a deadline loomed, her mind wandering and her mood darkening. Concerned about his wife, Mike had tried his utmost to lighten her spirits and had racked his brains to think of a suitable tonic.

"So that's when he came home from work with a kitten." Suzie smiled and unpinned a photograph of Oscar from her kitchen noticeboard before handing it to me. "Nothing could fill the void of losing my parents, of course, but he thought I might like a little companion."

"He's a beauty," I said, staring at his enormous mint-green eyes.

Suzie had been somewhat skeptical—she'd never owned a cat before—but when Oscar arrived, with his marbled brown coat and his snow-white whiskers, she was smitten. As she'd lifted him from his carry case, he'd immediately begun to purr and had raised his front legs, gently pawing at the sleeves of her cardigan.

Her new chum would sit on her lap as she typed, rub against her ankles as she made lunch and curl up beside her at night, like a big, fluffy comma. Whenever she had an emotional lull, her feline friend seemed to detect this, nuzzling closer into his owner's neck or purring with increased volume. He also had a habit of pouncing on her slippers and nibbling at her toes, which would send her into fits of giggles. Much to Mike's delight, Suzie and Oscar soon became inseparable.

"He sounds like a wonderful cat," I said, prompting my client to nod forlornly.

Once I had gathered the required information, I prepared to commence the search. Suzie agreed to stay at home—she was exhausted, and ten days of fruitless searching had clearly taken its toll—and I promised to keep her posted about any significant developments.

"Thanks, Colin," she said, blinking back tears as she handed me a wad of MISSING CAT leaflets that she had printed herself. "I just want my Oscar back."

4

The Catalyst for Change

Finding this missing cat was paramount and, as I walked back out into the bright April sunshine, I opted to begin the search in Suzie's garden. The two-meter drop from the kitchen window to the patio would have prevented Oscar from jumping back into the house; I'd investigated a few similar cases and reckoned that, in a quest for safety, security and warmth, he'd probably sought refuge close by. Judging by the lack of confirmed sightings, it was highly likely that this was a case of accidental lock-in and that the cat had most probably become trapped in an outbuilding.

With the help of some cooperative neighbors and shop owners, I gained entry to as many gardens, sheds and garages as I could. It proved to be a time-consuming affair, since many of the stone-built, thatched-roofed cottages in this genteel village had long, snaking driveways threading through large, sprawling gardens. More frustratingly, when I finally reached the doorstep, I'd often find that the occupants weren't in, meaning that some potential hideaways remained under lock and key.

By mid-afternoon I'd drawn a blank—there was simply no trace of Oscar—and as time ebbed away my hopes of finding him began to fade. Every minute mattered when a cat had been absent for such a long period of time, as I knew only too well, and I braced myself for a tough conversation with Suzie.

One particular property continued to pique my interest, though. Occupying the largest plot in East Meon, this large converted farmhouse boasted a swimming pool to the east, a tennis court to the west and—more pertinently—a spacious shed to the rear.

I had already visited the house twice that morning, but on both occasions the driveway had lain empty and my knocks on the door had gone unanswered. However, as I began to make tracks to Suzie's—it must have been about four o'clock—I noticed a sporty blue BMW parked on the drive. I jogged up the cobbled driveway, rapped the shiny brass knocker, and crossed my fingers. After a minute or so, the door creaked open and I was faced with a fair-haired fifty-something female dressed in skinny jeans and a leather jacket.

"Good afternoon." I smiled, introducing myself and holding up a leaflet. "I'm searching for a missing cat, Oscar, and I'm wondering if I could have a quick peek in your shed?"

The lady fixed me with a glacial stare.

"It's a pool house, not a shed," she replied, in a cut-glass accent. "And, in any case, there's no need for you to go inside. I've seen all the posters around the village, and I've searched it myself. There's no cat in there, I can assure you."

I wasn't convinced. Thirty years spent in the police force or as a private detective had equipped me with an array of finely tuned interpersonal skills, and my built-in lie detector was now bleeping like crazy. The woman had turned her back toward the shed while talking to me, had provided me with information I hadn't asked for and, most crucially, had broken eye contact at the precise moment she'd mentioned searching the place. I was convinced that she hadn't been near it for weeks, which made me all the more determined to gain access.

"I'd really like to have a quick look, if you don't mind . . ." I asked politely.

The woman defensively folded her arms and slowly shook her head.

"It'll only take five minutes, I promise," I added hastily, while flashing her a friendly smile. "Oscar's owner is distraught and just needs to know what's happened to him one way or another. I'd be ever so grateful."

Her mood seemed to thaw momentarily and, with a resigned sigh, she headed off down her hallway, reappearing with a silver key dangling from her forefinger.

"But I shall be coming with you," she said, arching her eyebrows, "and you'd better be as quick as you say."

She opened the shed and ushered me in, albeit reluctantly. To the right, illuminated by a shaft of sunlight, was a large plastic box full of pool accessories: deflated lilos and rubber rings, snorkels and flippers. A metal shelving unit on the shadier, left-hand side of the shed—sorry, *pool house*—housed some terracotta plant pots and some loosely stacked hanging baskets, the latter separated by pale green jute liners.

"As you can see," said the woman, returning to her icy self, "there's no cat in here."

Suddenly, out of the corner of my eye, I noticed one of the hanging baskets wobbling slightly. Then I heard a faint rustling, accompanied by a feeble mewing sound. Within seconds, a tiny paw had poked itself out of the wire basket, causing Mrs. Frosty-Pants to let out a gasp of shock. At first sight his fur appeared to be black, and my heart sank, but as the animal clambered out of his dark corner, there was no mistaking that distinctive coat and those huge green eyes. *Oscar.*

Looking gaunt and bedraggled, he took a couple of faltering steps before collapsing at my feet. I carefully scooped him up and—without exchanging a single word with the woman, who was probably cringing in embarrassment—I cradled Oscar in my arms and exited the garden. Apart from a half-hearted claw at my fleece, the cat offered little resistance. The poor fella was far too frail to sense any kind of stranger-danger.

I walked over to my car and gently placed the trembling kitty on the passenger seat, tenderly brushing away the cobwebs from his matted fur. I slowly drove over to Suzie's, calling ahead to inform her I'd found her cat but stressing that we needed to take him to the vet immediately. She was waiting for us at her front gate, anxiously clasping her hands to her chest.

"My Oscar!" she gasped as she opened the passenger door.

For her, it was both the best-case scenario and the worst. While she was utterly overjoyed to see her precious pet alive—he'd survived, I reckoned, by licking the condensation off the shed windows—she was greatly distressed by his frail, skeletal appearance. His sky-high temperature, bone-dry nose and glassy eyes confirmed that we were dealing with a very poorly cat who needed urgent medical attention.

Suzie tenderly lifted Oscar from the car seat, as if he were made of porcelain, before nestling him into her lap. Her head remained bowed during the twenty-minute journey to the veterinary surgery and, as I stopped at a set of traffic lights, I noticed tears rolling down her cheeks. Other than giving me directions to the vet's, she barely said a word.

I dropped them off at the surgery—a concerned nurse was already waiting at the entrance—and I parked up nearby. Inside the building I found Suzie sitting alone, in the middle of a row of blue plastic chairs.

"Oscar's being seen by the vet now," she said. "It'll be about half an hour before they complete the examination."

"Would you like me to stay with you?" I asked.

"That's so kind," she replied, "but Mike's already on his way."

A few minutes later Suzie's husband rushed into the reception area, and I took that as my cue to leave them be. I bid my farewell and set off back to Sussex.

My head was pounding as I drove home. I was angry at the woman who had failed to search her shed and furious at myself for not finding Oscar earlier. I felt totally gutted that I couldn't have done more for Suzie; seeing her so upset had been hard enough, but suspecting that there was worse to come left me feeling so helpless.

Damn . . . if only I'd got to him sooner, I told myself, slamming my hand against the steering wheel in frustration.

Suzie called me with an update the next morning. The vet had diagnosed severe dehydration—Oscar had lost over fifty percent of his body weight—and this, combined with malnutrition, had led to significant organ damage. I knew from my previous experience of recovering trapped cats that Oscar would have survived by breaking down the cells in his body, a process known as catabolism, which would have put an enormous strain on his liver and kidneys.

While the cat remained stable and sedated at the surgery, his only chance of long-term survival was a swift transferral to a specialist treatment center in London. The vet couldn't offer any guarantees that this course of action would work, however, or whether the ailing Oscar would even withstand the two-hour journey. Suzie was adamant, though.

"It's going to cost me a fortune, Colin, but he's worth it," she said. "I promise I'll keep you posted."

When she rang me for the second time that weekend, her quivering voice told me all I needed to know. Oscar's condition had deteriorated overnight—his kidneys had begun to fail—and she'd been summoned to the surgery to make the decision that every pet-lover dreads. As he'd lain curled up in her lap, her beloved Oscar had been put to sleep and their beautiful bond was broken.

I tried to say the right things to Suzie—that she'd made the correct call, that she'd been with him when he died, that she'd given him a lovely life—but no platitude could begin to alleviate her overwhelming grief. I sensed that the untimely loss of Oscar had unearthed the deep-seated trauma of her recent bereavement, too. An image of my own brother, David, flashed through my mind, and I felt dreadfully sad that Suzie had experienced so much pain in such a short space of time.

When his wife, inevitably, became choked with emotion, Mike took over the conversation.

"It wasn't the happy ending she wanted, Colin, but Suzie's so grateful for your help," he said. "Had you not found him, she wouldn't have been able to say a proper goodbye."

I put down the phone, leaned back in my chair and gazed out of the window. Bramble Hill Farm's lush meadows were speckled with daisies, clover and buttercups. Beyond them, the Wey and Arun Canal glinted like a silver ribbon along the horizon. Up in the sky, a lone buzzard circled around the treetops, poised to seize its prey.

Contemplating this rural idyll normally filled me with comfort and joy—it was a blessing to have my HQ located here—but on this occasion I felt only frustration and sadness. As far as I was concerned, Suzie had put her trust and faith in me and, despite my best efforts, I'd failed her. Had my tactics been more effective and strategic, poor Oscar could have been recovered hours earlier, and that might well have made all the difference. I had taken far too long to comb each garden and I needed to find a more efficient way to search, without compromising on quality.

You can't let this happen again, Colin, I said to myself. *Something needs to change.*

So, on that springtime Sunday morning, I made a pledge. It was time to put my long-standing idea into practice. It was time to test my trailblazing concept once and for all.

It was time, I realized, to finally find myself a cat-detection dog.

In order to find more felines in the short term, however, I decided that UKPD had to start studying cat behavior in much finer detail. Sam, who knew just how devastated I'd been following Oscar's case, was in full agreement.

"Now that we're not handling as many dog thefts, there's no reason why we shouldn't devote more of our resources to cats," she said one Friday afternoon as we enjoyed an end-of-week drink in the Red Lion pub in Shamley Green.

"The only way we're going to become more effective, though, is by working at the coal face, as it were," she added. "We need to get up close and personal with cats. We need to watch what they get up to, where they go, who they interact with, why they go missing."

My colleague was spot-on. Our results hadn't been great, and there was surely more work that we could do to understand a cat's mindset and to track its movements. Over the course of the evening we hatched a plan, a far-reaching strategy aimed at equipping ourselves with as much knowledge and information as possible.

"Let's call it the Red Lion project," said a grinning Sam as we clinked our glasses.

For the next few weeks we pored over numerous cat-behavior books, studied reams of academic papers and watched a wealth of films and documentaries. In the meantime, Stefan kept the private-investigation side of my business ticking over nicely.

This initiative, we decided, would constitute an innovative, groundbreaking experiment. To provide us with a real insight into cat behavior, we'd identify some willing cat owners and, with their consent, affix small GPS tracking devices to their pets' collars. We would then monitor the data, which would aim to address some pertinent questions: where did cats go when they left their homes, and what did they get up to?

First and foremost, we had to choose a decent location for our research.

"Why don't we do it here, in Shamley Green?" said Sam, taking a sip of her Chardonnay.

"Yeah, why not?" I replied. "I think it'd be perfect."

Quintessentially English, it boasted a large village green, a lush cricket pitch and a variety of quaint shops and eateries, including the renowned Speckledy Hen Café. Crucially, it also had an unusually high density of cats, something I'd noticed while working there on previous investigations. Everywhere I'd turned, I'd seen cats staring out of windows, sitting on doorsteps or moseying along the pavement.

The next step was to recruit some volunteers, so Sam and I displayed posters in shop windows, delivered flyers to local households and posted messages on local social media sites.

"Are you a cat owner?" they stated. "UK Pet Detectives is seeking a better understanding of feline behavior and we'd love YOU to get involved . . ."

Ten interested parties made contact, and we eventually slimmed it down to three. We purposely chose some largish cats who could easily carry the GPS devices on their collars: Monty, a docile silver Maine Coon; Shamley, a female tabby who'd lived in the village for ten years; and Branson, a long-haired ginger tom named after a rather successful businessman who'd once resided nearby. This lightweight piece of kit was around the same size as a matchbox but, even so, was probably too bulky for a smaller breed like a Siamese or a Devon Rex.

"Let's hope it's all worthwhile," said Sam, smiling, on day one, crossing her fingers as we set off to the owners' houses, where we'd show them how to fit the cat trackers. If things went to plan, we'd retrieve some useful and valuable information.

What we didn't realize at the time, however, was that we'd unwittingly chosen the three laziest cats in Shamley Green. A week or so later—and much to our disappointment—the data analysis at UKPD HQ showed that these slovenly moggies had hardly moved a muscle. Shamley, the most active of the trio, would plod to the bottom of the garden each morning, where she'd sit on the shed roof for a few hours, sunning herself and guarding her territory. After loosening her bowels in a neighbor's garden, she'd then return to her kitchen for lunch, have a snooze on the sofa, then repeat this whole eat-poop-sleep cycle in the afternoon. In terms of the project's remit, this level of inactivity was deeply unsatisfactory.

Then we had a stroke of luck. The editor of a local glossy magazine, *The Guildford*, had read a piece about UKPD in a regional newspaper and requested an interview with us. I agreed, but only on the proviso that we could mention our Red Lion project, with the intention of attracting more participants. The article certainly had the desired effect, because within days of publication we'd managed to recruit a dozen more volunteers.

"We'd love to get involved," said a local schoolteacher who'd called us up in response to the piece. "Our little Sheba is hardly ever indoors, and it'd be fascinating to know what she gets up to."

Some villagers kindly allowed us to set up cameras in their

homes and gardens to record their cats' comings and goings, and I also installed a number of ground-level motion-sensitive "field cameras" around the village in order to follow any roaming felines.

At long last, we began to collect some fantastic data. Our new cohort of cats was infinitely more lively and, as Sam and I observed the film footage and analyzed the GPS range maps, we began to piece together some marvelous information. We learned an awful lot about cats' day-to-day behavior, habits and movements and, critically, the circumstances that led them to migrate or go missing. Some cats, we noted, reacted adversely to a change within the household—the arrival of a new baby, perhaps, or even a room being redecorated—and others were driven from their usual territory by an aggressive cat encroaching on their home or garden.

Amazingly, Sam and I also discovered that a few of the Shamley Green cats had come up with an ingenious solution to avoid conflict with each other; they were effectively time-sharing their territory. It tended to be a more dominant cat that patrolled a particular patch during daylight hours, we observed, followed by a more submissive cat once darkness fell. Our equipment was able to track an American Bobtail called George, for example, who prowled around a quiet cul-de-sac from morning to afternoon, scent-marking trees and fences as well as loitering beneath bird feeders. Several hours after George departed the area, a skinny Siamese called Skog (a so-called Chocolate Point, with a distinctive brown nose) appeared to patrol the same territory, slinking under hedges and skulking around gardens. We then saw him sniffing nervously at George's marking points—and adding his own unique scent signature—before disappearing around sunrise. By ritualistically depositing their own distinctive perfume, these felines were effectively publicizing their identity and their movements, as well as posting clues to their health, age and diet.

"It's a kind of social media for cats," I said, grinning, as we replayed this illuminating footage.

"Haha . . . that's an interesting way of looking at it," said Sam, grinning, too.

Some of the most remarkable cat's-eye-view footage captured the activities of so-called "intruder" cats, who habitually snuck into neighboring properties to seek food and shelter. We watched intently as one particular cat, a plump British Blue called Norman, sat at the end of his driveway every morning, his eyes focused on the neighbors' opposite. This couple left for work at 6:30 a.m. each day and no sooner had they departed than Norman would stroll across the road, enter the kitchen via a cat flap, pilfer some of their own cat's food and pad around their house like he owned the place. About half an hour before the couple were due home, he'd re-emerge from the back door, amble over the road and rejoin his "parent" household. Both sets of owners were astonished, but amused, when I played back this revealing footage.

"The cheeky so-and-so," Norman's owner remarked. "No wonder he's so tubby." The cat's routine continued unabated, although I gather some additional supplies of cat food exchanged hands.

Not all intruder cats were so docile, though. A few weeks into our Red Lion project our attention was drawn to a slightly unkempt, long-haired, gray-and-white cat, who seemed to be entering a multitude of houses. He had the tell-tale brawn and swagger of an unneutered tom and was making a real menace of himself as he lorded it around the village. He muscled his way into cat flaps or open windows and proceeded to ambush other cats, gobble up their food and, for good measure, spray his urine up the walls in an attempt to claim his territory. Such was his strength and stature, Sam and I christened him Titan.

One unfortunate family unwittingly locked this formidable cat in their utility room, having mistakenly adjusted the settings on their cat flap so that he'd been able to enter, but not exit. When the family returned home late following a day trip, they were confronted with a trashed room and a livid cat. Titan had not taken kindly to being locked in and had gone berserk; a Venetian window blind was hanging off its hinges, the contents of a laundry basket had been shredded and the place stank of rancid cat pee. They couldn't open the back door quickly enough, breathing a huge sigh of relief when Titan fled into the night.

Another poor family, while snuggled up on the sofa watching *Finding Nemo*, were horrified when a testosterone-fueled Titan burst into their lounge, hurtled across the room and attempted to ravage their beloved pedigree Persian on the hearth rug. Both cats were snarling, clumps of fur were flying, and the father was badly clawed while trying to drag Titan off. The parents and kids were left traumatized, as, no doubt, was the object of his lust. Indeed, this female cat went missing soon afterward—a common response to such shock and distress—but, thankfully, she returned home a few days later.

Despite his destructive and dominant tendencies, over time I became strangely fond of this roguish rapscallion of a cat. I used to enjoy tracking him as he patrolled the village—I could often pinpoint his whereabouts via the motion-sensitive cameras—and I often found myself wondering about him. Was Titan a feral cat who had always lived in the wild? Or was he a stray cat who'd once had a home or perhaps still had an owner somewhere? Suspecting it was the latter, I decided to investigate.

In the first instance, I plastered dozens of DO YOU KNOW THIS CAT? posters around the area, in the hope that any owner would recognize him. Then, in order to build a comprehensive profile of our feline intruder, I interviewed all the neighbors who'd reported sightings of him and analyzed footage from our array of cameras. I was able to glean that he was frequenting five separate households, all of which owned cats that he could either fight with, mate with, or—very rarely—socialize with. There was only one property he visited on a daily basis, though, a neat bungalow owned by Valerie, an amiable woman in her late sixties. She was a committed cat-lover—she owned Max, an elderly Burmese male—and had developed a fondness for the sinewy gray moggy, who'd regularly pop in for a snack or a snooze.

"Funnily enough, I've never had any problems with him," she said, when I'd described Titan's unruly behavior. "He always seems pretty settled here, and Max is too decrepit to cause him any bother. In fact, I'd say they get on really well. He's quite the softie when he wants to be."

Valerie had become very attached to young Titan and was clearly hankering after adopting him. I gently explained to her, however, that I felt it was my duty to try and trace his background, which might allow me to return him to his rightful owner—if indeed he had one—and to restore some stability to his life. He also needed to be neutered sooner rather than later; stray or feral cats were more susceptible to disease, and any animals that he scrapped with, or mated with, would be at serious risk of infection. The "snip" would also reduce the aggressive tendencies that had alarmed a handful of local residents.

With all that in mind, Valerie allowed me to set up a humane cat trap in her kitchen one evening—basically, a large, airy plastic-coated cage with some food as bait—so I could contain him with ease. Then I'd take him to the vet's for a health check, and to ascertain if he was microchipped.

Valerie called me at eight o'clock the following morning.

"I think you need to come over, Colin," she whispered. "I've got a rather bad-tempered cat in my kitchen."

The incarcerated Titan was none too pleased to see me, hissing angrily and swaying his bottlebrush tail as I advanced toward him. Luckily, I managed to calm him down with a handful of cat treats and a few soothing words and was able to transfer him to a much comfier carry case.

Just as I began my journey to the vet's, I received a call from Sam, who'd not long arrived at the office. It seemed a lady called Mrs. Lewis had left a message on our answerphone the previous evening, stating that she'd seen my poster on a noticeboard and claiming that Titan belonged to her.

"She says his real name is Milo," said Sam, "and she reckons he went missing from Bramley six months ago."

The village was only a ten-minute drive from Shamley Green and I knew it well.

"Right, okay," I replied. "I'll drop the big fella off at the vet's and I'll go and pay her a visit."

Mrs. Lewis, a mum of two in her thirties, greeted me at the doorstep and led me into her kitchen. She rummaged in a drawer and produced a photograph of a brawny gray cat—it was unmistakably Titan—before telling me how distraught her children had been when he'd gone missing and how they'd given up hope of ever seeing him again. She also explained that his disappearance had coincided with one of their three female cats (whom Titan had got pregnant) giving birth to a litter of six kittens.

"I think he just had too many wives and too many kids." She smiled. "It was as if he'd said, *Right, this is too much, I'm packing my bags and I'm outta here . . .*"

"That's actually a classic trigger for a cat to go missing," I replied, explaining how cats were extremely sensitive to changes to their environment and how all the fuss and upheaval in the household could have caused him to migrate to a new territory. Mrs. Lewis then told me that most of the kittens had since been rehomed and that the eldest "wife" had not long passed away.

"Suffice to say that it's much calmer and quieter here these days," she said, "so we'd love to have Milo back."

I offered Mrs. Lewis a couple of nuggets of advice: first and foremost, it was high time to get the cat neutered—many of his behavioral issues were connected to his "intact" state—and, secondly, she should try to curb the number of cats in the household, because that had probably triggered his disappearance.

Titan, aka Milo, was soon reunited with his elated family, bringing an absorbing investigation to a satisfying close and finally answering the questions that had nagged me for weeks. While not a feral cat, this tom wasn't a typical stray, either, since he'd not been abandoned and he'd, technically, had a home. I preferred to regard him as a "returned-to-the-wild" cat, insofar as he had previously lived happily with humans but, following a specific trigger, had been displaced from his own territory. He had then chosen to swap his domestic lifestyle for a nomadic existence, selecting Shamley Green as his new "manor" since its glut of cat-owning households guaranteed him plenty of food, females and fighting opportunities.

I bade farewell to Titan and made my way back to Bramble Hill Farm. While I was pleased to see him back with his family, I couldn't help but wonder how long this willful, wayfaring moggy would remain there.

To all intents and purposes, the Red Lion project had been an incredibly worthwhile exercise. Invaluable data recorded by our trackers and cameras had enabled us to obtain a fresh insight into cat behavior—their secret lives, if you will—and had cast new light upon the issue of feline migration. Armed with this newfound knowledge, UK Pet Detectives was able to take on more cases of lost and missing cats and our recovery success rate soared to over sixty percent. For me, however, that still wasn't high enough—I couldn't bear our occasional failures—and I knew I needed to shift things up a gear.

5

A Pioneering Project

The seed of my cat-detection-dog idea had been sown during my teenage years in 1970s England. Having spent my early life in Malaysia and Singapore—my father was an engineering officer in the Royal Navy—my family had returned to the UK when I was twelve years old, settling initially in the Gloucestershire town of Cheltenham before moving down to Fareham, in Hampshire. My passion for the great outdoors had been nurtured in the rainforests of the Far East and it continued when we relocated to England. Whether it was exploring the Cotswold Way or combing the south coast, I very much enjoyed observing the local nature and wildlife.

My parents and grandparents were huge natural-science lovers, too, and actively encouraged my hobby. At Christmas, and on my birthday, they presented me with beautifully illustrated reference books like the *Hamlyn Animal Encyclopedia* and David Attenborough's *Zoo Quest* series. I devoured them all, page by page, absorbing facts and figures about homes and habitats, senses and communication and movement and migration. My own pursuit of knowledge knew no bounds, and I'd regularly bring home creatures that I'd caught during field trips, such as newts, lizards, grass snakes and slow-worms.

"You've had them two days, son, best take them back now," Dad would suggest, as a selection of small insects and amphibians writhed around in homemade vivariums. "They belong in the wild, son, not in your bedroom."

My elder brother David and I would also spend much of our school holidays up on Cleeve Hill Common, a sheep-farming area that loomed high above Cheltenham. Working there was a very good friend of my grandfather's—Alec—a self-styled "countryman" in his late sixties who kept an eye on the farmers' land and their livestock. Aware that we were nature lovers, Alec often allowed my brother and I to accompany him and would drive us up to Cleeve Hill in a battered, bottle-green Austin Gipsy, its beige canvas roof pulled on or peeled off depending on the weather. This jeep-like vehicle had a distinctive smell of dog, sheep and pipe smoke; Alec's tobacco had a honeyed, pine-cone tang, and David and I would often come home reeking of it.

Bouncing around in the back of the truck would be a couple of black and white collies—the most skillful and traditional of sheepdogs—who'd help to corral the animals and rescue them from perilous situations. Sometimes Alec would receive a call to say that a sheep had fallen down a quarry, for example, or had trapped its leg in a cattle grid, and the Gipsy would be hastily cranked up.

"Ready for action, lads?" he'd ask, our adrenaline coursing as we squeezed into the passenger seat. "A daft old ram's got himself stuck in a stile, so we'll need to go and untangle him."

I hero-worshipped Alec. His knowledge of the local area was unrivaled (he knew every hill, dale and dirt track) and no one understood collies like him. He doted on those dogs—he'd talk to them with such tenderness, as if they were his own sons—and, in turn, they repaid him with their utmost trust and loyalty, responding dutifully to his every call and command. Alec worked his dogs hard, but he also loved them deeply; it was a dynamic that I found truly mesmerizing.

Throughout my childhood, a procession of pets passed through the Butcher household, including a variety of dogs, cats, hamsters and mice (the latter were smuggled into the house without my parents' knowledge and hidden in my sock drawer, where they used to escape with annoying frequency). My mum and dad developed a serious soft spot for shih-tzus, and I'd often return home from school to discover another cute golden-coated puppy bounding around the back garden, picked up that afternoon from our local branch of the RSPCA. My parents always took on rescue dogs—for them, it was a matter of principle—and would never visit specialist breeders or pet shops.

"Every dog deserves a second chance," Mum would say, scooping up the latest addition to our family and giving him an affectionate nuzzle.

One such pooch was Gemini, a silver and white shih-tzu who was so clever that he was able to recognize all the names of his favorite toys when we called them out. He also got on famously with our resident cat, Mitzy, a confident and incredibly affectionate two-year-old tortoiseshell, and these furry friends would often snuggle up together in Gemini's fleecy dog bed. Mitzy was an adorable little thing, with sage-green eyes and a distinctive snow-white coat splodged with black and orange. In between her many naps—like most cats, she slept for up to sixteen hours a day—she had a habit of following me around the house, meowing for my attention and beseeching me to play with her. I was more than happy to oblige; she clearly favored me over my three siblings, and Mum and Dad were often too busy restoring our old Victorian house to have the time to run up and down the stairs with a catnip mouse.

On a wintry Saturday in November, however, Mitzy vanished into thin air. We thought it strange that she'd not surfaced for her lunch—she loved her food and had a plump little belly to show for it—and when there was still no sign of her the next morning, our fears began to mount. David and I organized the family search party, scouring our back garden, rummaging through hedgerows and, when that came to nothing, knocking on neighbors' doors. We spent an entire Sunday evening drawing MISSING CAT posters with our colored pencils then attached them to lamp posts and tree trunks.

"Don't worry, boys, she'll probably return of her own accord," said my mother, but as the hours turned into days—and the outdoor temperatures plummeted—my hope waned. Gemini seemed to sense the gray cloud over our household, too; our dog appeared more stressed and anxious than usual, running haphazardly around the house, stopping occasionally to scratch, whimper and look up at us dolefully.

"Poor Gemini," I lamented, giving him a big bear-hug. "He's missing Mitzy as much as we are."

The following Thursday, almost a week after our cat had gone AWOL, the family was sitting in the lounge watching *Top of the Pops,* my sister Lynn's favorite program. Gemini was crouched in the corner, whining and pawing at the carpet.

"I wish he'd stop doing that," grumbled my mum. "We only laid that a month ago and it's already threadbare."

As a long-haired leather-clad woman belted out her latest chart-topper, I became distracted by a sudden noise from across the room.

"Hey, I'm sure I just heard a meow," I said, sitting bolt upright. "Turn the volume down, Dad."

We all listened intently for a couple of minutes, but heard nothing.

"It was probably Suzi Quatro hitting a high note," grinned Dad, whacking the sound back up.

Moments later another loud, distinctive meow emanated from the corner of the lounge and a light bulb went off in my head. Our clever shih-tzu, with his superior scenting and hearing skills, was indicating that our cat was down below, hence the constant moaning and scratching. The poor dog had probably been trying to alert us for days and we just hadn't read the signs.

"MITZY'S UNDER THE FLOORBOARDS!" I screeched, dashing over to the corner. "That's why Gemini's been acting so weird."

Mum sprang up from the sofa, put her hands on her hips and glared at my father.

"This is *your* fault, you silly sod," she hissed.

"What d'you mean?" replied my startled dad.

"You took up the kitchen floor last weekend, didn't you? The cat must've sneaked in when you weren't looking."

My father had indeed been replacing some crumbling water pipes the previous weekend, and Mitzy had evidently slipped in before he'd nailed the floorboards back down.

"But I hardly moved from the kitchen," said Dad somewhat sheepishly. "And surely I would have noticed her—"

"Clearly not, Geoff," responded my mum indignantly. "You'd better go and get your toolbox. That poor little thing needs to see the light of day."

Chaos ensued for the next hour as we heard an agitated Mitzy scampering off in different directions, her subterranean movements being closely tracked by Gemini, his ears pointing north, his snout pointing south. My father, armed with a claw hammer, ripped back carpets and wrenched up floorboards as David and I poked torches through the gaps, cajoling our cat with cries of "Mitzy, *ch-ch-ch* . . . Mitzy, *ch-ch-ch* . . ." As all this unfolded, Mum cradled my baby brother Rian in her arms, watching on with horror as her house was torn apart.

A growling Gemini then indicated that Mitzy had reached a cul-de-sac beneath the downstairs loo. As our dog corkscrewed around in excitement, Dad carefully jemmied up a floorboard and, after a few tense moments, out crept a befuddled, bedraggled little cat, encrusted with dirt and grime and sporting a noticeably slimmer tummy. Rian's gleeful yelp of delight, followed by a peal of laughter, said it all. Gemini had found Mitzy and our gray cloud had lifted.

The whole experience made a lasting impression on me. Watching my brainy dog find my beloved cat was one of the most amazing things I'd ever seen and, unbeknownst to me, had imprinted a grand idea on to my psyche. It would take another four decades before I was able to fully explore its true potential.

As we approached the winter of 2014, I felt the time had come to launch the second phase of my cat-detection plan. A specialist scent-recognition dog would not only complement our Red Lion project but would also complete my team, enhance our service, and—most important—increase our chances of finding these missing pets. This would in turn bring joy and relief to their owners and, hopefully, avoid tragic outcomes like poor Oscar in Hampshire, which continued to haunt me. I was utterly convinced that it was a viable concept; if a police canine could be taught to detect a specific drug or firearm, I saw no reason why a sniffer dog couldn't be trained to isolate the odor of a particular cat. In my mind, it was eminently doable.

I was under no illusions, however; I knew that I wouldn't be able to complete the project alone and that I'd need some expert help along the way. A good friend had once advised me that, in order for a great idea to work, "You first need the know-*how*, and then you need the know-*who*," and it was with that simple equation in mind that I set myself to the task, aided and assisted by the ever-helpful Sam. Although I had a vast experience of dogs—I'd always had them in my life and I'd owned and trained a succession of rescues—I was aware that I lacked expertise in the science of canine behavior and scent recognition.

Throughout 2014, I studied these subjects voraciously, reading hundreds of academic books and papers (American dog expert Roger Caras was a favorite author of mine) and watching countless documentaries on television and on YouTube, including those featuring famed British naturalist Desmond Morris.

I learned all about the evolution of the canine olfactory system, for instance, reading with interest how African wild dogs would single out a sick or vulnerable kudu or impala and chase it for miles. If the animal made it back to the safety of the herd, the dogs would then track it by focusing on its unique scent signature, ensuring they didn't waste valuable energy by chasing the wrong animal.

I also discovered that the array of scent glands dotted around a cat's head, paws and tail exuded one-of-a-kind pheromones that were entirely unique to each animal. Conducting this kind of research added more weight to my big idea and made me keener than ever to take it forward. Sam and I would spend hours discussing everything we'd learned, which gave us much food for thought.

"Just think, Colin, if all goes to plan, you could have yourself the UK's first cat-detection dog," I remember her once saying. "How brilliant would that be?"

I took advantage of my contacts book and client list, too, firstly, to ascertain whether there was anyone in the region who could help me find and train a specialist dog (or point me in the direction of someone who could), and, secondly, to gauge a cross-section of opinion regarding the basic thrust of my idea. What I hadn't expected, however, was to hit a brick wall of apathy, negativity and downright hostility.

A contact of mine kindly put me in touch with a gun-dog breeder from Petersfield, but when I paid her a visit to talk through my idea (in fairly vague terms, since I didn't want anybody to pinch it) she gave me the shortest shrift imaginable.

"I can't see that *ever* working," she sneered, "and if it is such a good idea, don't you think an established dog trainer would have done it by now?"

Okay, maybe it's never been done before, I remember thinking as I walked back to my car, my hackles rising, *but that doesn't mean it can't be done.*

Not only that, other dog trainers failed to return my calls and emails, and a Kennel Club official rudely implied that I didn't possess the expertise to take on a project of such magnitude. Another so-called expert took great pleasure in telling me that sniffer dogs were better equipped to search for people rather than cats, since humans were more heavy-footed and therefore easier to trace.

"Felines are hunters, Mr. Butcher, so they creep around very quietly and don't tend to disturb the ground," he said, shaking his head condescendingly. "And, because they're covered in fur, they don't shed as many skin cells as we do. For those reasons, cats would be very, very hard to locate."

"Well, let's just say I respectfully beg to differ," I replied, biting my tongue.

The same individual also questioned whether a scent-recognition dog would be able to pinpoint one particular cat within a community of hundreds, since he reckoned that they all "had the same smell." However, my extensive reading and research—together with the findings from my Shamley Green Red Lion project—had already convinced me otherwise.

Later that summer, at a Sussex county show, I struck up a conversation with a field-trials organizer, a famously pompous old bloke who laid on simulated shoots for gun dogs. He gaped at me in disbelief after I'd outlined my concept to him.

"What on earth are you talking about?" he bellowed. "Dogs *chase* cats, they don't bloody *find* them. I think you're wasting your time, as well as mine. Now, if you don't mind, I've got a trophy to present . . ." He then stomped off, grumbling something about "damned time-wasters."

I even contacted Surrey Police's dog-training center in Guildford, hoping they might be interested in a PR-friendly joint venture. I would fund the specialist tuition for the sniffer dog—I'd already ring-fenced a small budget for my cat-detection project—and the force could take the credit for the outcome. The sergeant virtually laughed at me down the phone.

"I can't say that missing cats are a priority of ours," he said, barely able to hide his amusement, "so I really don't think it's something we'd be interested in."

This sardonic response shouldn't have surprised me, I suppose; police officers could be quite cynical at times, and the sergeant was probably too set in his ways to see how the project could benefit his dog section. To him, no doubt, I was a deluded pet detective touting some hare-brained idea that might damage their professional reputation. Perhaps the curse of Ace Ventura had struck again.

I drove back to Cranleigh feeling demoralized, but not defeated.

Waiting for me at home that night—and bracing herself for the inevitable rant—was Sarah. She and I had first met in September 2012, when she'd been working as an area manager for a homeware retailer. One day, I'd popped into the Guildford store to buy myself a new wok and couldn't help but notice the smart and attractive blonde standing near Customer Services, clipboard in hand. Sarah and I had got chatting, I'd cheekily asked her out for a drink and, within a few months, she'd moved into my house in the nearby village of Cranleigh.

Unusually for me, though, there weren't any animals roaming around my place at that point in time. I was still mourning the loss of three beloved rescue dogs in the space of eighteen months—Tess the German shepherd and my two Rottweilers, Max and Jay—and I'd decided to have an extended break from pet ownership. Three heart-rending visits to the vet's in quick succession had taken its toll and had left me feeling distinctly fragile.

I occasionally fostered animals, however, as part of my UK Pet Detectives remit. Invariably, they were recovered stolen dogs whose owners were untraceable or abandoned cats who were waiting to be rehomed. It was during one such stopover—when I'd provided temporary sanctuary for Bracken the springer spaniel—that I realized Sarah wasn't the world's greatest dog-lover and, given the choice, much preferred cats. Exceedingly house-proud, painstakingly tidy and immaculately groomed, my girlfriend, it seemed, didn't take too kindly to doggies and their detritus.

"Ugh, Colin, there's mud *everywhere* . . ." she'd wailed when Bracken and I had returned from a soggy walk in the woods, leaving a trail of mucky paw- and footprints along the hallway.

"And there's dog hair *all* over the kitchen, for goodness' sake!" she'd exclaimed. "It's *revolting* . . ."

While Sarah had known about my cat-detection-dog plans from day one, I think, deep down, she'd doubted it would ever come to fruition and had been secretly quite relieved about that. On this particular evening, though—as I licked my wounds following the Surrey Police snub—she kept her feelings well hidden.

"Everywhere I turn there's a knockback, Sarah," I moaned, slumping into the leather sofa and pouring myself a large glass of Chablis. "I'm trying my best to move things forward, but all I get is skepticism and small-mindedness. It's really bloody dispiriting. Everyone is telling me it's a crazy idea and that I'm wasting my time, but I know it can be done."

"You're not throwing in the towel, are you, Colin?" she asked, knowing full well that I wasn't the kind of bloke who gave up easily.

"No chance. If anything, it's making me more determined," I replied. "I just need to find somebody who believes in me, and who believes in my idea. They must be out there somewhere."

They were indeed, most notably in the guise of a dog-lover called Anna.

While my "pet project" ate up much of my spare time, I still had to manage my private-detective agency, and I continued to handle animal-related cases and crimes. One afternoon, I received a call from a woman asking if I could possibly investigate the suspicious death of her Welsh terrier, Molly. A well-regarded dog trainer-cum-canine expert—and weekly radio broadcaster—Anna had relocated from central London to rural Shropshire in order to give Molly, to whom she was absolutely devoted, a better quality of life. The dog had been diagnosed with cancer a few months previously and Anna felt that the fresher air and calmer environment would boost her pooch's health, and perhaps even prolong its life.

A few weeks after moving into her little cottage, Anna was asked to attend an important work-related conference in Brussels. Mindful of Molly's poor health, she was reluctant to place her in kennels and instead asked a local dog-walker to mind her for the weekend. The lady in question, Jill, also worked as a part-time gardener, and she and Anna had become quite friendly since her arrival in the village.

"You may as well stay with Molly in the cottage," my client had suggested. "She likes her creature comforts, and she'd really love your company."

Anna worried throughout the conference—she very rarely left her terrier's side—and she couldn't wait to fly home that Sunday. Upon her return, however, Jill was nowhere to be seen. Not only that, when Molly wandered over to greet her owner, she didn't seem her usual self. Her movement appeared incredibly labored and lethargic—like she was wading through treacle—and her tail hung limply behind her. A deeply concerned Anna was unable to contact Jill by phone, but eventually located her at the local garden center.

"Oh sorry, Anna, I forgot to mention . . . Molly fell off the sofa and bumped her back," said the dog-walker somewhat nonchalantly, before claiming that a family emergency had taken her away from the cottage that afternoon.

Over the next forty-eight hours, Molly's condition worsened. Anna took her to the local vet, who diagnosed a severe blow to her back end, which had caused a tail dislocation and a hip displacement. The little dog was dosed up with painkillers, but her health quickly deteriorated and a fortnight later, sadly, she passed away. The vet couldn't say for sure whether she had died of the cancer or her injuries—or a combination of the two—but, either way, Anna was devastated.

"Colin, I know it won't bring Molly back, but I just want you to establish the truth," she said, her voice cracking with emotion down the phone line. "I need to know what really happened to her while I was away."

It proved to be a long, intricate investigation that included studying text messages and CCTV, as well as carrying out a forensic examination of the cottage. It soon became apparent that Jill had lied repeatedly about Molly. Her falling-off-the-sofa story was highly implausible—the cushions were far too low to have caused serious trauma—and, taking into consideration the vet's comments, the most logical explanation for Molly's injury was that she'd been thrown or kicked down the stairs. The prime suspect was a friend of Jill's, a local man who it transpired had gained access to Anna's cottage while she was away. I was unable to establish his exact motive, unfortunately, but clues hinting toward behavioral problems, added to certain forensic material, suggested that he was the perpetrator of this cruel act.

While there wasn't enough evidence for a civil or criminal prosecution, my client was satisfied to have obtained a few answers to her questions and to have achieved some kind of closure.

"I've just got to try and block out the bad thoughts, Colin, and cherish the good times," said Anna forlornly. "I'll never, ever forget Molly—she was my best friend—but now I feel I can finally let her rest in peace."

Anna and I went on to become firm friends. She was wonderful company—I loved her constant stream of dog anecdotes—and, when she moved back to London, we regularly met up for coffee. It was during one such get-together, in a Notting Hill café, that I raised the subject of a cat-detection dog.

"Listen, Anna, I've got this idea," I said. "Everyone else seems to think it's some kind of pipe dream and that I've totally lost the plot, but I'd really value your opinion."

Not only did my friend think it was a fabulous concept, she was also confident she knew an organization that could assist. She had once worked on a PR strategy for a Milton Keynes–based charity, Medical Detection Dogs, whose staff were doing pioneering work with specialist scent-recognition canines and had successfully trained up a number of medical-alert assistance dogs. These amazing creatures used their ultra-sensitive noses to detect minuscule changes in an individual's personal odor, which enabled them to spot certain warning signs. If one of these dogs was allocated to a Type 1 diabetes sufferer, for example, it would be trained to sense dangerously high or low blood sugar levels and would alert the patient to this medical event by either jumping up or licking, or both. Similar canines assisted people with Addison's disease—an endocrine disorder—or those with severe food allergies.

"These dogs are phenomenal, Colin," remarked Anna. "They don't just change lives, they save them."

According to my friend, MDD was also conducting on-site trials with specialist bio-detection dogs. Astonishingly enough, these animals were being trained to detect certain cancers by odor alone—via samples of breath, urine and skin swabs— the hope being that, one day, they could assist with the clinical screening of the disease. For this innovative research, the charity had recruited working breeds that possessed excellent noses and a natural hunting instinct—such as Labradors and cocker spaniels—and had allocated between six to eight months to train them. All the dogs lived in the homes of staff or local volunteer fosterers (never in kennels) and were loved and cared for as part of a family.

"MDD could be just what you're looking for," said Anna. "I can't promise anything, obviously, but I can certainly set up a meeting."

I met Dr. Claire Guest and Rob Harris—the driving forces behind Medical Detection Dogs—on Wednesday, 25 September 2015. Claire, an eminent academic in the field of animal behavior and scent recognition, was the charity's chief executive officer. Rob, the bio-detection project specialist, was a highly regarded expert in canine olfaction. He had trained a multitude of dogs to detect all manner of things, ranging from SIM cards smuggled into prisons, to dry rot in historical buildings, bed-bug infestations in hotels and illegally trafficked ivory.

"It's all about taking what a dog does naturally and honing it into a unique skill," said Rob when I quizzed him about his impressive career portfolio. "What's great, though," he added, "is that the majority of these dogs don't view their work as a chore.

They see it as a fabulous game of hide-and-seek that they absolutely love playing and which they get rewarded for."

They both listened intently as I presented my case, with Anna at my side for moral support. When I finished speaking and closed down the PowerPoint, they glanced at each other and nodded.

"In principle, I definitely think it's something we could help you with," said Claire. "It's an excellent concept, Colin, and—if done properly—I reckon it could be potentially groundbreaking."

It took every ounce of restraint not to punch the air and yell, *"Get in there!"* just like I did whenever Chelsea FC scored a goal at Stamford Bridge. I couldn't believe what I was hearing. It was a eureka moment for me. I felt like leaping up and dancing around the room, and it took all my effort to remain seated.

"I think it's a really exciting challenge," Claire went on, "and, as an animal-lover myself, I really admire the reasons behind it. A dog that finds cats . . . I mean, what's not to like?"

She also explained that, if things went to plan, they'd consider drafting in a contact of theirs—Astrid, a scent-matching expert from Chile—for the dog's laboratory-based training. They told me that she'd just finished working on a special assignment with the German police force which had involved training sniffer dogs to match scenes of crimes with specific offenders. If a burglar robbed a bank and dropped a glove, for example, this evidence would be seized by an officer, contained in a controlled environment and presented to the canine. The animal would attend the police line-up and, if it detected a scent match, would sit down in front of the suspect in question. While this procedure couldn't conclusively prove guilt, it had become a vital component of the evidence package.

"Astrid is astoundingly good at what she does; in fact, I'd say she's among the best in the world," said a smiling Rob. "I'm sure she'd love to work in tandem with us."

This was music to my ears. Like Astrid's training technique, my specialist detection dog would also be expected to distinguish one-off scents. Each search would involve the recognition of a cat's unique individual odor, unlike drugs dogs, for example, who were generally exposed to the same narcotics day in, day out. With this in mind, I had a feeling that Astrid's expertise would prove to be vital.

As we wrapped up the meeting I felt like pinching myself. At last, and thanks to Anna's intervention, I'd met some brilliant people with "can-do" attitudes who'd actually bought into my idea. I had clicked with a group of pioneering professionals who were prepared to help me push boundaries and overcome hurdles in order to create something fresh and innovative.

"So, are we in agreement?" I asked somewhat cautiously.

"Yes, I think we are," replied Claire. "Let's make this happen."

Now that I'd joined forces with MDD—and had completed that "know-*how*, know-*who*" circle—it was time to make an important decision. We needed to pinpoint the ideal canine breed for our project. Over the years, I'd encountered working dogs of all descriptions, not only within the police force and the pet-detective arena but also by visiting various field trials, game shoots and county shows in the southeast region. I was forever picking the brains of owners and breeders so that I could build up a picture of my ultimate working dog, whether it was chatting to the owner of a Labrador at a Hampshire shoot or quizzing the handler of a springer spaniel at Heathrow Airport.

My research was based on a two-pronged hypothesis. Firstly, what would be the most effective and efficient dog from my perspective? Secondly—and crucially—what would be the best dog in the eyes of a missing (and possibly traumatized) cat?

As its prospective handler, and in my capacity as a pet detective, it was imperative that I found a dog that had a natural-born instinct to search. Claire had suggested the vizsla breed—a Hungarian pointer with incredible air-scenting ability—but I reckoned it would be too big; our dog needed to be small enough to squeeze itself into confined spaces. It also needed the energy

and endurance to embark upon lengthy, time-consuming assignments, which would often involve an element of travel.

Trainability was a key factor, too. If this dog was going to
be taught highly technical skills at MDD, it was essential that
it was extremely alert, intelligent and quick-witted. Personality-
wise, our ideal breed also needed to have a sociable and compli-
ant temperament in order to interact happily with different types
of people within a variety of settings and scenarios.

As regards the cat's-eye view—and without stating the blind-
ingly obvious—the last thing we needed was an overly noisy dog
or an animal that would frighten felines, prompting them to bolt
or retreat. For this reason, it was imperative that we found a quietish dog that had no previous negative experience of cats. In my
experience, any puppies that saw adult dogs growling and barking at cats would invariably copy and learn that behavior, and it
was virtually impossible to untrain that response.

To summarize, I had to consider the dog's appearance (preferably small, so as not to be overbearing or intimidating); the noise
it would make (quietish, with no inclination to bark at animals or
people when excited); and its personality (even-keeled, without
any aggressive tendencies).

"Well, that's the German shepherds, rottweilers and blood
hounds out of the running, then." Sam smiled as I weighed up
the various options in the Bramble Hill Farm office one morning.

Eventually, I managed to whittle it down to three breeds: the
Labrador, the working springer spaniel and the working cocker
spaniel. But which one would I finally plump for? As Sam did a
little drumroll, tapping her index fingers on her desk top, I made
my decision.

"It's going to be . . ." I said, then paused dramatically, like a
reality-show presenter before a big reveal, "the working cocker
spaniel."

"Excellent decision," replied my colleague, who, like me, was
a huge fan of these lively and affectionate animals.

Working cockers seemed the natural choice, and the more

I'd seen them in action, the more convinced I became that they were perfect for the role. They were compact and agile creatures with oodles of grit and stamina, epitomized by my favorite police sniffer dog, Rainbow. I had also witnessed their amazing abilities during game shoots, where I'd seen these gun dogs deftly flushing out and retrieving pheasants and partridges. There was a slight element of personal bias, too, since my sister Lynn and brother Rian had both kept cocker spaniels as pets—albeit those of the "show" variety—and I'd grown incredibly fond of them as a breed. In addition to their good looks, they were incredibly smart, very tactile and excellent problem-solvers.

"And what about gender, Colin?" asked Sam.

"Female, definitely," I responded.

As part of my research, I'd asked dozens of handlers why they'd opted for a male or a female and, generally speaking, it seemed that cocker spaniel bitches had superior longevity and fewer post-training problems than their opposite numbers. Both factors pretty much swayed my opinion.

"And tail docked, or undocked?" asked my assistant.

This practice—which involved the removal of portions of a dog's tail, sometimes for purely cosmetic reasons—had been outlawed under the Animal Welfare Act of 2006. Some exemptions still remained, however, usually appertaining to working dogs whose wagging tails might get snagged and shredded by brambles and would therefore be susceptible to injury and infection. My opinion on this was unyielding, though.

"Undocked, Sam," I said, confident that I'd never use this dog to flush out game and would never knowingly deploy her in any areas that might cause injury.

So I'd ticked off most things on my detection-dog "wants" list—working cocker spaniel, female, undocked tail—but another important stipulation remained, a prerequisite that I felt incredibly strongly about. It was a subject I broached during the first proper planning meeting at MDD, which took place in November 2015. Claire, Rob and I had been discussing the qualities of working cocker spaniels—they'd wholeheartedly agreed

with my choice of breed, thank goodness—as well as the training techniques that would be employed once we found the right
dog. We were just about to break for coffee when I decided to
drop the bombshell.

"I know this is asking a lot, guys," I said tentatively, "but when
we come to source our cat-detection dog, I'd really like her to be
a rescue."

My colleagues took a few moments to consider my neatly
pitched curveball.

"A rescue dog?" said Rob, raising an eyebrow. "Are you sure
that's a good idea?"

"I'm positive it is," I replied. "It's a matter of principle, more
than anything, and something I just feel compelled to do. Now
let me explain why . . ."

~ 6 ~

A Remarkable Rescue

My devotion to rescue dogs had taken root in the Far East. The urban streets of Malaysia and Singapore, where I'd spent my early childhood, were teeming with feral animals, most of whom spent their existence scavenging for food, scrapping with one another or seeking shade in the sweltering heat. My brother David and I were captivated by these scraggy street mutts, and would often smuggle food from the family larder, sneaking past my mother to pilfer fish and chicken leftovers. We would then dash outside to feed these titbits to the dogs, squealing with delight as they hungrily gorged every last morsel.

Every now and then, however, when the streets were completely overrun with strays, the dreaded dog van would turn up. Dozens of hounds of all shapes and sizes would be ruthlessly snatched from the street and thrown into the vehicle, never to be seen again. Witnessing these incidents would break our little hearts—especially if it involved one of our favorite dogs—so David and I would often take matters into our own hands. Whenever we learned that the "dog killers" were in town, we'd stuff our pockets with stolen snacks, using them to lure our canine chums away from danger.

"Follow us, you dozy dogs!" we'd yell, darting down narrow alleyways in our shorts and flip-flops, scattering rice balls and bacon rind behind us. I wished I could have rescued every single street stray—my desire to protect them was intense—but my parents only let David and me keep one dog, an adorable rice-colored mix-breed with wolf-like ears. We named her Honey and she became a much-loved family pet.

In the late 1960s Singaporeans and Malaysians hadn't yet embraced the concept of rehoming or rescuing an animal. If a dog was unable to serve a function—either as a guard or a herder—it was deemed surplus to requirements and was often abandoned on the streets. Once, during the monsoon season, my father and I had made a futile attempt to save a sackful of puppies from drowning in a ten-foot-deep storm drain and I vividly remember watching on, helpless, as these poor wretches were sluiced away in the flood water.

"There was nothing we could have done, Colin," said my father, as hot, angry tears rolled down my cheeks. An ardent dog-lover himself, this pitiful sight must have greatly upset him, too.

"But it's just not *fair*, Daddy!" I'd cried as he'd led me away, draping a fatherly arm around my shoulder.

I remember collapsing on to my bed when I got home and making a private, personal pledge to myself. I was going to do all I possibly could to help life's unwanted animals, both now and in the future, and would never, ever, *ever* buy a pet if I could attempt to rescue one instead.

Back at Medical Detection Dog's Milton Keynes office, I outlined my long-held, deep-rooted principles to Claire and Rob. Every single dog owned by myself or my family had been a rescue, I told them, and I had no plans to deviate from this core value. I also took the opportunity to explain to them that, through my work in the police and as a pet detective, I'd come across far too many abandoned and neglected dogs, the sight of which had never ceased to torment me. On the flip side, I'd also encountered dozens of wonderful animal shelters and rescue centers who were devoted to rehoming unwanted animals and I was forever committed to their cause.

"I appreciate that this has probably come as a fly in your

ointment, guys," I said, "but I hope you understand where I'm coming from."

"Oh, totally, Colin, and I can't really argue with your sentiments," replied Rob. "I'm more than happy to go down the rescue route," he added, "but it might make our search for the right dog a lot longer, and a lot riskier. But, hey, let's give it a go."

Rob and I duly set ourselves to the task. He contacted his many friends and associates within the dog world and I put the feelers out, too, liaising with animal shelters and speaking with former UKPD clients to ask if they knew of any suitable canine candidates. One such person—a woman whose stolen dog I'd recovered in Farnham—alerted me to Willow, an eleven-month-old working cocker spaniel living in Scotland whose family could no longer look after her. The dog's details were scant but encouraging; by all accounts, she was fit, friendly and had no discernible issues with cats.

By sheer good fortune, Rob happened to be traveling north of the border that same week and agreed to call in on Willow. Any high hopes I'd had were dashed, however, when he debriefed me over the phone.

"I'm sorry, Colin," he sighed, "but she's not the one you're looking for."

Rob explained how, as soon as he'd walked through the front door, poor Willow had run off in the opposite direction before cowering under the kitchen table. Despite his efforts to coax her out, the timid little thing had refused to move a muscle.

"We need the kind of dog that tries to climb on top of a table, Rob, not hide underneath it," I said, while sadly crossing Willow off the list.

Our quest continued apace, but with zero success. Over a period of twelve weeks Rob and I assessed half a dozen other rescue spaniels, most of whom showed serious potential on paper but none of whom cut the mustard in reality. Either they displayed the wrong temperament—too shy, too snappy or too lazy—or they were too hostile toward cats and other animals.

As time marched on, I began to seriously doubt my own judgment. My precious project—in which I'd invested so much time, thought and effort—seemed to have reached a dead end.

"Going down the rescue-dog route doesn't seem to be working," I lamented to Sarah one evening, having returned home from yet another fruitless dog visit. "To be fair, Rob warned me that it wouldn't be easy. Perhaps it's time for me to get real and broaden my options a bit."

"Maybe you're right," she replied, momentarily looking up from her *Marie Claire*. "If you're not careful, Colin, you could be waiting forever."

I hastily convened a meeting with Claire and Rob, at which I suggested—albeit reluctantly—that we should probably extend our search to include reputable breeders. If necessary, the small budget I'd allocated to the project could be used to secure the right dog, even if she wasn't the rescue that I'd pinned my hopes upon.

Within a couple of days, Rob had received a tip-off about Sasha, a beautiful light tan bitch whose Carlisle-based breeder had a surplus of working cocker spaniels. Unlike our previous candidates, she'd sailed through the preliminary assessment, and the next course of action was an intensive, week-long aptitude test. All the signs pointed toward Sasha being our perfect dog, and I was incredibly excited.

I arrived at MDD's headquarters the following Monday—the scheduled start of the trial—only to be greeted at the entrance by an ashen-faced Rob.

"Bad news," he said. "Sasha's not coming."

Her owner had withdrawn her at the eleventh hour, citing a chronic car-sickness problem that she'd "forgotten" to mention. I very much doubted that this was the genuine reason, though; I strongly suspected that the breeder had either secured a better price for her dog or had told a fib about Sasha's history that she feared was about to be exposed.

We were back to square one, and I felt utterly devastated. I wasn't going to give in, though, and was more determined than ever to succeed. Having run my own businesses for over a decade and managed a plethora of projects, I'd learned to expect hold-ups and setbacks as par for the course. Experience had taught me that seeing an important mission through to a fruitful out-come was simply an application of effort.

Later that day I went for a long walk around the farm, just to clear my head and recharge my enthusiasm.

There HAS to be a dog out there, I remember thinking to my-self as I wandered along the canal tow path. *It's simply a case of finding her.*

A few weeks later, while I was searching for a missing Labrador in the New Forest, my phone rang. It was Rob, sounding a little more upbeat than he had of late.

"Quick question, Colin . . . you've not totally given up on the rescue-dog idea, have you?"

"No, of course not. That was always Plan A, Rob."

"It's just that I've been online and I've seen a dog that I really like the look of."

"Whereabouts online?"

"Gumtree."

"*Gumtree?!*"

Over the years, the buying and selling website had become a popular online marketplace for dogs and an associate of Rob's had alerted him to a black working cocker spaniel bitch being ad-vertised as a giveaway. Aged around ten months, she'd had three owners in her short life, all of whom had apparently struggled to cope with her unruly and uncontrollable behavior. It was a stressed-out single mother in the East Midlands who had finally reached the end of her tether and had posted on the Gumtree website.

NEEDS A GOOD HOME, the advert had succinctly stated. OWNER CANNOT COPE.

"Now, forgive me for sounding negative, Rob, but—"

"Colin, I know exactly what you're going to say. This dog

sounds like trouble. But just bear with me on this one. I'm driving up this afternoon to see her, and I'll ring you later."

"What's her name?"

"Molly. Her name's Molly."

Molly. The same name as my friend Anna's dearly departed dog. *That's a good omen,* I thought to myself, comforted by the fact that fellow dog-lovers often experienced these spiritual, serendipitous connections.

"Right, first the bad news," said Rob, when, as promised, he called me with an update. My shoulders sagged as I braced myself for yet more disappointment.

"Molly's very, very demanding. She's been badly deprived of love and affection. She suffers from terrible separation anxiety. She barks like crazy when she's frustrated. She steals food from people's plates and pinches treats from their pocket. And she's one of the most willful, wayward and stubborn dogs I've ever met."

"And the good news?" I replied despondently.

"I reckon we've found our dog, Colin."

I rarely found myself lost for words but, on this occasion, I was stunned into silence.

"Yep, you heard me correctly," said Rob, laughing. "Molly's amazing. Sharp as a tack. Bags of energy. Brimming with confidence. She's exactly what we're looking for."

I slowly rubbed my forehead, trying to absorb Rob's glad tidings.

"Don't get me wrong, Colin, she's a dog who'd need an incredible amount of training, but I honestly think she could be perfect for the role."

"This is the best news I've had in ages," I said, allowing myself a little smile.

"But there's one thing I need to run past you," Rob added, "and it's something I've thought about long and hard. If we do take Molly off Gumtree and bring her to MDD, I think it's only right that you agree to adopt her once her training's finished, and that would have to be regardless of the outcome, Colin, or her suitability for the role."

"Okay," I said, my mind whirring as I collected my thoughts and processed this unexpected development. It sounded like poor Molly had experienced a wretched start to life, and casting her aside for failing to make the grade would be pretty heartless. Adopting her "blind" would be a risky decision, considering everything Rob had just said about her—there were certainly no guarantees that we'd be well suited—but it was one that I was prepared to make. I had spent much of my adulthood offering sanctuary to "problem" pets with troubled pasts and was quite sure that, with all the love and care that I could muster, I'd be able to give Molly the stable home she craved, regardless of whether or not she became my cat-detection dog. The decision was, as they say, a no-brainer.

"Sure, I'll take her on," I said, visualizing myself and Sarah living in a menagerie of adopted spaniels, none of which had the ability to find lost cats.

Rob secured Molly's ownership, sorted out the paperwork and arranged for her to be transferred to the MDD center. Since my home in West Sussex was two and a half hours away—too distant for a daily commute, particularly with a dog in tow— Molly was to be placed with a local foster family. I had been pleased and reassured to discover that the charity's strict no-kennel policy meant that all dogs in training were temporarily accommodated in a loving home; this would encourage them to feel as safe and as secure as possible, which would ultimately aid the whole process.

"While we don't know a lot about Molly's history, the fact that she's had numerous owners is bound to have had an impact on her wellbeing," said Rob, "so it's really important that she feels happy, settled and wanted."

These foster families, I learned, were highly experienced canine-carers who approached their role with great professionalism. They realized from the outset that the placement was temporary—it could be weeks or months, depending on the duration of the training program—and they closely adhered to the guidance and direction given to them by MDD. While they were expected to offer a high standard of care and attention, the foster families were discouraged from forging close bonds with these working dogs, in view of the fact that they would subsequently be handed over to a permanent owner, or primary handler. I gathered that many of the carers were MDD employees who enjoyed the benefits of having a dog in the evenings and weekends while being able to drop them off at the training center during the day.

I would make arrangements for a visit to Milton Keynes once Molly had settled in at MDD and had ensconced herself with the foster family. In the meantime, Rob emailed me a digital photograph of her that he'd taken during their first encounter. Sporting a mop of unkempt, shaggy black hair and aiming a moody, defiant stare at the camera lens, I couldn't help but chuckle when I clicked on to it.

"Have you seen this?" I grinned when I showed Sarah the photo later that evening. "She looks like a member of Black Sabbath."

"Bit scruffy, though, isn't she?" she replied, raising her eyebrows.

Tellingly, perhaps, I immediately set Molly's photo as my phone's screensaver. Whenever I caught myself looking at it, or whenever I showed it to friends and family, I felt all tingly and warm inside. This dog gave me good vibes and I could hardly wait to meet her.

When I first clapped eyes on Molly she was careering around the grounds of Medical Detection Dogs HQ, catching tennis balls that staff members were launching from various directions. The way she sprinted, crouched and leaped to ensnare those furry lime-green orbs was a joy to behold and, without even knowing this dog, I already felt a distinct sense of pride.

"Just look at her ability to focus, Colin. It's phenomenal," said Rob, who, like me, had been admiring her from afar. "And as for her energy levels . . . well, they're off the scale."

Half an hour later he was ushering me into a nearby Porta-kabin, where I'd finally be meeting Molly face to face. Unusually for me, I was beset with nerves—I felt like I was attending a final interview for a high-powered job—and as the minutes ticked by my head began to pound and my heart began to thump. Molly and I *had* to feel some kind of connection, otherwise things were in danger of going horribly awry.

Suddenly, the door creaked open and Molly shot into the room, trailed by Rob's colleague, Astrid, who'd recently returned from her German assignment. I was immediately struck by the dog's bright, sparkly eyes and by the self-assured way she stuck her shiny black nose in the air. She had clearly had a decent groom since the Black Sabbath photo—her coat was clipped, combed and glossy—and she looked a picture of health and happiness.

"This is one *fantastic* animal, Colin," remarked Astrid in Spanish-accented English. It emerged that she'd already spent some time with Molly, performing a few simple exercises in the training lab, and had already become smitten.

"Do let me know if you ever change your mind about adopting her," she winked, "because I'd gladly take her off your hands."

Molly then began to scoot around the cabin, sniffing each dusty corner, sussing every inch of space, sizing up every human. When she finally caught sight of me, perched tentatively on an office chair, she paused for a moment and tilted her head curiously.

Who are you, *then, mister?* she seemed to be saying. *Why are you here? What exactly are you going to bring to my world, huh?*

"Hey, just look at that, Colin." Rob smiled. "I do believe Molly's weighing you up."

I purposely didn't call her across or crouch down to say hello. I knew how perceptive dogs could be about human behavior and I didn't want to transfer any feelings of unease or apprehension.

Instead, I just stayed put, remained objective and held her gaze, while a multitude of thoughts swirled around my head.

Well, well, young lady, I mused. *What are you thinking? D'you reckon we can work together? Are you ready for a fabulous journey?*

Rob and Astrid were highly amused at this mutual sussing-out.

"I'm not sure which one of you is going to make the first move, here," chortled the Chilean. "It's like watching a Mexican stand-off."

As it happened, it was Molly who broke the stalemate. She slowly sidled over to me, gently nudged the side of my thigh with her snout and, much to my amazement, deftly sprang into my lap.

Yeah, I think I like the look of this fella, seemed to be the gist of it. She shuffled her bottom into a more comfortable position. *I reckon I can work with this guy . . .*

I nuzzled in close, ruffled her neck and looked across at Rob and Astrid, who were beaming like a pair of proud parents.

"I think Molly's made up her mind," I said, smiling, as she moved around to face the two of them. "And I reckon I have, too."

I finally had my dog—I just knew she was The One—and the feeling of relief was intense. It had been a long, hard slog to get this far, and it had left me feeling emotionally exhausted. During the previous two years barely a day had passed that I hadn't thought about my project, and my obsession had exacted a heavy toll on my business and on my home life. Some of my private-eye clients had closed their accounts, complaining that they'd been unable to get hold of me. Also, there'd been countless weekends when Sarah had been left home alone while I'd met with various canine experts. On many occasions I'd returned to Cranleigh feeling incredibly grouchy, having been told by yet another person that my idea didn't measure up. To her credit, Sarah had been incredibly supportive, patiently listening to all my gripes and grumbles.

The day I met Molly, however, I returned home brimming with glee.

"You'll never guess what, Sarah, but I've found my dog," I grinned, hugging her close and planting a big kiss on her cheek. "The search is finally over. Molly's absolutely amazing and, all being well, one day she'll be here with us . . ."

"That's great. I'm *so* pleased," my partner replied, not entirely convincingly.

That night, I made a point of phoning Anna. She had been closely following my progress and knew all about the trials and tribulations I'd faced. I also felt that I owed my friend a great deal, since she had introduced me to Claire and Rob in the first place.

"You won't believe it, Anna," I said. "Molly is just perfect. Beyond my wildest dreams, in fact."

"I'm so thrilled for you, Colin," she replied. "And I know MDD will do a marvelous job with her. There's no way they'd agree to train up Molly if they didn't think she was the right dog."

For the next half an hour we chatted all things Molly, focusing particularly on her health and wellbeing. Anna's expertise in this regard was second to none, and she offered me so much invaluable advice and guidance, regarding the right nutrition for working dogs, for example, and dealing with canine separation anxiety. By the time I'd hung up I'd amassed a long list of the things that I needed to consider and all the topics I needed to familiarize myself with.

At last, I thought, leaning back in my office chair. *We're finally getting somewhere . . .*

For the duration of her training—the projected timescale was six months—Molly would remain at MDD in Milton Keynes and continue living with her foster family in the evenings and at weekends. Under the expert guidance of Rob and Astrid, she would be taught how to scent-match through exposure to a host of different odors and would learn how to discriminate between them. As for me, I was allowed to visit Molly regularly to observe her in action, after which Rob would give me a progress report. I would also get the chance to spend some quality time with her—lots of walks, chats and tennis-ball action—in order to get to know my dog better.

Molly performed brilliantly at MDD and adapted beautifully to her training program, yet within a few months she began to develop some worrying behavioral issues away from the HQ. Since her arrival, Molly had become very close to Astrid (perhaps too close, I'd noted) and, it transpired, had suffered severe separation anxiety when the Chilean had left the charity to pursue other projects. While the MDD experts were able to manage Molly's fretfulness at the center, her foster carers faced enormous problems at home. Being a very willful dog, she'd started to bend rules and take liberties—jumping on the sofa, pinching food off tables and ignoring commands—and was effectively displaying the same disobedience that had driven her previous owner to Gumtree. This regression, we all realized, needed to be curbed before it jeopardized the whole project.

"There's no way a badly behaved, ill-disciplined Molly will be able to work in the field," I said to Rob. "This needs to be nipped in the bud. And sharpish."

A canine behavioral expert who worked for MDD on a contractual basis—the aptly named Mark Doggett—was drafted in to correct Molly's conduct and, in order to restore some balance to her life, she was transferred from the foster home to Mark's full-time care. She would reside in his house in the West Midlands with his two pet dogs, where she'd be taught to adapt her behavior and to adhere to strict boundaries, far away from any distractions. As regards her scent-match training, Mark—under the guidance of MDD—would continue this regimen away from the center, essentially building upon the excellent foundations already laid by Rob and Astrid.

This intensive one-to-one therapy would last for at least three months, which meant that the final handover—when Molly was due to join me permanently—would have to be postponed.

While I was deeply disappointed at this development, I agreed that it was the correct thing to do and was prepared to remain patient. I'd waited so long for this project to materialize and I was in no rush to get it wrong.

Molly's transferral to another carer was far from ideal, but when I watched Mark interacting with her for the first time I was convinced that she was in safe hands. Not only did he have a brilliant understanding of Molly, he also had a massively calming effect upon her and I could see exactly why MDD had decided to assign him to this role.

Mark also encouraged me to pay regular visits to his Birmingham home (I'd often drop by after a progress meeting with Claire and Rob) and he was more than happy for me to take Molly off for a long walk, just the two of us, man and dog. I savored every moment we spent together, and found each goodbye incredibly difficult.

Initially, Mark's progress with Molly seemed slow-going and his weekly reports appeared to identify a litany of problems.

"What I'm trying to do is pinpoint the issues that are stimulating Molly's disobedience so that I can address her negative behavior," he told me during one phone conversation, explaining that he was employing a rewards-based system in order to encourage her to act in a positive manner. For instance, during play sessions with Mark's pet dogs, Molly would be ordered to wait her turn, something that she found very difficult. However, if she did as she was told and curbed her friskiness and impatience, she'd be rewarded with some tennis-ball-related fun and games.

Indoor rules and regulations were paramount, too, in order to restore some decorum and discipline to her behavior. She wasn't allowed in the master bedroom or upstairs, for example, or in the kitchen when food was being eaten or prepared.

Fortunately, by month two, Mark confirmed that my little cocker spaniel was finally making fantastic headway; she was responding well to her behavioral training, and—much to my relief—was continuing to achieve excellent results with her scent-matching sessions.

This breakthrough meant that Claire and Rob at MDD were happy to set a date for the big handover: Friday, 23 December 2016. However, before I could bring Molly home for good, we were both required to undergo a fortnight's intensive training together in Milton Keynes. It was literally a pass-or-fail fortnight, certainly not a case of "Now you're trained, off you go . . ." Unless Molly and I could prove that we could work as an effective unit, the MDD seal of approval wouldn't be bestowed on us and, as a result, my project would be in jeopardy.

During this crucial two-week period we spent a great deal of time in various locations near the training center, starting at nine o'clock prompt every morning. Mark or Rob carefully demonstrated Molly's intricate odor-detecting techniques and, in addition, taught me how to lay on simulated searches by concealing different scent samples in a variety of outdoor environments. Each task became progressively more complex; early in the fortnight we'd asked Molly to detect a single scent sample in a small garden, for example, but toward the end of the itinerary we'd hidden the target scent in a large farmyard, together with two contrasting samples that Molly had to disregard. She completed every task with ease and, as she heeded my commands with aplomb, I felt my own confidence levels soaring. It wasn't just Molly that was being tested, after all; I was being constantly watched and assessed.

"Where did you think you went wrong that time, Colin?" Mark would ask, peering over my shoulder. It was all incredibly intense.

Following each training session—and while Molly enjoyed a well-deserved breather—I'd sit down with Rob or Mark to go through some theory. They would share their expertise and bolster my knowledge, explaining how scent profiles could be impacted by meteorology and topography, for example, or outlining the intricacies of a working cocker spaniel's olfactory system. We covered a wide range of topics, including the correct use of voice tone during searches, the application of certain types of play and the benefits of implementing a rewards system.

As the fortnight progressed, and as Molly began to realize that this Colin fella was going to play a significant role in her life, my detection-dog-in-waiting and I became even closer. The MDD team were extremely heartened by the deep bond we'd forged—our mutual affection was there for all to see—and they were delighted to witness us working in harmony. It felt like Molly and I had been buddied up like a traditional detective duo—think Cagney and Lacey, or Morse and Lewis—and everyone was thrilled to see my sidekick and me hitting it off so well.

"Your teamwork is outstanding, Colin," said Mark, as we drove to a nearby wood one morning for yet another practice session, while Molly sat in her dog crate, champing at the bit. "Having that deep understanding of each other was always going to be key, but from what I can see, you've both cracked it."

At the end of each training day Molly and I would travel to my parents' home in the Cotswolds, which was only forty minutes' drive from the center. They had agreed to let me stay with them during the fortnight—from Monday to Friday—and were particularly keen to meet the latest addition to the Butcher household.

Wow, this is exciting! Molly seemed to say, as we drove away from Milton Keynes following our first full day together at MDD. *Where are we going? Who are we meeting?*

As I'd expected, Molly turned on the charm with my parents, but they knew a challenging dog when they saw one.

"Goodness, she's got plenty of energy, hasn't she?" remarked my mother, with admirable understatement, while Molly bounced off the kitchen cupboards and surfaces in hot pursuit of a brand-new tennis ball. "Does Sarah know what she's let herself in for?"

"Sure," I said, smiling nervously.

By the end of the first week, my parents were exhausted—Molly had struggled with the change of environment and had proved to be rather high-maintenance—and their kitchen floor was carpeted with black dog hair. Being devoted animal-lovers themselves, however, they didn't care one jot.

Halfway through our training fortnight, on a bitterly cold Friday evening, I brought Molly home to Cranleigh for the first time. Prior to her arrival, I'd made a number of essential adaptations in the house in order to make it as dog-friendly as possible. I converted our downstairs utility room into Molly's own little den, a place where she could retreat for some peace, quiet and solitude. Then, despite Sarah's resistance ("Surely it only needs *one* place to sleep, Colin?"), I placed a selection of deluxe dog beds in the warmest parts of the house. I also ordered in plenty of Molly's favorite foodstuffs (including treats of raw black pudding, raw beef jerky, hot-dog sausages and Cheddar cheese) and, after a visit to my local pet store, I topped up my supply of dog toys and playthings.

Keen to devote as much time as possible to Molly while she settled in, I'd carefully adjusted my work routine, too, canceling all appointments or investigations that required me to be away from home for more than a few hours. Also, I chose not to book a foreign holiday for a period of six months, since I was loath to be parted from Molly at this vital stage in her life. That went down like a lead balloon with Sarah, who, for the previous four years, had spent most of February relaxing by my side at our friend's East Caribbean villa.

Suffice to say that my girlfriend wasn't overly impressed when she arrived home from work that Friday night in December. Molly and I had spent the whole day conducting training searches in the Buckinghamshire countryside, wading through streams and crawling under hedges, and had both ended up decidedly wet and whiffy. I was in the process of cramming the clammy contents of my holdall into the washing machine when I heard Sarah's key turning in the lock and her stilettos tip-tapping down the hallway.

"Oh my god, this place *reeks!*" she exclaimed, standing in the kitchen doorway, looking pristine in a navy-blue business suit and cream blouse.

"Hi, sweetheart." I grinned and gestured toward a mud-spattered Molly, who was spread-eagled across my raincoat. "Look who's here!"

I walked over to peck my girlfriend's cheek, only for her to recoil in horror.

"Look at the state of you both!" she shrieked. "You're absolutely covered in muck. And please . . . what the *heck* is that smell?"

"It's just wet dog, darling. It'll vanish once Molly dries out, I promise."

"That thing needs a bloody bath. It stinks," she said, glaring at Molly, and then at me. "And so do you."

She placed her leather handbag on a kitchen chair before turning around to hang up her jacket. Quick as a flash, my mischievous mutt stuffed her wet snout into the bag and proceeded to rummage around, dragging out a purse and a packet of tissues. She settled on the latter and began to shred its contents gleefully.

"I thought you said this dog was trained?" yelled my horrified girlfriend, swiping her bag off the chair.

"She's just a bit inquisitive, that's all," I answered meekly, as Sarah flounced out of the kitchen, slamming the door behind her.

Molly cocked her head to one side before blinking at me with woeful eyes.

What did I do wrong? Why doesn't that lady like me?

"Don't you worry, Molls," I whispered, retrieving the drool-soaked tissues. "This is all new to Sarah. It's nothing personal. She just needs a bit of time to get used to you. But here's one piece of advice: steer clear of ladies' handbags, eh?"

I patted her head affectionately and she snuffled my palm in return.

"Anyway, missy, let's get you in the bath." I said. "Sarah's right. You *do* stink."

I hardly got any rest that night. Molly whined constantly when-ever I tried to pad back to my bedroom for some sleep, and she seemed very tense and anxious. The MDD team had already briefed me on what to expect, advising me to give my dog plenty of love—and lots of latitude—as she slowly acclimatized to her new environment.

"Allow her to bond to you, Colin, because she's desperate to do so," said Rob. "Do whatever it takes to make her feel safe and secure."

I ended up dragging a duvet to Molly's den so that I could stay with her throughout the night. I lay quietly beside her bed, calming and comforting her until she curled herself up and closed her eyes.

The following week I was finally allowed to bring Molly home on a permanent basis. She and I had passed our two-week test with flying colors—at times it had felt as rigorous as my Royal Navy air-crew training—and she was good and ready to be trans-ferred to my care. MDD was bustling with Christmas spirit—it happened to be their annual work party that afternoon—and Molly and me were met with a sea of smiles (and a trickle of tears) as we bid a fond farewell to all the staff, who showered Molly with dog treats and me with mince pies. My dog stuck to my heel the whole time, like a clingy toddler.

I'm not leaving your side, Dad, she seemed to be implying. *I'm going nowhere . . .*

We then made a detour to Claire's office. She had, of course, played an integral role from start to finish, enabling the whole project to take place at her busy center and allowing me to work with her incredible in-house team. She had been instrumental in connecting me with Astrid, too; this pioneering scent-matching expert had been absolutely pivotal to Molly's unique training program, painstakingly applying the same scientific techniques to a working cocker spaniel that she'd used with the German police force's sniffer dogs.

"It's been a total privilege to play my part, Colin," beamed Claire, "and suffice to say, you've got an extraordinarily special dog on your hands."

As she said this, Molly held out her paw for Claire to shake, and I'm pretty sure I noticed my colleague blink away a tear.

"Goodbye, Molly." She smiled as we exited her office. "I wish you all the luck in the world."

Back outside, I spotted Rob and Mark chatting beside the huge training field which, over the past nine months, had become Molly's favorite playground. They both waved when they saw us ambling over and laughed as they watched Molly vanish under a nearby hedge, reappearing with a moldy old tennis ball between her gnashers.

"Whenever I watch Wimbledon, I'll always think of you, Molly," grinned Rob, gazing at her with a mixture of pride and affection, while I stood there with a lump in my throat.

"You guys have been fantastic," I said, embracing them both while manfully attempting to disguise the tremor in my voice. "You've gone above and beyond, you really have, and there's no way I could have done this without you."

Their combined knowledge and experience had propelled this project forward, and I would be forever in their debt.

"You've got yourself an exceptional dog there," replied Mark, crouching down low to give Molly a heartfelt hug. "She's one in a million."

"Thanks for believing in us, Colin," added Rob. "It's been a pleasure working with you both."

A few minutes later I was driving out of the car park and, as I took a long look at this fantastic center of excellence, I found myself casting my mind back to the events of the previous spring. Molly and I had arrived here separately, unsure where the future was going to take us, and now we were leaving as a team, embarking on an amazing adventure together.

My car phone was abuzz with well-wishers during the journey back to Cranleigh, whether it was Sam calling from the UKPD office, my father ringing from the Cotswolds, or my son, Sam, ringing from his student digs in Manchester. So many friends and relatives had been following Molly's progress and they were all thrilled to learn that she'd graduated with honors and was coming home.

As we passed through the Chiltern Hills, Sarah rang to finalize arrangements for our Christmas break. We had made plans to join my parents and siblings (and their assorted spaniels) at a wonderful dog-friendly hotel, the Lygon Arms in rural Worcestershire.

"I've started to gather Molly's things together in the hallway," she said, "but if you think we're traveling in *my* car with all that dog hair, you're very much mistaken."

Using my dog's forename instead of "it" was a promising development, I reckoned, but I was under no illusions: Sarah still needed a lot of winning over.

As the skies began to darken, I hit some holiday traffic and the car ground to a standstill. With no imminent sign of movement, I switched off the engine, peered into my rear-view mirror and began to talk to Molly. I chatted to her for a good twenty minutes as she stared at me through the back panel of her travel crate, her tail occasionally whacking against the sides.

I told her how much she was going to enjoy Christmas in the Cotswolds, and how the whole Butcher family was so looking forward to meeting her. I told her that, once New Year was upon us, I'd be taking her over to Pet Detectives HQ—to the lovely Bramble Hill Farm—where she'd be able to play in the meadows, frolic through the woods and practice lots and lots of searches. And while we waited for the traffic to subside, I told her about some of the dogs I'd known and loved in my life:

the street strays of Singapore; the cat-seeking Gemini; my best buddy, Tina; and latterly the much-missed Tess, Max and Jay.

"But now I've got *you*." I smiled, gazing at Molly's reflection in the mirror as she attentively cocked her head to one side. "You've worked so hard, my gorgeous girl, and you've made me so very, very proud. And just think . . . in a few weeks' time we might have found our first missing cat. How *amazing* would that be?"

Boof-boof-boof-boof went her tail against her crate, like some sort of doggy Morse code.

A few moments later the cars began moving and our journey south continued. Molly and I were homeward bound.

7

Skills and Drills at Bramble Hill

Having Molly home for good was the best feeling in the world. We had spent an idyllic Christmas at the Lygon Arms—my dog had been feted and fussed by staff, guests and the entire Butcher family and had coped remarkably well with the attention—but it was with a certain sense of relief that, on New Year's Day, I unlatched my front door in Cranleigh. With the festivities nearly over, it was time to devote some serious one-to-one attention to my new little housemate.

"Home, sweet home, Molls," I said as she loped off down the hallway, snuffling the skirting boards.

"Don't let her mark the walls, Colin," said Sarah coolly, before heading to the bedroom to unpack her suitcase. "Oh, and her feet need wiping."

"Molly has *paws*, honey, not feet," I replied.

"Well, whatever they are, they need cleaning or else she'll dirty the carpet."

I glanced at my forlorn-looking dog, who had clearly sensed Sarah's antipathy.

I wiped my paws on the way in, Dad . . . she seemed to be saying. *I am* trying, *I promise . . .*

Also accompanying us that day was my twenty-year-old son Sam, who'd opted to spend the final week of his holiday with me before heading back to Manchester University. He had first met Molly at Medical Detection Dogs the previous autumn—it had been love at first sight—and he was more than willing to stick around to help her settle in. December had been a disruptive month for my little cocker spaniel (she'd traveled between three shires, had stayed in many different places and had met countless new faces) and it was time for her to obtain some much-needed stability.

Sarah returned to work—she was palpably relieved to escape the Molly-related mayhem—and Sam and I stayed at home to help our dog acclimatize. My son was an absolute godsend, as it happened, and spent much of the week chatting to her in the kitchen or playing catch in the garden, alleviating her angst and helping to make her feel as safe and secure as possible. He and I had been devoted to our pets down the years—"Care first for those who can't care for themselves" had been a long-standing fatherly mantra of mine—and I was so pleased to see that my love of animals had rubbed off on him, too.

Molly was loath to leave my side in those first few days, which, considering the upheaval she'd suffered, was hardly unexpected. As a rescue dog who'd had a string of owners—followed by a long spell at MDD—separation anxiety was the likeliest of consequences. There were various manifestations of this insecurity, I discovered. When I greeted her in the morning, for example, she'd respond by nibbling the inside of my palm, like a puppy nursing her mother, which was her way of keeping me close and reinforcing our bond. By allowing her to do this, I was effectively letting her know that I'd always be there for her and, unlike her previous owners, would never abandon her.

I found that she constantly followed me around the house, too, nervily jumping up whenever I tried to leave a room and, moments later, suddenly appearing at my heel. All I could do at this stage was try and pacify her. I would crouch down low, avoiding any unexpected movements, and would stroke rather than hug her (like many dogs, she didn't like the feeling of being smothered).

"Molly, sweetheart, I'm just going to the hallway to pick up some post," I'd say, sotto voce. "I'll be back in two shakes of your tail, I promise."

She would invariably pad after me, though, her expression lovelorn, and for that first fortnight I just went with the flow and let her follow me around. Thereafter, however, I spent a lot of time training Molly to understand that my exiting a room wasn't a negative act. If I planned to pop out of my home office to make a coffee, for example—and Molly was lying yards away in her bed—I'd quietly attract her attention, telling her to "stay" and rewarding her with a couple of small treats before I slowly opened the door. Within a few days the penny dropped and her stalking behavior dissipated. She soon realized that I wasn't leaving her forever and that she could count on my return. To help her feel close to me at all times, I draped each of her beds with one of my fleeces or sweatshirts, too, confident that my unique scent "signature" would create a sense of comfort.

Fundamentally, our future success as a partnership—either as pet and owner, or as fellow sleuths—would rely on Molly investing her trust in me and understanding that I wasn't going to let her down. I didn't know much about Molly's history, but I knew enough about dogs to realize that she still felt vulnerable and that she was emotionally scarred by some bad memories. If I noticed her flinching at a sudden movement in the kitchen, for instance, or shuddering as the garage door slammed shut, I'd get in close and offer her reassurance. I could only assume that someone had once lashed out at her or had locked her away in an outhouse.

"It's okay," I'd whisper softly, gently cradling her head in my palms. "You're safe with me, Molly, and I'll always be here for you. Always."

Having had previous experience of rescue animals, I knew that, while dogs tended to live "in the moment," in some cases it could take a long time for a mistreated animal to erase painful experiences. The best way to manage that situation was, I'd found, to provide my dogs with unlimited, unconditional love and affection, layering on those good memories in order to stifle the bad.

I also introduced regular indoor play sessions to keep her

occupied, heeding Mark's advice to split her toys into two boxes. Box One contained Molly's comfort toys, which she was allowed to keep by her bed and which she could play with at all times (she became particularly fond of a squeaky rat, which she'd drag around the house). Box Two contained Colin's toys, however, and was kept on top of the fridge-freezer, well out of Molly's reach. These playthings could only be used on my terms and my dog was under strict instructions not to keep them, run away with them or rough them up. She would often sit in the kitchen and whine plaintively in their direction, but I had to stand firm.

"It's about instilling discipline," I remember Mark telling me. "Molly's a very headstrong dog and she's got to understand what's off limits."

While she'd been at MDD, Mark had taught Molly a long list of unique dog commands—some for day-to-day usage, some work-related—that my son Sam and I were obliged to learn and deploy. Indeed, Mark had customized a whole new lexicon for her, in an attempt to address the disobedience that she'd shown at her foster carers' home. There, she'd blatantly ignored standard instructions like "Sit" and "Down"—she'd willfully done the opposite—and had also developed a worrying aversion to the word "No." The latter had no doubt arisen from her carers' flexible discipline techniques, coupled with the fact that this sneaky little pooch had learned how to soft-soap them.

Her carers had admonished her with a sharp "No" whenever she'd jumped up to pinch a Hobnob off a plate, for instance, but after five minutes' worth of pawing and whining they'd acquiesced and offered up the biscuit as a treat. Naturally, Molly soon began to associate this purportedly negative command with a positive outcome; to her, "No" essentially meant "Yes."

Prior to the big handover, therefore, Mark had decided to reconfigure Molly's entire command system by embedding a brand-new set of words and erasing a legion of others. So "No" was replaced with "Ah-ah"; "Sit" became "Stay"; "Hup" denoted

"Jump up here"; and "Off" meant all four paws on the ground. He'd also tailored some working commands, too, designed to be used during field drills and real-life searches.

Sam and I spent hours practicing these new words and phrases with Molly.

"Ah-ah," I'd say, wagging my finger as she jumped on to a chair, and she would meekly sit back down when she realized I meant business.

I was frequently on the phone to Mark in those early days, since I was keen to understand Molly's various habits and behaviors. This included a trait she'd developed indoors, shortly after Sam had returned to university. Most evenings would find Sarah and me chilling out in the living room, either reading, watching a film or catching up with emails. Once we'd settled ourselves on to the sofa, though, Molly would detect that the focus had shifted away from her. Affronted, she took to repetitively pacing around the house, embarking upon a two-minute circuit that took her around the back of the sofa, along the living room wall, around the dining-room table, past the large bookcase, in front of the TV, along the fireplace, behind Sarah's chair and then finally back to me again.

Molly would perform about twenty laps, negotiating corners like a canine Lewis Hamilton, until she became so puffed out she would flop into her bed. Once she regained her breath, however, she'd start the circuit all over again and, despite my efforts, couldn't be placated or distracted.

"How the heck am I supposed to concentrate on this film?" griped Sarah one Saturday evening, as a panting Molly obstructed the TV screen for the fifteenth time. "It's driving me insane, Colin. Can't you do something about it?"

My suggestion to mount the television on the wall was met with an icy stare.

"Okay," I said meekly. "I get the message. Leave it with me."

The following Monday I rang the Mark Doggett hotline.

"Molly's definitely attention-seeking—and she may well be missing Sam, too—but there are ways you can break this Grand

Prix circuit," said my canine-behavior mentor, before outlining a strict plan of action.

For the next few nights, instead of sitting on the sofa—where she'd circle me like the Native Americans around General Custer—I'd sit reading my book with my back against the living room radiator or against the dining-room wall. My outstretched legs immediately presented her with a physical obstacle that interrupted her flow, threw her off kilter and allowed me to divert her attention with a toy for a couple of minutes. Mark's advice to hide her favorite beef-jerky snacks along her "course" to break her repetitive behavior worked a treat, too. She would soon become distracted by the scent, try to locate the snack and, when she succeeded, she'd receive a serious fussing from yours truly. Soon enough, the intensity of the circuits slowed down and they eventually came to a halt.

"Thank heavens for that," sighed Sarah with some relief one night, having finally watched an entire movie, uninterrupted, for the first time in weeks.

If I was going to keep a strong-willed dog like Molly in check, I needed to establish some rigid house rules. I knew I'd only be asking for trouble if I didn't lay down the law and set some parameters.

After much contemplation, and after consulting with Mark, I decided to give her freedom to move around most of the house, with a couple of no-go areas. She wasn't allowed to enter either of our two bathrooms—unless I was giving her a post-walk bath—and she was also forbidden from entering the master and the guest bedroom. I spent hours training her to recognize these particular boundaries, and even made them more conspicuous by covering the metal carpet thresholds with two widths of silver-gray gaffer tape.

"Ah-ah, Moll-yyyy . . ." I'd say if she ever attempted to trespass. "*Ah-aaaah.*"

Molly being Molly, though, she would constantly—and quite

literally—try to cross the line. Sometimes I'd spot her lolling in the hallway on the legit side of the gaffer tape, a meter or so away from our bedroom. Then, when she thought I wasn't looking, she'd slowly outstretch her paw so that it touched Checkpoint Colin and, bit by bit, shuffle her body forward.

"Moll-yyyyy," I'd scold, and she'd retract her paw immediately, like it was attached to a spring. Then, moments later, out of the corner of my eye, I'd spy her long black snout edging toward the threshold.

"*MOLL-YYYY . . .*"

It was a constant battle of wills between Molly and me, and sometimes it took a gargantuan effort to maintain the upper hand. Watching her perpetually testing these boundaries was highly entertaining. She was a determined young scamp, but I knew that if I was going to keep her safe during live searches, she'd have to obey and understand my commands. "No" meant "No" (or, in Molly's case, "Ah-ah" meant "Ah-ah").

Jumping on to our comfy leather sofa was also off limits, but that didn't stop Molly trying to push her luck. Sometimes she'd take advantage of dark, wintry nights, especially if my reading lamp was the sole light source, to stealthily creep up on to the settee, unnoticed. Five minutes later I'd glance to my left, only to catch sight of a pair of beady eyes glinting beside me.

"Oi, off you get, you cheeky minx!" I'd say, laughing and giving her a gentle nudge.

I also had to be extra vigilant whenever I watched football on the TV, too, because whenever I became distracted—celebrating a Chelsea goal, perhaps, or disputing a dodgy penalty decision— Molly would clamber up on to the sofa while I was otherwise engaged. She was a smart little cookie and a master problem-solver, and her sneakiness knew no bounds.

I was particularly strict about my dog's domestic eating habits. Following her evening meal, Molly would be walked for half an hour and then, while Sarah or myself prepared our own dinner, she'd be settled into her living room bed. In common with every dog I've owned, I never, ever let her watch me eat and refused to feed her any leftovers from my plate. For me, this was a baseline no-no. Experience and research had taught me that canine behavioral patterns often stemmed from "chaining"— when their brains associated a series of events with a positive outcome—and this could often be used adversely.

For example, if you regularly allowed your dog to watch you cook, watch you eat, and then gobble up the uneaten scraps off your plate, she'd invariably condition herself to recognize that the sequence of the cooking aromas, plus the clatter of pans, plus the setting of the table, plus the sight of you eating, would equal a tasty reward. As a consequence, your dog would plague and harangue you at the table and end up exhibiting a form of begging. This was far from ideal, of course, especially if you'd invited over some dinner guests or had planned a romantic supper for two with your other half.

Keen to stay in Sarah's good books, I did all I could to keep Molly in check at home.

"Molly's been nice and quiet, hasn't she?" said Sarah, after I'd prepared a nice, romantic three-course meal, while my fed-and-walked dog snoozed contentedly in her bed. Perhaps the strawberries and champagne had made my partner feel more loved-up than usual, but I was pretty sure I detected a hint—just a smidgeon—of affection.

There was no denying that Molly's first few weeks at home were rather testing. No sooner had I eliminated one behavioral trait than another would appear—it was like a merry-go-round of dog problems—and I was regularly on the phone to poor Mark, or my pal Anna, asking for advice and guidance.

Soon we were faced with another hurdle to overcome. Molly had limited experience of urban areas—she'd spent her early years cooped up in kitchens and garages, I suspected, before being transferred to MDD in rural Buckinghamshire—and she needed to acclimatize herself to busy public places. Aware that this wasn't going to be straightforward, I approached things step by step, firstly taking Molly for short walks in Cranleigh High Street, then building up to longer trips into Guildford town center. I researched all the dog-friendly venues in the area, gradually exposing her to a variety of shops, cafés and restaurants that could assure us of a pleasant welcome.

Initially, Molly was totally over-stimulated by all these fresh sights, sounds and smells and would bounce around like a hyperactive Haribo-fueled toddler. She would create havoc in any eateries we visited, making a mad dash to greet every customer who walked through the door, wrapping her lead around my calf as she did so and almost cutting off my blood supply. I learned that she had an aversion to bars and public houses, too. Sometimes she'd refuse to even enter certain premises, and on other occasions she'd stick to my side like glue, often panicking if she lost sight of me. I raised my concerns with Mark, and we concluded that one of Molly's changes of ownership had probably taken place in a pub. This must have been a deeply traumatic experience for her—she might have arrived with one owner and left with another—and it was one that I was determined to help her overcome. I needed her to understand that, although there'd be occasions when I'd have to leave her alone, she could always guarantee my return.

Mark and I devised a strategy to expose her to as many pubs as possible, and to apply some relaxation techniques once she got there. During the first few visits Molly watched me like a hawk, tracking my every move. She gradually began to unwind, however, and it wasn't long before she could last a full minute without checking on my whereabouts.

Some trips out were more successful than others, though. One Sunday afternoon Sarah and I decided to brave a local canine-friendly pub, The Wisborough, with Molly in tow. While we both had a bite to eat, Molly sat obediently under the table, her lead coiled securely around Sarah's chair leg. As we tucked into our desserts—sorbet for me, cheesecake for Sarah—some other diners, accompanied by a large, handsome Irish Setter, took a table across the open-plan eating area. Unbeknownst to us, they'd come armed with an egg-shaped, treat-filled plastic toy to keep their pooch occupied.

Then, just as Sarah got up to pay a visit to the loo, I answered an important phone call from a client. Sussing that I was distracted, Molly took the opportunity to career across the pub in a bid to grab the amazing dog toy she'd spied from afar. Sarah's chair was still attached, its legs scraping loudly behind her, but the darkness of Molly's coat—together with the pub's dim lighting—made the whole thing look like a furniture-flying scene from *Poltergeist*.

"Andy, I'll call you back," I hissed to my client.

With her prey clamped firmly in her jaw, Molly charged back—upending a couple of pints of beer as she did so—and dropped the toy at my feet, provoking a few loud guffaws from fellow patrons. The landlord wasn't remotely impressed, however, emerging moments later with a mop and bucket while carping about irresponsible owners and their uncontrollable dogs.

"*Bad girl*, Molly," I admonished, blushing from head to toe, before returning the toy to a rather startled-looking Irish Setter.

On a fresh and frosty afternoon, Molly enjoyed her very first visit to Bramble Hill Farm.

"Something tells me you're going to love it here, Molly," I said, fixing her gaze in my rear-view mirror as we neared the sandstone farmhouse. As soon as I released her from her dog crate she tore across the driveway, scattering gravel as she went, before hurtling into the large meadow facing the farmhouse. She zoomed around its perimeter in a joyful gallop, springing over frozen puddles, gulping down the chilly air and disturbing a pair of hooded crows, who cawed their displeasure at the unwanted intrusion. I watched on from the York-stone patio and smiled contentedly to myself. Over the succeeding months, Molly and I were destined to spend hours and hours at Bramble Hill, yet she already looked like she belonged there.

On the command of "Molly, come," she scampered back with a *Wow, Dad, this is FUN!* look on her face, whereupon I re-hooked her leash and attached her training harness.

"Let's go and explore," I said, flicking the ice crystals off her paws and wiping the water droplets from her whiskers, then leading her further down into this 500-acre estate. I was keen to familiarize my dog with all the various wildlife scents (she needed to be able to distinguish them from cat odors during searches) so our first port of call was a field known as Fox Cover, so called because—in the warmer months—it housed a vixen's breeding earth. Molly had a good old sniff around, poking her snout into the broad hole and doubtless picking up the faint scent of the previous season's fox cubs, as well as that of the small mammals they'd feasted on. We then sauntered over to a labyrinth of rabbit warrens—which Molly studied and snuffled with interest—before heading over a dense area of woodland, our arrival putting to flight the resident pheasants and wood-cocks, who set off toward a thicket of silver birch.

As the sun began its gradual descent and the clouds started to scud across the sky, I guided Molly toward my favorite place in Bramble Hill Farm. Shepherd's Rest was a small ridge located at the dead center of the estate and was easily identifiable by the presence of two ancient, majestic oak trees that had loomed large in the area for centuries. With its calm and peaceful set-ting and its panoramic views across the valley, it had become my little haven, my own private sanctuary, the place I visited to clear my head and blow away the cobwebs.

I perched myself on a large, flat tree root and rested my back against the trunk. A tired-looking Molly plodded over and plonked herself down, leaning into me for comfort as the winter breeze began to sharpen. We quietly surveyed this lovely vista for a good ten minutes, until a flurry of activity caused Molly to spring to her feet. I felt her muscles flinch and her heartbeat quicken as a trio of roe deer broke cover from the woodland and gawkily traversed a footpath before grazing on the lush wet grass.

I put a comforting arm around her warm little body, drew her close and saw two friendly brown eyes gazing up at me.

"Isn't this lovely, Molls?" I said, as a wave of emotion washed over me. Here I was, in my favorite spot, with my yearned-for dog, and—at that precise moment—without a care in the world. True, there had been days when Molly had been extremely challenging. Since moving in she'd destroyed a variety of clothing and soft furnishings and had caused a few accidents around the house, albeit nothing that couldn't be cleaned or replaced. Overall, however, she'd made excellent progress with her scent-match training and the good days had far outweighed the bad.

While Molly and I still had a long way to go before we could truly call ourselves a team, the future was looking very promising, and things could only get better. All things considered, having Molly in my life was all shades of wonderful.

Molly's second phase of field training, this time with me as her handler, began in earnest in mid-January 2017. If my dog and I were going to find some missing cats—and offer genuine hope to their distressed owners—I needed to be absolutely certain that Molly was on top of her game before she was deployed, and before I could obtain the all-important "proof of concept." I spent hours in the office devising a varied program of aptitude tests, skills exercises and mock-searches, many of which had been drilled into us by Mark and Astrid at MDD.

"You need to be so inventive and imaginative with these searches, Colin," Mark had said at the time, "and you must never forget how smart she is."

He went on to explain that, in order to find the sample, Molly would do her utmost to track my scent and, for me to combat this, I'd either have to walk around in different directions while I planted it or ask someone else to do the deed instead. Before we could start these practice searches, however, I had to obtain some genuine cat-hair samples. Initially, I'd asked some feline-owning friends and neighbors to oblige, but knocking on doors to obtain fur clumps from cat beds soon became quite time-consuming.

It was Sam who decided to telephone Battersea Dogs and Cats Home in south London. Not only did this world-famous animal-rescue center house a plethora of cats of varying breeds—we needed samples from as wide a spectrum as possible—they seemed more than willing to grant my rather unusual request.

"Happy to help, Colin," the manager said, smiling, when Molly and I arrived at their bustling center one morning. The open-plan, modern-looking entrance led to a large circular reception desk and there were shelves of dog toys everywhere. It was canine heaven. The staff couldn't believe how feline-friendly Molly was, admitting that they'd never met a dog that had no inclination to bark at cats, or to chase them. They were also intrigued about the cat-detection project—most particularly the scent-recognition process—but were equally impressed with its *raison d'être*.

"If Molly's going to be finding lost cats, that'll mean fewer of them will end up here, in all sorts of distress," said the manager. He explained that some of their cats had been brought to them from outside the London area and, since they hadn't been microchipped, it was unlikely they'd ever be reunited with their owners.

Molly and I waited patiently in reception as the staff—wearing sterile gloves, so as to avoid cross-contamination—visited some resident cats to collect the samples, gently rubbing pieces of cloth around the cats' faces in order to gather as much hair and scent as possible. Plastic bags were sealed and marked: Bag A was the "target" sample, which I would split into two parts, one part to hide and the other to present to Molly as the source sample. Bag B was the "environmental" sample that would enable Molly to discriminate the missing cat's scent from the background scents associated with the cat's home.

"I can't tell you how much I appreciate this," I said, when the manager emerged carrying a shoe box stacked with polythene bags. I popped a generous donation in their collection box and also purchased half a dozen secondhand cat carriers. It was the very least I could do for this army of animal aficionados.

Back at Bramble Hill Farm, winter gradually yielded to spring and Mother Nature seemed to yawn, stretch and slowly awaken. The frosted ground began to soften underfoot, the bare branches started to bud and the clearings became a white-yellow sea of snowdrops and crocuses. The farm contained plenty of nooks, crannies and bolt-holes—from rotting logs and drystone walls to disused hay barns and derelict stables—and the following morning I asked Sam to hide a target sample somewhere within this sprawling estate. It was what I called a "blind search," meaning that Molly and I had no idea where the sample was hidden and would have to work closely as a team to find it.

Then it was time to introduce Molly to the matching "A" sample, which had been transferred to a sterilized jam jar, in order for her to perform the scent match. I released her from her crate, controlling my body language, lowering the tone of my voice and carefully choosing my words so as to communicate that it was now time for work, not play. I attached my dog's work "uniform"—a bright yellow reflective harness—slipped her black-pudding treats into my utility belt then crouched down low beside her.

Carefully unscrewing the jam jar, I issued the unique command that Mark and Astrid had taught me at Medical Detection Dogs.

"Toma," I said, which was the signal for Molly to inhale the cat scent. She poked her nose into the sample jar, sniffing and snuffling for a few seconds in order to invite the aroma into her finely tuned olfactory system. She had performed this routine hundreds of times at MDD HQ but, judging by her fervent tail-wagging, she seemed thrilled to be back in action.

In a clear voice I then said, "Seek . . . seek!"—the command to find the cat scent—before letting her off the leash.

Within fifteen minutes, Molly had searched an area the size

of a football pitch and then, at the entrance of a small potting shed, she suddenly flung her body to the ground and performed the "down," her trademark "found it" signal which she'd been taught at MDD.

I've done my job, Dad . . . she seemed to be saying, focusing her eyes on mine.

"Brilliant work, Molly," I said, my upbeat gestures causing her to leap three feet off the ground repeatedly (I called these her "super-jumps"). Once she'd devoured her much-deserved reward, I gave her an extended play session with her favorite tennis ball, which was becoming balder by the day.

Each session at the farm became a new learning experience for both of us. Every search had a different objective—a trickier hiding place, maybe, or different weather conditions—and, slowly but surely, I increased their intensity and duration.

I also began to use real-life cats. Before I could deploy her on genuine missing-pet cases, I needed to be completely sure that Molly behaved appropriately in their presence and remained suitably calm, quiet and discreet.

"Would you mind awfully if I borrowed Pepper for a couple of hours?" I'd ask a friend, assuring them that their cat would be kept safe and secure and would at no point be released from its carrier. I would then hide the cat in a stable or hay barn for a bouncing Molly to locate in due course.

I captured many of these searches on a Go-Pro camera, which I'd strap to my chest, trying my best to keep up with Molly. I would analyze the footage afterward, focusing in on any plus points that could be repeated or any slip-ups that could be eliminated (on my part as well as my dog's). Then I would email the video clips over to Mark at Medical Detection Dogs for his comments; occasionally, I'd follow this up with a visit to Milton Keynes, where he'd assess Team Molly's searching skills at close quarters and attempt to iron out any glitches. This level of scrutiny could be immensely daunting; sometimes I felt like a *Strictly Come Dancing* contestant whose every step was judged and critiqued by the resident expert.

Molly's success rate was phenomenal—she, memorably, found one cat sample deep in the base of a hollow fruit tree, where it had fallen after I'd hidden it much higher—and on the rare occasions that she failed to complete the scent match it was generally my fault. Once, I accidentally mixed up the samples, and another time I failed to sterilize the jar properly, effectively exposing Molly to two different cat scents. I always knew when I got something wrong because Molly would make a strange whining sound and sit down before me, as if to say, *Come on, Dad, get your act together . . .*

A real sense of solidarity started to grow between Molly and me and that vital circle of trust began to strengthen. I had always been keen to emulate the man-and-dog teamwork I'd witnessed in my past, whether it was Alec the countryman marshalling his collies on Cleeve Hill or John the handler mobilizing Rainbow for Surrey Police. Both men had shown me how to bond and connect with a working dog; they had illustrated the joy and satisfaction you can derive from bringing the best out of an animal and by maximizing its natural-born talents. Success relied on working as a team and trusting each other implicitly.

Forty years had passed since my windswept mornings on Cleeve Hill but Alec's words of advice remained lodged in my psyche.

"An animal's love, trust and loyalty aren't given freely or easily, young man," he'd told me in his Gloucestershire drawl. "They have to be earned."

As Molly grew in confidence, both indoors and outdoors, I decided to take her on some selected work assignments—a succession of "bring your dog to work" days, I suppose. I chose appropriate dog-friendly venues to meet my private-eye clients, advising them beforehand that, if they wished to continue using my investigation services, there'd more often than not be a lovely cocker spaniel at my heel. Most of them were very accom-

Molly and Me—the perfect pet-detective duo

Molly's first meeting at Medical Detection Dogs (MDD)

Me and Sam at Pet Detective HQ

Molly relaxing with one of the cats
she searched for after a training
search at MDD

The brilliant Mark Doggett
with the first cat that Molly
found during training at MDD

Molly endured training in all
conditions, even through the winter

Rusty, shortly after being reunited with his owner

Titan, aka Milo, who was missing for six months, after he was reunited with his owners

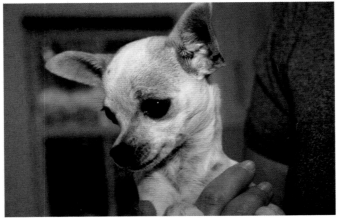

Mouse, a few days after she was recovered

A fluffy Buffy before she was stolen (*Courtesy of Renu Williams*)

Buffy, at time of recovery (*Courtesy of Renu Williams*)

Molly indicating that she had found Chester

Molly and her inflamed chest after the snakebite

Newton with his owner
shortly after being recovered

A neat and tidy Newton two weeks after he was found

A watchful Cuddles at home with her owner after recovery

Molly proudly indicating that she's found a missing cat

Tom on the road to recovery with metal pins in his broken leg

Sarah and Molly—friends at last

The treasures that Molly found
on Hampstead Heath

Columbus at home after his ordeal (*Courtesy of Katy Thatcher*)

modating and were super-kind to Molly, although I'm sure a few thought I'd completely lost the plot.

Molly, as it happened, became a useful asset, a nifty sidekick and my canine equivalent of Dr. Watson. If I needed to observe a specific house or office, for example, or survey a particular neighborhood, it was much easier to blend in if I was casually dressed and walking a dog on a lead. As a private eye, you had to become part of the environment and to look as if you belonged there and, with a cute dog at your side, suspicions were much less likely to be aroused. Some canine-loving crooks would even strike up a conversation.

"What's the little lady's name, then, eh, mate?" they'd say, sidling over to give Molly a friendly pat as I surreptitiously concealed my recording device. "Well behaved, ain't she?"

Yes, I felt like saying. *So well behaved that I heard every tiny detail of your dodgy dealing, sir . . .*

Molly's presence undoubtedly helped me to break down barriers and lower people's guards, a case in point being a divorce-related job that I took on. A legal firm had asked me, on behalf of their client Henry, to obtain so-called "proof of occupancy" relating to a property in Chelsea. A gentleman was contesting the hefty allowance he was obliged to pay his ex-wife, Olivia, since he suspected she'd set up home with a wealthy new partner and was failing to declare the additional household income. She, on the other hand, was claiming that James, her co-habitee, was merely a "lodger." I was tasked with unearthing the truth.

I duly put the house under surveillance. While I saw no sign of a lodger, I quickly established that Olivia employed a female student to walk her wire-haired miniature dachshund, Sherbet, in Burton Court Park each morning. At precisely 8:30 a.m., I noted, this girl would carefully tether the dog to a railing, grab an espresso from a nearby refreshments cart, take a seat on a wooden bench and enjoy a ten-minute breather.

One morning, Molly and I just happened to be sitting on the other end of the self-same bench as the girl sipped her coffee.

All I had to do was wait for my dog to make her move. She simply couldn't resist a meet and greet, and it wasn't long before she padded along to the other end of the bench to say hello.

Good girl, I thought, seeing her nudge the student's leg with her snout. The young woman began to make a fuss of her, telling me that cocker spaniels were her favorite breed before untethering Sherbet and going on her way. We engaged in more friendly chat the next day, and even more the next, and by the end of the week I'd learned that her boss was enjoying a live-in relationship with a well-off hedge-fund manager who'd often jet off to Dubai for business trips. He was so wealthy, the student told me, he was even paying the rent on the apartment, as well as the salaries of three domestic staff.

My simultaneous investigations revealed that James was quite a sneaky and devious chap; he'd park his sparkling new Aston Martin in a neighboring street, remove his suit jacket and tie, then walk the short distance to the house, entering the property via a private courtyard at the rear. The following week, with Molly by my side, I obtained some crucial CCTV footage of this carry-on, which I copied on to a memory stick and sent to Henry, along with a covering report. The next day he called me, buzzing with excitement over the evidence that I'd shared.

"I can't believe it," he said. "We've had another PI firm on this assignment for over three weeks and they couldn't find a thing. How did you manage it?"

"I've got a brilliant partner," I replied. "She's the best in the business."

"Well, whoever she is, she's an absolute star. Will you say a big thank-you from me?"

"Of course I will." I smiled, patting Molly on the head.

Molly also assisted me with my general pet-detective work, too, often acting as a smokescreen if I was investigating a fraudulent animal charity or a negligent boarding kennel. She accompanied me on a couple of missing-cat searches too, the incidences of which were increasing as the temperatures rose and more pets ventured outdoors. I didn't ask her to perform any scent matching, though, and chose not to advertise her special abilities to my clients, my rationale being that we were in the midst of our skills training at Bramble Hill and still had much to absorb and refine.

Essentially, I still needed to establish Molly's safe parameters or—as I sometimes referred to it—her "operational envelope," a term I'd become familiar with while flying with the Royal Navy. For instance, how effective would my dog be when she was searching in built-up areas, as opposed to open ground? Could she search in wet conditions or snow? How many breaks would she need, and for how long? These, as well as other factors, could have an impact on her ability to find and match the scent of a missing cat.

One thing I knew for sure: Molly's unique talent could be deployed only when both she and I were good and ready. Within a few weeks, that was indeed the case, and Molly and I would find ourselves experiencing our first proper live search, successfully locating Rusty on that momentous February afternoon.

8

Phillip, Holly and Mischievous Molly

Once Molly had lived in Cranleigh for six weeks, a stark reality began to dawn on Sarah. This frisky young cocker spaniel was a permanent fixture, not a passing phase, and in the blink of an eye we'd morphed into a household of three. This huge upheaval hadn't been easy for my other half—Molly could be demanding and disruptive, akin to many change-resistant rescue dogs—and I could hardly blame her for feeling somewhat sidelined. From Christmas onward, our romantic date nights, weekends away and trips abroad had remained firmly on the backburner while my new dog had commanded my attention and sapped my spare time.

By the same token, though, Sarah genuinely appreciated my love for Molly—as well my long-time passion for the cat-detection project—and so had shown remarkable patience and forbearance. No doubt there'd been much gritting of teeth and biting of lips in the process, though, since she was the first to admit that she wasn't a natural dog-lover. Sarah didn't even make that much of a fuss when Molly gnawed the heels of her brand-new boots; she just quietly presented me with a bill for a replacement pair.

"I know this has been hard for you, Sarah, and I know your nose has been pushed out of joint a bit," I said, as we curled up together on the sofa one evening, while Molly lay on the Persian rug chewing her favorite toy.

"Well, there's the understatement of the year," she replied with a wry smile.

"I do think Molly's behavior's improving, though, darling. She's starting to feel so much more settled now, and those teething problems seem few and far between."

"Mmmm . . . maybe . . ."

I affectionately ruffled my girlfriend's long blonde hair.

"You never know, one day we might even be able to drop her off at Mum and Dad's and we can go to that hotel you like in the Cotswolds."

"Now that would be lovely." Sarah nodded. Her grin, however, slowly faded into a grimace as Molly suddenly regurgitated a wad of part-chewed grass and spat it out on to the rug. (My partner had sported a similar expression the previous day, when she'd found a jet-black dog hair standing to attention in her tuna niçoise and had virtually Frisbee'd the plate into the dishwasher.)

"Molly, that's gross," I frowned, rolling up a newspaper to shovel up the gunky green mess. Sarah just sighed and shook her head. Molly looked up at us both, probably wondering what all the fuss was about.

There was no doubting that my dog still detected a certain *froideur* from the other female in the house. As the weeks had passed, I'd watched with interest as she'd tried—and generally failed—to worm her way into Sarah's affections, following her around the house or staring wistfully at her in an attempt to break the deadlock.

Okay, lady, so I know I'm not going to get the same attention from you that I get from Dad, she seemed to say, her eyes saucer-wide, *but how could you possibly not love a dog like me?*

As the head of one of the UK's foremost pet-detective agencies, I was accustomed to receiving a variety of media requests. News outlets would often interview me about my line of work or ask for my comments regarding contemporary pet-related issues—

the growth of illegal puppy farms, for example, or the scourge of dog theft. Sam and I occasionally arranged for some of UKPD's successful cases to feature in the local press and in pet magazines, too, which would print articles alongside photos of beaming owners cuddling their recently recovered fur-babies. It was a win-win situation, really; fifteen minutes of fame for my clients and their pets, feel-good content for the respective publications and fabulous PR for my service.

Radio and television also came knocking, too, and in early 2017 I received a request to appear on ITV's *This Morning*. Having first aired in 1988, it is one of Britain's most enduring and successful daytime TV shows and it was an opportunity I surely couldn't refuse.

"We're running a piece on the rise of dog thefts in the UK, Colin," explained the program researcher, "and we'd really appreciate some insight and opinion from a proper pet detective."

Presenters Phillip Schofield and Holly Willoughby would interview me on the *This Morning* sofa, and there'd also be a live link-up to a former client of mine, Hayley, whose pet chihuahua had been snatched the previous October. Mouse (so named because of her size) had eventually been recovered—albeit in a very sorry state—thanks to a painstaking UKPD investigation.

"Sounds great," I replied. "I'd be delighted to come on."

Sam agreed to take care of Molly while I was in London—my colleague would be glued to the TV at Bramble Hill Farm, no doubt—and I began to look forward to my prime-time chat with Phillip and Holly.

On the eve of transmission, however—not long after I'd returned from a very muddy practice search with Molly—I received another telephone call from the researcher. It transpired that one of the *This Morning* guests had let them down—some actor or singer, I think—and in order to fill the gap they'd decided to allocate more time to the canine-theft feature.

"We've given you a double slot now, so we were wondering whether you'd like to bring your dog, Molly, along with you as well?" she asked. "I hear she's a bit special—finds cats, doesn't she?—and I'm sure our viewers would *love* her."

I was somewhat taken aback by this conversation, and ummed and aaahed for a few moments before I made up my mind. While Molly's trailblazing recovery of Rusty had caused a few ripples via word of mouth, I genuinely hadn't realized that news of her unique talent had spread further afield. It was my intention to shield Molly from the media spotlight for the time being, since I wanted us to have a few more successful searches under our belt and my dog still had much to learn. Despite maintaining this low profile, though, I'd still had to deflect inquiries from intrepid local reporters who'd already heard rumors about a Surrey-based pet detective and his amazing rescue cocker spaniel. Some had cottoned on to our partnership when, during Molly's stint in Milton Keynes, Medical Detection Dogs had put out requests to local people for cat-hair samples, causing the journos to dig a little deeper.

"So what d'you reckon, Colin?" badgered the researcher. "Is it a possibility? I need to let the director know in the next few minutes, you see . . ."

"Oh, go on, then," I said, perhaps against my better judgment.

"You don't need to worry," she said. "We've had many pets and animals on the show, so we're past masters at this."

As soon as I put the phone down I flung Molly straight into the bath. She couldn't be meeting Phillip and Holly stinking of duck pond.

We arrived bright and early at ITV's South Bank studios the following day and were ushered straight into the *This Morning* green room. I grabbed myself a coffee and soon got chatting to a fellow guest, a leading heart surgeon, who was extremely taken with Molly and appeared captivated by her story. Ten minutes into our conversation, however, a dog for the blind, Luna, and its handler had entered the green room—the program had been following the labradoodle puppy's progress for months, apparently—and the little cutie wanted to play with Molly. This was the last thing I needed. I had aimed to keep Molly totally calm before we went live on air and this puppy was beginning to wind her up.

"I think we need to keep them apart," I suggested to Luna's handler, as both dogs barked at each other. "They're getting a bit too excited, aren't they?"

Fortunately, it was soon time for Luna to head to the studio, leaving behind a very hyper cocker spaniel and one very stressed owner.

Five minutes later a member of the production team directed us to their contingency studio, which, being virtually identical to the main *This Morning* set, was used as a back-up if there were any technical hitches and also as a holding area for guests prior to their broadcast slot. While it was a far quieter environment than the claustrophobic green room, any hopes of calming Molly down evaporated when a young runner on the show bounded in with a boxful of dog toys. No doubt he thought he was being helpful. My heart sank, however.

"I . . . I . . . I'd prefer it if you perhaps didn't show her those. She'll become over-stimulated; she'll go bananas . . ." I stuttered, my voice trailing off as I realized that the damage had already been done. Molly's hypersensitive nose had immediately detected the familiar smell of bendy rubber bones and fuzzy tennis balls and she was now geared up for some fun and games.

"No need to worry; there's plenty of space for her to play," grinned the runner, ignoring my grimace and gaily launching a ball across the room. "We've had loads of dogs in here."

Molly let out an excited yelp and hurtled toward her prey but came to an abrupt halt as she reached the full extent of her leash. She then performed a cartoon-like sprint-on-the-spot, straining to reach a pristine new tennis ball that was a couple of yards away. I had to slowly reel Molly back to the sofa, as if I were trying to land a giant fish.

"Lively, isn't she?" nodded the runner as I gave him a murderous stare.

Just at that moment the floor manager walked in, trailed by a cameraman holding his finger to his lips in a *ssshhhh* gesture. A camera lens was shoved in my face and an audio feed boomed out from the adjacent studio.

"When we come back after the break we're going to meet a real-life pet detective and his dog, Molly, who's been trained to find cats," said the familiar voice of Phillip Schofield. *This Morning* viewers from Penrith to Penzance will have then witnessed the camera panning to a fifty-something bloke with a sweaty brow and a rictus smile trying desperately to rein in a crazed cocker spaniel. It was an inauspicious start to our star turn on primetime TV, and—believe me—it would only get worse.

"Time for you to have a quick chat with the presenters and to get you settled on to the sofa." The floor manager smiled and gestured for us to follow him.

My dog is anything but "settled," I felt like saying. *Thanks to Mr. Runner over there, my dog is as high as a bloody kite . . .*

Holly Willoughby was charming. She seemed genuinely pleased to see us—she was a dog-lover herself, telling me all about Benny, her French bulldog—and she made a point of thanking me for bringing along Molly at such short notice. Phillip, however, didn't appear quite so cordial. Granted, Molly continued to be jumpy and skittish (she was still hankering for the toys in the other studio) and I might have seemed slightly stressed, but he just looked on, silent and stony-faced, as I chatted with his co-presenter. No doubt his years of experience had alerted him to what looked like a very troublesome dog. All the while, I was trying to pacify Molly—I kept ruffling the nape of her neck and stroking her silken ears—but the little minx wasn't having any of it.

The ad break finished, the familiar *This Morning* jingle rang out and then we were live, beaming into the front rooms of millions of UK households. Phillip and Holly introduced me as a "real-life pet detective" and proceeded to quiz me about the rise in dog theft, asking me how their viewers could best keep their pooches safe and secure. I advised against walking dogs at dusk—in my experience, many were stolen at this time of day— and suggested that animals should never be left alone in cars or town centers. I also emphasized the importance of training dogs to have excellent recall skills and recommended that owners should remain extra vigilant should there be a spate of thefts involving their specific breed.

". . . and always contact the police in the first instance if you're convinced that your dog has been stolen," I added, "as they are obliged to investigate these cases."

They then quizzed me about Molly's ability to hunt out cats; I answered as succinctly as I could, but it was hard to remain focused with a wired and wide-eyed Molly straining at the leash.

"What's she after?" asked Phillip, clearly concerned, when Molly began to whine loudly.

"She's after the dog toys from next door," I replied, through gritted teeth.

"You can let her off her lead, if you like," suggested Holly. "She can go and play."

"Ooh, no, she wouldn't come back," I said with a nervous smile. "She'd get lost in the studios and I'd never see her again."

They probably thought I was being precious, but what they didn't realize was that I rarely let Molly out of my sight—the only other people who walked Molly were Sarah, my son Sam and my colleague Sam—and the idea of her running amok in the cavernous South Bank studios filled me with dread.

As we soldiered on with the interview—with a fractious Molly attempting to climb on to the blue L-shaped sofa—I detected some unease behind the scenes. The director was concerned, apparently, that I was holding Molly too tightly on her leash—I really wasn't—and was fearful that it would prompt an avalanche of viewer complaints. I can only assume that a voice in Phillip's earpiece instructed him to take Molly off my hands, because he suddenly jumped up from the sofa and grabbed her lead.

"You two carry on, I'll look after Molly," he grinned, before taking her off the set and out of my eye-line. My protective instincts kicked in, and for a split second I contemplated running after Phillip and demanding my dog back. But then I realized I was in the middle of a live transmission and that there was no other option but to keep calm and carry on. Beneath the cool veneer, however, I was panic-stricken.

Where's my dog? yelled a voice in my head. *Where the hell's my dog?* My blood ran cold as I visualized Phillip accidentally letting go of the leash and my precious cocker spaniel getting lost within the maze of corridors or becoming trapped inside an empty studio.

After a couple of torturous minutes—by then I was sweating from every pore—I spied a black flash of fluff darting back into the studio and diving underneath the sofa. A somewhat frazzled-looking Phillip followed in Molly's wake and reclaimed his seat next to Holly.

Phew, I thought. *Molly's safe.*

". . . and let's now link up to a former client of Colin's, whose dog was targeted by thieves," said Phillip, as images of Hayley sitting at home in Hampshire with her tiny chihuahua on her knee were beamed into the studio. Emotively and eloquently, she described the traumatic chain of events that had seen poor Mouse being stolen to order from her boarding kennels and explained how we at UK Pet Detectives had helped to reunite her with her dog by identifying the thieves and eventually making contact. It was a dreadfully upsetting case that had resulted in my client having to effectively buy Mouse back from the offenders, who were threatening to sell her at a car-trunk sale. The little mite was emaciated when we recovered her—she was barely recognizable—and had also suffered a broken tail and fractured jaw. Hayley had burst into floods of tears when she'd seen her pitiful state.

As Hayley solemnly recounted this appalling tale to the nation, however, she had to do so amid a soundtrack of grunts and snorts as Molly noisily explored the underside of the *This Morning* sofa. If that wasn't embarrassing enough, my dog then made a beeline for Holly and began to snuffle around the hem of her long, salmon-pink skirt.

The blonde presenter burst out laughing.

"She's licking my feet!" she exclaimed, screwing up her face, while Hayley—who didn't have a clue what was going on—looked totally bewildered.

"She likes you," I said, immediately regretting how drippy that must have sounded.

Molly jumped on the sofa and crept across the back of it, her leash dragging after her. She then skulked behind Phillip and Holly, thwacking their necks with her long black tail as they attempted to read the autocue. And yes, the studio hands and camera operators may well have been guffawing, but I was dying inside. Molly had been billed as a supremely professional, highly trained detection dog, yet here she was, acting like an ill-disciplined toddler and adding to the annals of car-crash TV.

"Honestly, she doesn't do this at home," I said feebly, but I doubt anyone in the studio believed me.

"Talk about a scene-stealer," tutted Phillip, before, inevitably, winding up the interview. "Thank you very much, Colin; it's been lovely meeting you," he said, but I wasn't that sure he meant it.

As I drove out of the capital, with Molly sleeping soundly in the back of the car—and with my blood pressure slowly returning to normal—I called Sarah. A peal of giggles rang out through my speakerphone.

"Tell me the truth, Sarah. It was a disaster, wasn't it?" I said.

"Not at all," she replied, once she'd finally stopped laughing. "It was brilliant television, Colin. Molly was hilarious, and I bet the viewers *loved* it."

"You sure about that?"

"'Course. It was like watching *Morecambe and Wise* in their heyday. Molly was the funny, slapstick one and you were the serious straight man. Honestly, it was TV gold."

I spent the rest of the journey home reflecting on a bizarre morning and—much as it pained me—questioning my own judgment. I concluded that, in hindsight, I probably should have left Molly at home and out of the limelight. I had wanted to show her off, I suppose, like a proud parent, but by doing this I'd overlooked the fact that, deep down, she was still an excitable young rescue dog and was naturally prone to mischief. She, like many pets, was never going to comply to the rules and regulations of a live TV studio and it had been unfair of me to expect anything more.

"I'm so sorry, Molls," I lamented as her snores rattled around her crate.

Fast-forward a few hours, however, and it became apparent that Sarah's judgment had been spot-on. Molly's antics had gone down a storm with the *This Morning* viewers and, much to my surprise, had also gone viral on the internet. Footage of my dog creating havoc had been posted on the show's YouTube channel, as well the *Sun*'s website ("She's Licking My Feet" was the latter's strapline).

That same evening, Sarah and I watched the interview again (I spent most of the time peeping through my fingers, I admit). Molly lay spread-eagled on the rug by my feet, having enjoyed a long, bracing walk in the woods followed by a bowl of her favorite dinner.

"Once a drama queen, always a drama queen, Molly," I remarked as she looked up at me with her Penelope Cruz brown eyes and raised a quizzical eyebrow, as if to say, *I can't help it if people love me . . .*

As we continued to watch TV, I noticed with interest that my dog was attempting, slowly but surely, to cozy up to Sarah. My girlfriend's attitude toward her still wavered between tolerance and ambivalence, but Molly was in no mood to abandon her charm offensive. I couldn't help but smile as I watched her rest her chin on Sarah's left sock and lean her head against her ankle, edging as close as she could before Sarah noticed and peevishly moved her legs away.

"Mark my words, you two will be cuddled up on this sofa one day," I grinned.

"Not a chance," scowled Sarah. "I'll leave all that stuff up to you. I'd prefer not to have dog hairs on my trousers, thank you very much."

Molly padded back to me, somewhat resignedly, and curled up on the rug.

Don't give up, sweetheart, I felt like saying to her. *She'll come around in the end, I just know it . . .*

I felt it was important that we kept up our search momentum—it would boost Molly's confidence, as well as my own—so when, a few weeks later, Sam took a call about a missing cat in East Sussex, I was keen to follow it up.

The client in question, Cat Jarvis, worked as a press officer for Cats Protection, a well-known cat charity, and had rung up the office in a state of blind panic, so much so that she could barely speak. Eventually, Sam managed to decipher that Phoenix, a beautiful Bengal pedigree, had disappeared without a trace four days previously. There always seemed to be an upsurge in such cases during March; the evenings were starting to become lighter, which meant that cats like Phoenix were staying outdoors for longer.

"He's trapped somewhere, I know it," wailed Cat, "and I'm so scared he's not going to survive."

Fortunately, I didn't have any case work planned that morning, so I was able to prioritize this as an emergency. An average week for us usually entailed about twenty new inquiries; some were time-sensitive—what I call "fast track" investigations—and others fell into the category of protracted or "slow burn" cases. I usually tried to have six investigations running concurrently, allocating my time to each one as and when it was needed, always keeping some time back to respond promptly to any crisis calls like Cat's. On top of this, I also had to ensure that Stefan kept me informed on the progress of our private-eye cases, many of which would run for several months at a time. This meant that I'd often work a six-day week, which wasn't exactly ideal.

Sam, Molly and I made the short trip to our client's home and, when she answered her front door, she promptly collapsed into my colleague's arms, her body shaking with sobs. While we were accustomed to dealing with traumatized owners, this lady was in a state of acute distress. She was dazed, disheveled and deathly white—the loss of her cat had clearly hit her hard.

It being a fast-tracked case, I'd not had the opportunity to obtain any background information from the owner. In an ideal situation, I'd have a thirty-minute telephone conversation with the client, obtaining details about the missing pet's health, diet, temperament, daily activity and behavior toward other pets and people. This fact-finding usually served to help me decide whether or not to take on a case and would also help me to select the best possible strategy. In this instance, however, the lack of context meant that we would be going in cold—not my preferred approach, by any means, but if Phoenix was trapped in a building (as her owner suspected), we needed to locate him as soon as possible.

Judging by Cat's emotional state, I realized that we'd have to address her trauma before we were able to extract any meaningful details about Phoenix and the circumstances of his disappearance. It was at times such as these that my policing experience came into play. As a detective inspector back in the 1990s, I and a colleague had devised a family-liaison initiative which facilitated the training of specialist Surrey Police officers as trauma counselors. They were taught how to deal sympathetically with distressed individuals—parents of a missing child, for example—while gently extracting information that would assist the investigation. Recruiting highly trained professionals to perform this sensitive role took the onus off detectives, allowing them to concentrate on the crime itself. Indeed, the initiative was so successful that it was rolled out to other police forces.

A few years down the line, and within the UKPD auspices, it seemed logical to offer the same support and counseling to distraught pet owners. I had learned over the years that some human brains found it hard to differentiate between the trauma of a missing child and a missing pet, and for that reason I applied exactly the same counseling techniques. I would give my clients the opportunity to pour out their grief and express their fears and, having unburdened themselves, they'd soon become calmer and more rational. With tact and diplomacy, I'd then ask the questions that would allow me to build up a picture of the pet's personality and proclivities and enable me to start coordinating the search. Usually, I could extract this kind of information only once their emotions were in check.

The one downside of this person-centered approach was that the client would often transfer their hopes and fears on to me, which would ramp up the pressure to get a result.

"I'm counting on you to end this nightmare. You're my last resort," was a common response.

This was exactly what happened with Cat, who, in the lounge of her 1930s semi, cried herself dry and beseeched me to find Phoenix. The shock of losing her cat had almost rendered her incapable—she was in a state of emotional shut-down—and, unlike most clients of mine, she hadn't mustered the strength to cover the basics. Her house-to-house inquiries, her distribution of posters and her use of social media had been somewhat disorganized.

"Seems like we're starting from scratch here," I whispered to Sam.

I decided to employ a Catherine-wheel-type search strategy that morning, starting from the inside and spiraling outward. I googled a map on my iPad, tagged Cat's house, plotted Phoenix's likely territory and identified the gardens and outhouses in that catchment area. I also took a sample of Phoenix's scent for Molly—our *pièce de résistance*, I hoped—in order to maximize the chances of recovery. My fragile client, bless her, had dissolved into tears when she'd presented me with her pet's hair-covered blanket.

Contrary to my advice—I'd strongly suggested that she stay indoors—Cat insisted on accompanying us on the search around the village. ("It'll make me feel closer to him," she'd said.) Our first task was to conduct door-to-door inquiries. We showed neighbors a photo of Phoenix—he was a stunning-looking cat, with distinctive marbled, grayish-brown markings—before quizzing them about his whereabouts and trying to establish a pattern of behavior. Just like my beat-officer days in Farnham, I tried to speak to as many neighbors and witnesses as possible.

"When did you last see him?" I'd ask. "Do you spot him regularly? And what time of day, roughly? Does he have a favorite little haven in your garden? Have you seen him with other cats?"

One particular front door was answered by a young woman in a dressing gown who took one look at me, then one at Molly, and gasped in shock.

"Oh my goodness!" she cried, before dashing to the foot of her stairs. "Kids, get out of bed, you'll never believe who's at our front door."

A pair of drowsy, pajama-clad children appeared at their mother's side, rubbing their eyes. They soon shook themselves awake when they saw the dog on the doorstep, mind.

"It's Molly!" they squealed in unison. "Molly the naughty dog!"

The kids and their mum were among the millions of viewers who'd seen Molly's exploits on *This Morning*, just a few weeks earlier. I allowed them to pet and stroke her for a couple of minutes—she adored the attention—and it was quite touching to see the children's joyful reaction. Molly's celebrity status was growing, it seemed.

"You'll have to get used to playing second fiddle, Colin," said a laughing Sam. "Molly's the star of the show now."

Once all the fan-worshipping had calmed down and the kids had returned to their bedroom, we asked about Phoenix.

"Oh, I know that cat. He's a gorgeous little thing," said the woman. "He usually crawls under my privet hedge and sits there for an hour or so, but I'm afraid I've not seen him since the weekend."

Other neighbors had similar accounts—he'd often sit on number 12's fence to observe a bird table and would bask on number 23's patio when the sun shone—but there'd been no recent sightings. This information—coupled with the fact that Molly hadn't detected a strong enough scent in any of their gardens—led me to believe that one of three things had happened. Phoenix had either been trapped, accidentally transported out of the area or killed. For Cat's sake, I dearly hoped it wasn't the latter.

After a pause for lunch—a takeaway Cornish pasty for the humans and a handful of biscuits for the spaniel—we resumed the search. I reintroduced Phoenix's scent to Molly and, as we ambled down a wide, leafy avenue, I noticed her becoming a little animated. Her trot quickened and her tail-wagging increased as we passed a huge fenced and gated property boasting a large, square garden and a couple of swanky cars on the driveway.

Seeing this house gave me a sudden, jarring flashback to the case of Oscar, the scared and skinny cat I'd found cowering in the garden shed of a similar house and who—heartbreakingly—had died shortly afterward. I'd held myself partly to blame for this—I felt that I'd not located him quickly enough—and my shortcomings had been the catalyst for finding a cat-detection dog like Molly. The fact that I was now working in tandem with this very dog, in order to try and rescue a cat in peril, felt both surreal and satisfying.

This is exactly *why I've got Molly*, I said to myself. *I can't go through another case like Oscar's. I need to get into this garden, pronto* . . .

With my dog getting more agitated by the second—she clearly had the scent in her nostrils—I walked over to the property's tall black gate and pressed the buzzer. No reply. I pressed it again, and again; still no reply. It was only when I leaned on the buzzer for a good twenty seconds that a voice finally crackled through the intercom.

"Will you please stop ringing the bell?" barked a woman with a broad Mancunian accent. "The residents aren't in at the moment."

"Sorry about that—I think there's a problem with your buzzer—but we're looking for a lost cat, you see, and a neighbor has seen it run into your garden."

It wasn't big, and it wasn't clever, but I often had to tell little white lies to gain access.

"I wish I could help, love, but I'm not allowed to let anyone in. I'm afraid I'm going to have to ask you to come back when the owners are home."

I wasn't taking no for an answer. There was no way that I was leaving until I searched this garden; Molly was indicating that Phoenix was close by and, if he was trapped somewhere, we needed to find him as soon as possible.

Somehow I had to get this person to the gate; it was never easy to tug on somebody's heart strings via intercom. I pressed hard on the buzzer for another twenty seconds.

"Will you *please* stop ringing the bloody bell?" she shouted. "You can't come in, I've told you."

"I'm not touching it," I lied, yelling over the incessant buzzing. "As I said, it appears to be stuck. I think you'll find it needs repairing."

"Oh, bloody Nora, just wait there," I heard, and the intercom clicked off.

My dastardly ploy had worked. The front door opened and a small, squat, dark-haired woman emerged, dressed in chef's whites. The occupants' personal cook, I assumed.

"You know what, I think I may have fixed it for you," I said, as she advanced toward us, wearing a puzzled expression. "This was jammed into the button," I fibbed, showing her a small metal washer that I'd fortuitously found on the pavement. "Bloody, kids, eh? Anyway, as I was saying . . ."

Then, before the little chef had the chance to scuttle off, I regaled her with the story of poor Phoenix and his perturbed owner and explained how Molly (who by now was whining in frustration) had detected a possible scent trail. Somehow, I managed to twist her arm—her sympathetic nods suggested she was a cat-lover herself—and she eventually unbolted the gate.

"But you'd better be quick," she said. "My bosses have been on a cruise and they're due back tonight. I'd get the flamin' sack if they found out."

"Cheers," I replied. "You're a diamond."

I let Molly off the lead and she shot across the lawn like a cannonball. She then leaped up acrobatically, arching her back, inhaling the air, gauging the scent source. My heart thumped when she veered off toward the westerly side of the garden and pelted toward the brick-built garage. Rarely had I seen her so focused. This was Molly on a mission.

Please let Phoenix be in there, I said to myself, following in her slipstream. *And please let him be alive.*

As I lifted open the giant garage double doors—they were unlocked, luckily—a waft of air hit my face, bringing with it the overpowering stench of cat pee. Within a millisecond, a quivering Molly had done the "down"—no surprise there—but, to the naked eye, there was neither sight nor sound of Phoenix. Not helping matters was the fact that the garage was full of clutter, from floor to ceiling. With Molly remaining still and silent, just as she'd been trained to do, I gently started to move the teetering items of furniture. I did so very gingerly, however, since I was petrified that it was all going to come noisily tumbling down, like a giant game of Jenga. As I gradually cleared some space, I must have released a vacuum of cat scent, because Molly suddenly slid over to the back of the garage and gave me another definitive "down." This time she also wiggled her bottom and shuffled her paws, which was usually a sure-fire sign of certitude.

I'm absolutely positive the cat is here, my dog was saying. *One hundred percent . . .*

With Cat at my side, and Sam and the chef looking on, I slowly crept toward her, moved an old, dusty golf bag to one side and—lo and behold—behind it sat Phoenix. The way he defensively sprang up, arched his back and hissed in anger told me he was very much alive and well.

I think the whole town must have heard his owner's shrieks of joy.

Afterward, the four of us stood among all that garage junk, chatting and laughing, as Phoenix cocooned himself in Cat's arms, thoroughly relieved to be back with his mum. Molly, meanwhile, spun round in tight circles, panting and squeaking, almost in celebratory fashion. The only things missing from this carnival atmosphere were fireworks, fairgrounds and a brass band.

Uplifting outcomes like these made me realize exactly why I'd trained Molly in the first place: to save cats' lives, to help distraught owners who could barely think straight and, ultimately, to reunite them with their lost pets. They had been my main objectives from day one, and to see everything come to fruition like this was simply marvelous.

News of my dog's brilliant cat-detecting exploits finally began to spread like wildfire—some local press coverage of Molly had been picked up by national newspapers—and, soon enough, we both received an invitation to attend Crufts, the world-famous canine show and exhibition. We had been asked to represent Medical Detection Dogs—an honor, of course, considering everything that Claire, Rob and Mark had done for us—and we'd also be the VIP guests of Natural Instinct, a well-known dog-food manufacturer.

"We're so pleased you're both coming," gushed a plummy-voiced press officer who rang to confirm our three-day attendance at Birmingham's National Exhibition Center. She seemed enchanted by our story (". . . a rescue dog that became a cat's best friend . . . how *wonderful!*") and she informed me that they'd already received dozens of interview requests from print and broadcast media, both national and international, many prompted by the *This Morning* footage.

"In fact, Channel 4 has been in touch this morning . . . they want to film Molly at Bramble Hill Farm and are wondering whether you would like to take part in a live chat on the sofa with Clare Balding?"

As she begged the question, an image of Molly slavering over Holly Willoughby's ankle briefly flashed before me. I reckoned that Crufts would be an entirely different proposition, however. I'd learned a lot from my ITV experience, and this time around I'd make sure that both Molly and I were much better prepared for the media attention.

"Count us in," I told the press officer. "It would be an absolute privilege."

On the day of the broadcast Molly and I traveled north to Birmingham, meeting up with my good friend Anna. Having worked extensively in canine-related PR and broadcasting, she'd suggested I draft a press release detailing Molly's journey from rescue dog to sniffer dog—including her brilliant recoveries of Rusty and Phoenix—which she'd roll out to the media in advance of the show. We wouldn't be able to fulfill every interview request—and I was reluctant to overwork and overwhelm Molly—so this was a good way of keeping everyone informed and updated.

As a result of this, the media buzz surrounding Molly was incredible and she was treated like a celebrity. Reporters were as keen to meet my charismatic little spaniel as they were to meet some of the show dogs and, wherever we went in the exhibition hall, we were stopped by people asking for selfies, photographs or cuddles (with Molly, of course, not me; I'd generally hover in the background, like her minder). She absolutely loved all the attention and adulation.

"What a clever, *clever* wee lassie," cooed a tweed-suited Scottish lady, gently stroking her head. "I've got three Persians back in Dundee, and I'd be heartbroken if any of them went missing. So keep up the good work, Molly, hun."

It was during Channel 4's primetime 8 p.m. slot, on the first day of Crufts, that we met Clare Balding on the sofa. She would be interviewing me, together with the CEO and co-founder of MDD, Claire Guest. This time I was determined that Molly would behave herself, bearing in mind that we were broadcasting live to an audience of millions of dog-lovers in the UK and across the globe.

I was already a huge fan of Clare's—she is a talented writer and a superb TV presenter—and I found her really warm and friendly. She made a big fuss of Molly prior to transmission and was highly amused when Molly tried to pilfer some of the food that the crew had hidden behind the sofa for her.

"I've hardly stopped all day, and I'm starving," she grinned, tucking into her sandwich, as Molly looked up at her with doleful eyes.

"Here, have a snack, greedy guts," I added, giving Molly a handful of her favorite beef-jerky bites, "and keep your paws off Clare's dinner."

With twenty minutes to go before transmission, however, my dog began to get worryingly frisky and I started to break out into a cold sweat. Fortunately, I had expert assistance on hand. The rest of the team from Medical Detection Dogs had left their exhibition stand to watch the filming—Rob and Mark included—and the latter was able to apply some simple calming techniques.

"Just walk her around, Colin, away from the crowds, and quietly chat to her. This should help to remove the anxiety. She can probably sense that you're also stressed, don't forget, so you need to stay chilled, too."

As it happened, I couldn't have hoped for a better interview. Clare was as professional as ever—she'd clearly done her research on scent-detecting canines—and Molly behaved impeccably throughout, snuggling next to me on the sofa and curiously eyeing the crowd of Crufts visitors that had amassed around the makeshift studio. As the show was beamed out to its worldwide audience, I talked about Molly's rescue-dog origins, explaining how I'd given this disadvantaged animal another chance at happiness and how she'd reciprocated by offering me love, loyalty and companionship. By investing my time, patience and dedication, not only had Molly been transformed into a scent-detection prodigy, she had also become a much-adored pet. Clare put me

at ease throughout; indeed, it felt more like a conversation between friends than an interview.

"Time to see this fantastic dog in action," she said, cueing up
the short film that had been captured at Bramble Hill Farm a
few weeks earlier. On a nearby monitor, I watched the footage of
Molly taking the feline scent sample and bombing over to a derelict barn to locate my neighbor's cat in its carrier, just as she'd
been trained to do.

"Wow," whispered Clare. "I've never seen anything like it."

I glanced over at Rob and Mark, both of whom were beaming
with pride.

I knew *exactly* how they felt. Our Molly was a superstar.

∼ 9 ∽

Bring Back Buffy

As a pet detective, I've handled hundreds of dog-theft cases. Over the last decade, sadly, it's become a colossal problem in the UK, largely due to the growing popularity of valuable "designer dogs," allied with the increasingly sophisticated methods employed by merciless thieves. Huge financial gains can be made by dog-napping, whether it's through extorting ransoms from traumatized owners, targeting an expensive puppy for breeding purposes or snatching pets out of spite or in relation to a messy dispute of ownership. It's a heinous, heartless crime.

Post-December 2016, when Molly and I had first joined forces, I continued to take on the occasional missing-dog investigation. I was very selective, however, and would agree to offer my services only if I felt confident that my safety, and that of my dog or my staff, would not be compromised. One such case will live forever in my memory.

In April 2017 I was contacted by a Sri Lankan woman, Renu, who informed me that her seventeen-week-old pet had been stolen from her house in the north London suburb of Willesden Green. Buffy, a beautiful white, golden-eared puppy—a rare cross-breed known as a Coton de Tulear—had been snatched one Friday evening while Renu had been dining at a local restaurant with her husband, Sachin, and her two sons, Harry and Freddie.

When they'd returned home, at about ten o'clock, Sachin had realized his blue BMW 5 Series was missing from the driveway.

"Renu, the car's gone," he'd said. "They must've gone inside to get the keys."

"Oh my god . . . oh my god . . . *BUFFY!*" his wife had screamed.

She had raced around to the back of the property, only to be confronted with a gaping patio door through which the robbers had forced entry into the sitting room. There, she'd discovered an ominously empty dog cot, in which Buffy had been snoozing contentedly when they'd gone for their meal. A frantic search of the house had revealed no trace of her whatsoever, but it seemed that she'd been the target of a pursuit; the poor little pup had soiled herself as she'd fled upstairs and a single bed had been upended by the thieves, perhaps as she'd cowered beneath it in fear. Not only had these cold-hearted burglars ransacked the property and stolen money, handbags and jewelry—as well as the car, of course—in all likelihood, it seemed they had also abducted an innocent puppy.

The family was utterly devastated. The sweet, lovable Buffy had become a huge part of their lives—almost like a third child to Renu and Sachin and a sibling to the boys—and the idea of her being alone, in danger, or no longer alive was just too awful for them to contemplate. To make matters worse, the response from the Metropolitan Police hadn't exactly been encouraging. The officers who arrived on scene the following day had been quite dismissive of the idea that the thieves had stolen the family dog.

"She's probably just run off," they'd shrugged, treating Buffy's disappearance with the same level of concern as they were Renu's missing handbag. "Give it a few days and she'll probably turn up in a neighbor's garden."

To them, the fact that she was a sentient creature was immaterial, and they weren't going to pull out all the stops to find her.

"But she's so vulnerable, and she's so dependent on me," Renu had wept, but she'd received scant sympathy in return.

Friends and neighbors rallied around, fortunately, launching a "Bring Back Buffy" campaign on social media, registering her details on the DogLost website and helping the family to display posters and distribute flyers. Renu's plight even attracted the attention of the *Evening Standard*: DEVASTATED MOTHER OFFERS REWARD AFTER PUPPY IS SNATCHED, ran the headline.

The publicity raised much-needed awareness and led to numerous reports of a "white, fluffy dog" in the Willesden Green area. Agonizingly for Renu, none of these pooches turned out to be Buffy; her hopes would soar with each promising sighting, only to be cruelly dashed when it became clear that these dogs were doppelgängers.

The weeks turned into months, and by the time May had arrived the family had begun to lose all hope of ever seeing their cherished puppy again. It was during a chance conversation with Buffy's breeder, however, that Renu had discovered that there was another option to pursue.

"My friend's dog was recovered by a pet detective, a guy based near Guildford," she'd said. "Why not get in touch with him? I mean, you've got nothing to lose, have you?"

"What, you mean like Ace Ventura?" a skeptical Renu had replied. "This is real life, y'know, not a Hollywood movie . . ."

It must have played on her mind, though, because within hours she'd accessed my website and given me a call.

Molly and I found ourselves knocking on Renu's door the following afternoon. An elegant brunette in her late thirties, Renu gave me a kiss on both cheeks—and Molly a hug—before ushering us into her bright, airy front room. Sitting on the sofa in their school uniforms were her sons, Harry and Freddie. Their eyes lit up like candles when my dog trotted in, sporting her usual wide, pink-tongued doggy-grin.

"Aw, she's *soooooo* cute," said Harry, the elder of the two, holding out his hand for Molly to snuffle while his younger brother chuckled beside him.

"I tell you what, lads, why don't you take her into the back garden for a run-around?" I smiled, winking conspiratorially at Renu. "She always needs to stretch her legs if she's been in the car a while."

"Really? Can we?" asked Harry, slightly tentatively.

"Of course," I replied, lobbing over Molly's favorite tennis ball.

The boys weren't to know that I'd brought her with me for a reason. During our phone call, Renu had revealed how much they'd both bonded with Buffy and how anguished they'd been following her disappearance. Her younger son, Freddie, had re-acted particularly badly, so much so that he'd made his mum promise that she wouldn't replace her with another dog. It would only get snatched by "nasty men," like before, he'd said, and this would make him feel "all sad and lonely" again. His despondency had broken his mother's heart, and she had hoped that a little canine therapy, courtesy of a cute cocker spaniel, might help the healing process.

As I watched Harry and Freddie dash down the garden after Molly, I was instantly reminded of myself and my brother David at a similar age, hot on the heels of our own family dog. My brother and I would have been utterly devastated had our be-loved pooch been so cruelly snatched from us, and I felt so sorry for these poor young boys. To experience such torment seemed horribly unfair.

With her sons out of earshot, Renu and I were able to address more serious matters. She ran through the events surrounding Buffy's disappearance, gulping down sobs as she revisited the awful memories of that fateful day.

"It's the worst thing that's *ever* happened to me, Colin," she said, shaking her head. "I don't give a hoot that the thieves have stolen the car and my jewelry, to be honest—they're replaceable—but I can't come to terms with the fact that they've taken my Buffy. My gorgeous puppy. My precious baby. Who would do such a thing?"

"Here, have a tissue," I whispered as her face crumpled and the tears streamed down her cheeks. I had comforted plenty of distraught dog-lovers over the years, yet witnessing their grief and suffering never got any easier. This poor woman was utterly broken.

"The thing is, I know there are some people out there who think I'm over-reacting, and who'll say, 'It's only a dog,'" she continued. "But they tend not to be pet owners. They think that unconditional love is just reserved for humans. They just don't understand."

Renu also revealed how Buffy's absence had prompted debilitating bouts of anxiety and depression—she'd become a shadow of her former carefree self—and, by her own admission, she'd been an "absolute nightmare" to live with.

"It's the not knowing that's tearing me apart, Colin," she said, biting her lip. "I can't get Buffy out of my head. Is she alone? Is she suffering? Is she dead? She's the first thing that I think about in the morning and the last thing I think about at night, and I won't be able to rest until I know what's happened to her."

I heard a bark from the back garden and craned my neck to check that Molly was okay. A giggling Harry was holding the ball aloft, teasing his doggy playmate, but Freddie was leaning against the wall with his head down and his hands deep in his pockets. My heart went out to the younger boy—I could read his mind—and it was at that very moment that I decided to take on the case. Since Molly's arrival, UKPD had focused primarily on finding missing cats, but Buffy's case had touched me. The pup's theft was hurting every member of this lovely family, and I believed I was the best chance they had of ever seeing her again.

I was very careful to manage Renu's expectations, however. Buffy had been missing for over three months and, with each passing day, the chances of finding her were becoming slimmer. I also knew that it would be an extremely difficult investigation and that I was going to need a few lucky breaks along the way. On the plus side, I'd successfully investigated hundreds of burglaries as a police officer (I'd be deploying my full range of sleuthing skills to try and trace Buffy) and my success rate for recovering stolen dogs was excellent. Not only that, I'd also have my intrepid canine assistant by my side. While Molly hadn't been trained to scent-match dog odors, she was more than able to help me with site searches, and—as she'd done many times previously—would be acting as a decoy during surveillance operations.

"I think of Molly as the Watson to my Sherlock, and the Lewis to my Morse," I said, which elicited a little smile from Renu. "And one thing's for sure: we're going to do all we can to bring Buffy home."

The following day I printed up some photos of the missing dog, as well as a stack of business cards featuring my contact details. For each investigation, I would use a different pay-as-you-go mobile phone number, a practice that I'd originally introduced to the private-eye side of my business but which I'd also decided to employ as a pet detective. Sadly, not every call I'd received in the past had been helpful or well-meaning; sometimes, the person on the end of the line would direct threats toward me or the animal I was seeking—especially if I was working on a stolen-dog case—and it made sense, therefore, to use a temporary SIM card that would be destroyed once the missing pet had been recovered.

My first task was to establish, with as much certainty as possible, that Buffy hadn't escaped during the burglary. With this in mind, I roamed the streets of Willesden Green and spoke to as many local residents as possible, focusing particularly on dog-walkers. Having the ever-friendly Molly with me made this infinitely easier—she was a brilliant ice-breaker—and I was able to strike up a number of useful conversations. None of the walkers, it transpired, had seen this distinctive little puppy on the evening of the burglary, or indeed, ever since. One close neighbor, a Barbour-jacketed gentleman with an elderly Airedale terrier, was particularly obliging.

"I walk my Jerry every night, between nine o'clock and eleven, and I go right past the lady's house," he said. "It's almost like I'm on sentry patrol—I stroll up and down the same road, at the same time—and I'm pretty certain I'd have seen that little dog running about."

"Thanks," I said, as Molly and Jerry bumped noses. "You've been really helpful."

His testimony—as well as the total lack of sightings of this distinctive dog—convinced me that the thieves had left the scene with Buffy in tow. And as I began to build up a picture of the crime and draw up a profile of the thieves, I started to suspect that it had been a planned and professional theft, as opposed to an impromptu, ad-hoc raid. Having perhaps staked out the property for weeks, and aware that the family often went out on Fridays, the offenders had specifically targeted Sachin's car that evening. When they'd come across Buffy, however— and had realized she was a pup with a price tag—they'd decided to snatch her, too. I wondered whether this pretty little dog had been opportunistically stolen to give to a gangster's wife, or a girl-friend, along with the handbags and the jewelry; it seemed quite odd that the household iPads and laptops had been ignored.

Due to a lack of forensic evidence at the crime scene and the failure to find the stolen BMW, within two weeks the Met Police had gradually scaled down their inquiries. I wasn't prepared to give up that easily, though, despite the passage of time, and I planned to approach this case with the rigor and diligence it deserved. Keen to obtain as much detail as possible, one morning I drove over to north London to meet Renu's husband and, over tea for two at a dog-friendly café, he gave me his version of events. Molly sat dutifully by my side, flinching with excitement every time a new customer entered and the bell on the front door tinkled.

"One thing I should have mentioned to you, Colin, is that when the car was stolen the fuel tank was virtually empty," said Sachin. "I'm pretty sure the burglars would've needed to fill it up straight away."

"Drink up your tea," I replied, galvanized by this golden nug-get of information. "We're going on a garage crawl."

With Sachin in my passenger seat, and Molly in her dog

crate, I visited a handful of local petrol stations within a five-mile catchment area of the family home. Rogues and robbers rarely paid for fuel, so I asked each manager to check if they'd had any so-called "pump and runs" involving a blue BMW on the day of the burglary.

"You know what, I think we did . . ." said one, flicking through an A4-sized diary before stopping at the date in question. "Yeah, remember it well. They filled up a whole tank, then sped off the forecourt. Three dark-haired lads. One getting the petrol, two others sitting in the car. I've still got the CCTV if you want to take a look?"

"Absolutely we do," I said.

The footage threw up two significant lines of inquiry. Firstly, the registration plates had swiftly been removed, the plan being to replace them with false versions. This—together with the fact they'd filled up the tank completely—suggested to me that the thieves intended to continue using the car themselves for the foreseeable future. Secondly, the images showed three young men—in their late teens, perhaps, or early twenties—who, in my eyes, looked Mediterranean or Eastern European in appearance.

The net seemed to be closing in on our offenders, and I could only hope and pray that the BMW would soon resurface. Only then, I felt, would I get any nearer to cracking the case, and to discovering Buffy's fate.

While I continued to circulate images of the missing dog and kept my ear firmly to the ground, a whole fortnight or so passed without any major leads or developments. There was another maddening case of mistaken identity, sadly, whereby a dog answering Buffy's description (and with the same name, apparently) had been spotted by a passer-by in a north London park. I had followed things up the next day, with Molly and Sam in tow, but it had become quickly apparent that—pardon the pun—we were barking up the wrong tree. Not only was this dog much older and plumper (it actually looked more like a Maltese terrier), we also heard its owner yelling "Poppy . . . come here, Poppy!" when it had scampered past us.

"I suppose Poppy does sound a *little bit* like Buffy," shrugged Sam.

"Yeah, only if you're wearing earmuffs." I sighed. "Time to give Renu the bad news."

Our client was understandably crestfallen when I called her—she'd felt really optimistic about this particular sighting—but it seemed she had some news of her own to relay.

"You're not going to believe this, Colin, but Sachin's BMW has been found," she said, explaining that it had been abandoned in Stoke Newington following an accident and towed to the Met Police car pound. Officers had checked it for forensic evidence but had concluded there was nothing of significance.

"By rights, our car-insurance company owns it now," added Renu, "but they've agreed we can examine it, too, if we want, before it goes off to auction."

"That's *fantastic* news," I replied. "I'm on my way."

Sam took Molly home to Sussex, and I met Sachin at the car pound, where we joined a motley crew of rogues and reprobates queueing up to reclaim their vehicles. It wasn't the most salubrious of places—the bulletproof windows and the NO VERBAL OR PHYSICAL ABUSE OF STAFF notices spoke volumes—and everywhere you turned there seemed to be spats and scuffles. Sachin's eyes widened as a bloke at the front of the queue was deemed too drug-addled to collect his Suzuki motorbike and was frogmarched out, kicking and screaming, by two police officers.

We were eventually ushered through a turnstile and into the pound itself. It was like a vast, out-of-town car supermarket, with line upon line of confiscated vehicles, ranging from flashy sports cars to total write-offs. Sachin's BMW was clearly in the latter category. It was a mangled mess of metal—the crash had been high impact—and, I assumed, would be sold off for parts only.

As Sachin chatted to the clerk, I began to search the car's

interior. Throughout my fourteen years as a police officer, I'd searched lots of stolen cars and every single search had resulted in the discovery of a crucial piece of evidence that had taken the investigation forward. You needed to be very thorough, and you needed to break the search down into four phases: trunk, hood, exterior and interior.

When I opened up the trunk I was surprised to find that it contained two new wheels (probably stolen) and a jerry can. I could only assume that the thieves had not risked taking the car to any more petrol stations and had opted to siphon their fuel from other cars. The presence of the two spare wheels suggested that the robbers were thinking about keeping the car for the foreseeable future.

The search of the hood, exterior and front interior drew a blank, however. It seemed I was dealing with a gang of professional crooks who had gone to a lot of trouble not to leave any forensic evidence behind that could lead to their identity.

Finally, I climbed into the rear passenger seats and had a good look around. Still nothing.

Come on, Colin, look harder, I berated myself. *There's always something . . .*

I cast my mind back to some of the previous searches I'd completed for Surrey Police and remembered one occasion whereby the car owner, a small-time drug dealer, had hidden his stash beneath his front passenger seat. Keen to comb every inch of Sachin's car, I decided to check the underside of Sachin's passenger seat, my heartbeat quickening when I felt something plastic and sticky. I gave it a gentle tug and, when I realized what it was, could hardly believe my eyes. There in my hand was a parking ticket bearing a registration number, a date, a time and—crucially—a location: the northeast London suburb of Stoke Newington.

"YESSSS!" I whispered to myself, performing a covert little fist pump. This was the significant breakthrough I'd been waiting for, the stroke of luck that would allow my investigation finally to gather some pace.

The clerk remained deep in conversation with my client so, while he wasn't looking, I furtively slipped the yellow notice into my pocket. A tad naughty of me, I suppose—I ought really to have informed the police—but the Met had shown little interest in this case and I reckoned I needed this cold, hard evidence more than they did.

Sachin was overjoyed with this momentous development—he realized how pivotal it could be—and after I bade him farewell I set about following the first of many lines of inquiry. A check on the false number plate revealed that the thieves had cloned it from an identical BMW on sale in a Birmingham car dealership, confirming my suspicions that the burglary had been planned. I rang the showroom manager, who said that he'd been somewhat perplexed by the deluge of parking tickets and court summonses he'd received from Hackney Borough Council. Due to data-protection law, however, he regretted he was unable to send me copies.

Undeterred, I asked Sachin to inform the council about the parking tickets related to his car and to ask if he could settle the payments online. *Bingo.* He was duly allocated a unique reference number which enabled him to access a grand total of five parking tickets on the internet, all of which had been generated in the Stoke Newington area.

"I think I can hazard a guess as to where the thieves live," I said, when he forwarded me the details.

Then, using my network of contacts, I identified, and then interviewed, the traffic wardens who had issued each parking notice. They were legally obliged to take photographs of offending vehicles in order to provide evidence of time and location—some wardens captured video footage, too—and as a result our investigation took another major leap forward. The biggest fillip came in the form of two separate photos, which revealed background images of two Afro-Caribbean men—mechanics, I presumed—who appeared to be working on roadside vehicles just yards away from where the BMW had been illegally parked.

These guys could be the best witnesses we've got, I thought to myself.

It was time to go undercover on the streets of northeast London. It was also time to draft in the assistance of Detective Constable Molly Butcher.

Stoke Newington is home to a huge Turkish community—the largest in Western Europe, in fact—and there was a distinct probability that the Mediterranean-looking men spotted at the petrol station were among their number. To secure the locals' trust (and to acquaint myself with the territory), I thought it would be wise for me to go incognito, so I ditched my UKPD fleece, donned my jeans and T-shirt, honed my north London accent and posed as a regular guy, casually walking his cocker spaniel along Stoke Newington High Street. As ever, with the gregarious Molly by my side, it was much easier to blend into the crowd.

Armed with a wad of "Bring Back Buffy" leaflets, I visited various shops, cafés and bookmakers, introducing myself as Terry, a friend of Renu's who was raising awareness about the dog's disappearance.

"The family don't want to get anyone into trouble, and they're not aiming to involve the police. They just want Buffy back," I told the proprietor of a Turkish barber's (I was particularly keen to get the message across that, should Buffy be recovered alive, there would be no repercussions). Then I proceeded to tug gently on his heart strings—a well-worn technique to get someone "on side"—by describing the devastating effect of the robbery.

"The whole household is heartbroken, as you can imagine," I said, as the barber nodded sympathetically. "My friend's worried sick, and her kids can hardly sleep at night. I don't know about you, mate, but I couldn't cope if *my* dog went missing."

The man looked down at Molly, who—as if on cue—tilted her head to one side and gazed imploringly at him. Meryl Streep would have been so proud.

"No, me neither. I'd be so, so upset," he said, his accent ly-ing halfway between Hackney and Ankara. "My French bulldog means everything to me. *Ev—ery—thing . . .*"

"Exactly," I replied, handing over a business card and a leaflet. "Please, if you have *any* information about Buffy's whereabouts, you must give me a call."

With my trusty sidekick trotting obediently at my heel, I continued with my door-to-door inquiries. Most of the resi-dents and traders we met were very helpful and promised to keep their eyes peeled, but the total absence of sightings in the district suggested that the puppy was either being kept indoors, had been whisked out of the area or was no longer alive. While the prospect of the latter was far too grim to dwell upon, at the same time I had to be realistic: there was always a risk that thieves would see a dog like Buffy as a liability—she directly linked them to their crime, after all—and would take action to end her life prematurely. But that was the worst-case scenario, of course, and I was determined to stay positive.

"Come on, Molly." I smiled, heading off to a nearby park for some tennis-ball-related fun and frolics. "You've worked incred-ibly hard today. Time for a well-earned break."

The following day I ramped things up a notch. Molly and I visited a handful of Stoke Newington community centers, affix-ing the Buffy posters in areas of high footfall and maximum vis-ibility. I'd also asked Sam to mock up a photo of Sachin's BMW, sporting the fake registration number, which I brandished at every opportunity in the hope that it would jog someone's memory. Then, I revealed my true pet-detective identity to a number of well-connected individuals—council officers and café owners, for instance—before asking them to spread the word far and wide.

My strategy was to reach the thieves through the commu-nity and to apply pressure on them. *Give Buffy Back* was my message, *and then I'll go away.* News would hopefully filter through to the perpetrators that I was on their case and that I was zoning in on their community. I needed them to feel the pressure.

Outside one such community hub I got chatting to a middle-aged Jamaican woman walking a frisky, yappy Jack Russell terrier. Dressed in a rainbow-hued robe and matching head wrap, she listened intently as I gave her the lowdown on Buffy's story, from the missing dog to the mangled car. I also happened to show her the traffic warden's images of the mechanics by the roadside, whom I was keen to identify as potential witnesses.

"That looks very much like Mr. Wilson and his son," she said, giving her dog's leash a sharp tug as he dashed toward Molly. "They fix a lot of the cars in the neighborhood, including my husband's. Nice gentlemen, I'm sure they'll be happy to help. Let me give you directions . . ."

Mr. Wilson's lock-up was sandwiched between two sprawling housing estates. As Molly and I walked past a sea of boarded-up shops and properties, many of them plastered with graffiti and fly posters, it seemed like a world apart from the bustling vibrancy of the high street, just a stone's throw away. Most passers-by wore hoodies and walked with their heads down—no nods or pleasantries here—and, rightly or wrongly, I felt myself holding Molly's lead extra tightly.

As I sidled over to the lock-up, a raucous game of dominoes was in mid-flow. Four middle-aged Afro-Caribbean men were sitting around a table—an upturned oil drum, to be precise—whooping, laughing, groaning and back-slapping as a succession of tiles were dramatically slapped down. One of them, wearing paint- and oil-spattered overalls, noticed me and Molly loitering with intent. I raised my palm in a "no, carry on, I'll wait" gesture.

Five minutes later the game had come to an end and three of the four men had gone their separate ways, leaving behind the man in the overalls.

"Mr. Wilson?" I asked, handing over my business card. "My name's Colin Butch—"

"The guy looking for the dog, yeah?" he interrupted. "My friend Rosie rang to say you might be paying me a visit."

I spent the next few minutes showing him all my photographic evidence. He confirmed that the traffic warden's image depicted him and his son—they often did roadside repairs in the locality—and I asked him if he'd ever noticed the blue BMW or, better still, had completed any repair work on it. The vehicle had probably been in a few scrapes before the recent accident, I explained, and there appeared to be two new wheels in the boot that were ready to be fitted.

His thumb and forefinger stroked the white bristles on his chin.

"I'm not aware of the car myself," he said, "but you might want to speak to my son about it."

I paused for a few moments, waiting for him to elaborate.

"He takes on some jobs that I wouldn't touch with a barge-pole," he sighed, "but some groups of lads can be, shall we say, a little persistent . . ."

His voice trailed off and he seemed unwilling to divulge any more details. Being a father myself, I recognized those protective, paternal instincts.

"I can promise you, Mr. Wilson, that no one's going to get into trouble. Buffy's owners would prefer not to involve the police. And it's my job to seek pets, not prosecutions."

My assurances seemed to placate him slightly.

"Andrew's working in the back yard," he said. "Let me go and have a chat with him."

I heard some muffled voices—it seemed a few sharp words were being exchanged—and soon enough Wilson Jr. emerged. A taller, slimmer version of his father, he sported baggy denim dungarees and a tool belt laden with wrenches and spanners. He leaned against the lock-up wall and stared at me blankly.

"I don't know anything," he said.

"*Andrew* . . ." admonished his father.

"I don't . . . know . . . anything," he repeated. "Now, can I get back to work, please?"

"Listen," I said. "As I've just told your father, no one's in trouble here. I just want to know if you've been in contact with some people I'm looking for."

He stared at his hobnail boots and shook his head.

"I'm not the police, okay? I'm a pet detective. I find missing animals. I'm working with a family who've had their beautiful little puppy stolen and who are absolutely bloody traumatized."

The boy briefly caught my gaze, before hurriedly looking away.

"All you need to do is to give them a call. To tell them that I'm on their case, and that, one way or another, I will find out what happened to Buffy."

Silence.

"And, if she *is* still alive, they need to either get in touch with me, or hand her in to a rescue center."

"*Andrew* . . ." repeated his father, more sternly.

"All right, all right," he said, throwing up his hands in exasperation. "So, they rang me to get their wheels changed. I didn't want their business. They're wrong 'uns. They're trouble. But they said they were going to pay me a daft amount of money. Couldn't refuse it in the end, could I?"

"So you've got their contact details then?" I asked. "And you can ask them about the missing dog?"

Andrew pulled out a pack of tobacco and rolled himself a cigarette, gave it a long suck and blew the smoke skywards. I knew he was stalling and I was ready for his answer.

"My phone's broken," he said unconvincingly. "I dropped it. Smashed it to bits. I can't get their number. Sorry."

"That's no problem." I smiled. "I've got software that can retrieve data from a broken handset. Either that, or I could ask a contact of mine to access your phone records."

He gulped hard—his Adam's apple protruded like a peach stone—before glancing at his father. I'd forced him into a corner, and he knew it.

"Make that call, Andrew, and make it today," I said, patting Molly, who went from sitting to standing. "Just do the right thing. Please."

Two days later, Molly and I were traveling home from Sevenoaks, having spent the afternoon trying to find a rare Sphynx cat called Andromeda, when I picked up a voicemail from Renu. Her squeals were so loud I had to turn down the volume on my speakerphone.

"BUFFY'S BEEN FOUND!" she yelled, and a thunderbolt of adrenaline shot around my body. "Two young lads handed her in to a dog-rescue center in Essex," she panted, barely able to get her words out. "The staff scanned Buffy's microchip and rang me. Sachin and I are on our way. Never thought this day would happen. Never thought I'd see her again. Thank you so much, Colin. *Thank you SO, SO much . . .*"

There then followed a few seconds of joyful sobbing—I welled up, too, I'm not ashamed to admit—before the message clicked off. I looked in my rear-view mirror and could see that Molly was shifting in her crate, seeking a comfortable sleeping position for the journey home.

"Well, well, well, Detective Constable Molly Butcher," I said, smiling. "Looks like we finally cracked our case."

I let out a deep sigh of relief. It had been a tough investigation, but Molly and I had solved it.

As soon as I got back to Cranleigh I rang the rescue-center manager to glean more information about Buffy's return. He told me that two teenage lads—from a nearby traveling community, he reckoned—had brought in the dog, and had left without saying a word. *Intermediaries*, I thought to myself. They had probably been given a back-hander by the perpetrators, who certainly wouldn't have wanted their faces caught on CCTV, and who'd clearly wished to wash their hands of the dog they'd stolen. I'd made Buffy such a well-known figure in Stoke Newington that she'd become too hot to handle and they'd chosen not to dispose of the dog in a more callous manner. On the face of it, destroying the "evidence" might have been the easier, safer option for them.

Buffy had been delivered to the rescue center in a terrible state, however. She had contracted a dreadful eye infection and had incurred friction burns to her nose, consistent with being confined in a metal cage. Her coat was matted, she was ridden with fleas and she was grossly underweight. But she was alive—thank heavens—and she was finally out of harm's way.

I left Renu and her loved ones alone for a few days—I felt it was important that they were given plenty of time and space with Buffy—but we kept in touch via text and email. The puppy had received a clean bill of health from the vet's, she told me, and had been washed, groomed and pampered for the first time in four long months.

I paid a visit to Willesden Green the following week. Watching Harry and Freddie running around the garden with their happy, healthy and fluffy little pooch was a sight to behold, and again reminded me of my brother David and I larking about with our canine friends in Singapore. I turned to Renu, who flashed me the most beautiful of smiles.

"I'll never forget what you've done for us, Colin," she said. "Our family is complete again."

"I couldn't have done it without Molly," I said, feeling a little overcome with emotion myself. I gave Renu a big hug, before waving goodbye to the boys.

As I put Molly back into her crate, she gently nudged my arm and looked at me with concern, as if to say, *Are you all right, Dad? Your eyes look a bit sad . . .*

I was, I admit, mentally exhausted. The Buffy investigation had taken several months to complete and I'd had to step up to the plate and show strength and confidence, even if, like Renu, I'd had my doubts about the outcome. Thank goodness I'd delivered on my promise, and Buffy was back where she belonged.

I looked down at Molly, who still seemed a little confused by my demeanor.

"I'm good, Molls, honestly," I said, ruffling the backs of her ears and kissing her snout.

~ 10 ~

Bluebell Wood

Although Molly's scent-detection skills were coming on in leaps and bounds—quite literally, in fact—it was still vitally important that we kept up our rigorous training schedule. There were always new techniques to learn and new hidey-holes to discover, and three or four times a week I'd take her over to Bramble Hill Farm in order to put her through her paces. Molly could often sense that we were off to HQ, and as I got everything ready at home she'd take up a position by the front door, usually sitting on my outdoor boots. As I pulled them on to my feet, she'd always gently place a paw on the leather, just making double-sure that we were venturing outdoors.

Sometimes I'd set Molly specific tasks at Bramble Hill, often based upon issues we'd encountered in previous searches. I would, for example, plant a cat-hair sample high up in a sycamore, to replicate the missing moggy she'd found holed up in a treehouse. Or I'd take her to areas where small animals roamed—beside the lake, or along the canal—to teach her to focus on the core cat scent rather than being distracted by the odors of ducks, rabbits or squirrels.

While Molly's progress over the past few months had been nothing short of phenomenal, it was vital that her scent-detection techniques as a working cocker spaniel—as well as my own dog-handling abilities—were constantly improved and refined. This very fact had been underlined by Mark, the canine-behavior expert who'd worked so closely with Molly prior to my ownership of her.

"You'll never, ever stop improving, Colin," he'd told me on handover day. "Every single search will throw up different tests and challenges, and you've got to learn from them all, even the disappointments."

Indeed, Molly and I had experienced a handful of unsuccessful cat searches that spring. In one such instance I had unwisely deployed her in fine rain and, despite her very best efforts, it had been impossible for her to match the animal's scent in the damp conditions. The search was ultimately fruitless and, not only did I get soaked to the skin (as did Molly), I came away feeling utterly dejected. On another occasion we'd been tasked with finding a farm cat named Spider but, upon arrival at the location, I discovered that all the barns and stables were packed with livestock. Unable to guarantee Molly's safety, we'd had to leave without searching a single building. I wasn't deluded—realistically, we were never going to locate every single cat—but I still felt down and disconsolate whenever we didn't get a result, even if it was beyond our control. I would use these setbacks as a platform for further learning, however, and would put in hours of extra training to compensate.

"We'll get it right next time, Molls," I'd say, as she tore off toward Shepherd's Rest, where, an hour earlier, I'd hidden a cat-hair sample in a hollow oak tree.

On one such training day—a breezy springtime morning—I was driving over to Bramble Hill Farm while an impatient Molly bounced and bobbed around her crate.

C'mon, then, Dad . . . she seemed to be saying, as keen as ever to have some fun and fill her lungs with fresh air. *Are we nearly there yet?*

Then my car phone rang, so I pulled into a lay-by and took the call.

"Hello, Colin Butcher speaking . . ."

There followed a pause and then the sound of muffled voices, as if the phone receiver was being passed from one person to another.

"Good morning, dear," replied a frail, elderly voice. "Are you the pet detective?"

"Yes, that's me."

"The gentleman with the dog that finds cats?"

"Indeed." I smiled, and Molly whined petulantly behind me.

"I'm afraid I may need your help. I've heard all about you and Molly, and my kind colleagues here at the cat charity have found your telephone number. It's my Chester, you see. He's gone missing."

The lady's name was Margaret, she lived near the Kent village of Hawkenbury and she'd seen neither sight nor sound of her cat for three long days. An eighteen-year-old tabby, with mackerel-patterned markings, Chester was largely housebound and his extended absence was hugely out of character.

"I've been worried sick," she said. "He's not getting any younger and I'm petrified that he's come to some harm."

She explained that she and her sister—both in their mid-nineties—were too infirm to search their large garden and that numerous attempts by local villagers to find Chester had drawn a blank.

"I simply can't bear it," she said, her voice faltering. "All I want is for my cat to be found, Mr. Butcher, and for me to know exactly what's happened to him. I don't suppose you and Molly could possibly help?"

"Firstly, you must call me Colin," I replied soothingly, "and, secondly, I'm sure that we can assist in some way. Ask one of your friends to text me your address and we'll be with you as soon as we can."

"Oh, that would be wonderful," she replied, sighing with relief. "That's just what I needed to hear."

I disconnected the call and turned to face my restless dog, who by now was emitting low growls of frustration.

"Change of plan, Molls. Training's abandoned. We're off to find Chester."

I collected my trusty assistant along the way (Sam had become accustomed to last-minute call-outs for hasty assignments) and, following a scenic drive through the Surrey Hills, we reached Margaret's village around noon. We'd had a fair bit of trouble locating our client's home—we found ourselves in a maze of narrow, blossom-laden lanes, with a dearth of house signs and numbers—and it was only when we spied a tiny old lady leaning on a rickety wooden gate, squinting at the car, that we realized we'd reached our destination. As we pulled up, she waved cheerily, unlatched the gate and gestured toward a long, snaking driveway.

I slowly wound down my window, noticing a rotting house sign on the ground. It was no wonder we'd had problems finding the place.

"Margaret?"

"Indeed it is. I'm *so* delighted to see you all," she said, as Molly yapped excitedly and thumped her tail against her crate. My dog was smart enough to realize that the sound of a stranger's voice usually indicated that a live search was imminent.

Peering through my windscreen, I spied a distant rooftop through a canopy of laurels.

"How's about hopping in the back seat, Margaret?" I asked. "Looks like a fair old trek to your front door."

"I'm fine, thanks," she replied. "The walk will do me good. Old dears like me need all the exercise they can get."

Fifteen minutes later Sam and I were leaning against my open trunk with the warm sun beating down on us, waiting for Margaret to emerge. Sitting between us, still in her crate, was an increasingly animated Molly. In these scenarios she would often tremble in anticipation, like she was shivering with cold, and would produce strange gargling noises from the back of her throat.

Come on, you two, my dog appeared to be saying. *Let's see some action . . .*

Facing us was Greenlea Hall, an imposing but dilapidated Edwardian mansion. The grandeur of its sash windows, its lofty gables and its white portico was somewhat diminished, I noticed, by flaking paintwork and crumbling masonry. Parts of the coppery-red brickwork had been dislodged by a gnarled and knotty wisteria and at the front of the house stood a huge stone fountain, riven with cracks and covered in lichen.

"I can't believe a couple of OAPs live here," said Sam, scanning this sizable Kent residence. "This place is *huge* . . ."

Finally, Margaret hobbled into view. Her long, silvery-white hair was tied into a loose ponytail and she wore navy cotton trousers teamed with a baggy sky-blue sweater.

"So let me have a look at Molly," she grinned, stooping low and peering through the grille. "Oh, what a *gorgeous* girl. And a very, very clever doggy, from what I've heard . . ."

Molly's gurgles and tail thwacks promptly went into overdrive.

"Oh, she'll *love* you for saying that," I laughed. "Flattery will get you everywhere with this little madam."

Margaret chuckled as she slowly straightened herself up.

"So, can I tempt you indoors for some tea and cake?"

I explained to Margaret that, while Sam and I would appreciate some refreshments, Molly would have to remain in the car until the start of the search. We had to be very careful not to expose her to any cat scent in the house; it might overwhelm her nostrils and hamper the search.

"I'll keep the trunk open for some fresh air, though, and I'll leave a couple of soft toys for her to gnaw. She'll be happy enough."

"Whatever's for the best." Margaret smiled, then ushered us toward her grand abode.

As we sat in her olde worlde farmhouse kitchen—a room that had probably remained unchanged in decades—I gave my client a potted history of Molly's story. At the far end of the kitchen, near an old Aga stove, sat two other cats, a sleek Abyssinian and a scruffy Maine Coon. Both were feigning a casual indifference, but I could tell by the odd flick of a tail and the twitch of an ear that they were more than aware of our presence.

"That's Simba and Sandy," said Margaret, gazing fondly at them, "although I have to say, they've not been themselves recently. They're both missing old Chester as much as I am."

All three cats had been strays, apparently, and were among the many lost or abandoned moggies that Margaret had sheltered and adopted over the years. Animal aficionados like this lady were my favorite type of client, it has to be said: kind, compassionate and utterly devoted to their pets.

Suddenly, the mahogany kitchen door swung open, causing Sandy and Simba to leap up in fright and shoot out of the cat flap.

"Did I hear her saying she *adopts* them?" guffawed a gray-haired lady, clad in beige nylon slacks and an olive-green fleece. "What nonsense. My sister steals the bloody damned things from our neighbors. She can't help herself. Loves those wretched cats more than she loves me."

"Oh, for goodness' sake, Kathrine," said Margaret, wearily shaking her head. "Colin, you've probably gathered that this is my sister. Please don't believe a word she says."

"Ah, so you're this detective fellow, are you?" she smirked, shuffling over and extending her bony hand. "A Hercule Poirot for pets, eh?"

She wasn't the first person to be amused by what I did for a living.

"Well, I hope you're not expecting to be paid, old chap," she continued, "because we haven't got a bean until the day I decide to sell this place. Not a bean."

"*Kathrine!*" cried her horrified sister.

"As it happens, I'm classing this visit as a training session for Molly," I responded, trying to stay measured. "I'm just happy to help your sister, to be honest."

"You'll probably be wasting your time, anyway," she harrumphed. "That animal's so decrepit it's probably dropped dead. Either that, or it's been flattened by a passing truck."

Margaret gasped and raised her hands to her flushed cheeks. *What a charmer*, I thought. *What an absolute charmer.* Sensing my mounting ire, Sam made a timely interjection.

"Colin, isn't it time for you and Margaret to go outside for the pre-search recce?" she said.

Sam knew that I always liked to have a safety-first sweep of the area beforehand, in order to identify any hazards that might endanger Molly's search: derelict outbuildings, rusty machinery or loose-lidded chemicals could be perilous.

". . . and while you do that, I can stay inside with Kathrine," she added with a wry smile. She had sussed, quite rightly, that I didn't want this overbearing sister sticking her nose in.

"Excellent idea," I replied.

Greenlea Hall, it transpired, was set in one of the largest estates in east Kent. Comprising a huge patchwork of lawns, fields and woodland, it also contained a smattering of dilapidated outbuildings and disused farm vehicles. Had Chester been a young, agile and independent cat, Molly and I would have definitely had our work cut out for us. But, in these circumstances, I didn't think a widespread search of the area would be necessary. My knowledge and experience of cat behavior told me that, taking into account his age, his frailty and his strong homing instinct, Chester would be found nearer rather than farther, and sooner rather than later.

"All things considered, Margaret, I'm pretty sure that Chester won't have strayed far," I told her.

"Oh, I do hope you're right," she replied. "Shall I show you around the gardens?"

Spanning the rear of Greenlea Hall was an impressive glass orangery which bordered on to a huge, moss-covered York-stone terrace dotted with assorted buckets, plant pots and watering cans. This opened up on to an extensive lawn—a quarter the size of a football pitch, I reckoned—beyond which lay stunning views across the county. To the right was an empty paddock (Margaret had been a keen horsewoman back in the day, she told me) and to the left was a traditional walled garden. It, too, had seen better days, judging by its gangly fruit trees and scraggy herbaceous borders. An unkempt patch of grass was studded with daisies and dandelions and edged by a row of bare-branched oaks on one side and a line of bushy, overgrown firs on the other. In its prime, this garden would have been a hide-and-seek paradise for a curious child or a serene sanctuary for a frazzled parent. Those days were long gone.

"Chester used to love watching the world go by in here," said Margaret, her eyes glistening with tears. "He'd loll around in the sunshine and watch the blue tits flitting about. He was far too slow and tubby to catch any, of course."

I asked if I could take a peek inside the ramshackle garage, which housed the couple's vintage Mini Cooper, as well as a stack of antiquated gardening tools. As I shifted a pair of medieval hedge clippers to one side, I spied a cluster of rusty bicycles, in size order, ranging from a toddler's trike to a teenager's racer.

"They all belonged to my daughter," said Margaret wistfully. "I don't like to throw anything away. I . . . well . . . I thought they might be needed one day."

She explained that Greenlea Hall had belonged to her parents and that she and her sister had inherited it some thirty years ago. "My sister can be very outspoken," she said. Relations between Kathrine and Margaret's only child had deteriorated, prompted by a huge row in which the former had accused the latter of meeting an "unsuitable" man and subsequently marrying "beneath herself."

"Elizabeth lives in Cornwall now. She'll only visit when it's just me in the house, which—with Kathrine's arthritis—is hardly ever these days," she said. "We speak, and we write, but it's not the same. I feel like a stranger to my daughter. It's *ever* so sad."

As she gazed into the distance, something about her expression seemed oddly familiar. And then it dawned on me. That same look of pain. That same sense of loss. It was like staring into the eyes of my mother, three decades earlier, following the passing of my brother David. He had only been twenty when he'd succumbed to pneumonia—his immune system had been shot to pieces after a ten-year battle with leukemia—and my parents had been left utterly broken-hearted. Although not entirely unexpected, his death had hit me massively hard, too. I'd grown up idolizing my cool, calm older brother; we'd had so many childhood adventures together and had shared so many passions, none more so than our enduring love of dogs. It was a crying shame that David had not lived long enough to know my Molly. I know he'd have loved her to bits.

Margaret and I—both deep in thought—continued our walk to the foot of the garden and, shielding my eyes from the bright sunlight, I surveyed this rambling mansion and its bedraggled grounds. Once upon a time, a great deal of love and labor must have gone into Margaret and Kathrine's dream family home. Now, sadly, it seemed that the place—and their friendship—had become run-down. I felt a sudden pang of sorrow for this delightful woman who, in her twilight years, seemed to be reaping most of her happiness from her pets, not her sibling.

"It's time for Operation Cat Sample," I said, smiling, and offered Margaret my arm for support as we strolled back toward the house. "And it's time to fetch the lovely Molly."

I *remained on* the terrace while Margaret retrieved Chester's favorite cushion, which, as instructed, she had kept away from Simba and Sandy and had left inside the house. Unfortunately, it was commonplace for cat owners to put their missing cat's bedding, favorite toy or litter tray outside in the garden in the mistaken belief this would encourage their cat to return. Sadly, this often attracted visits from other neighborhood cats, who would scent-mark these items, presenting the absent cat with yet another reason to stay away.

My heart leaped when my client appeared on the terrace with a large cushion balanced on her palms. At first I assumed it was made of mohair but, on closer inspection, I realized it was completely swathed in Chester's wispy beige fur. I felt like punching the air.

"I'm one of the few people in Britain who gets giddy when they see something covered in cat hair, Margaret," I grinned, thrilled that Molly now had the best possible chance of matching the scent and finding the pet.

Wearing latex gloves to ensure I didn't contaminate the sample with my own scent, I gently eased away several large clumps with a stainless-steel wire brush before carefully decanting them into one of my sterile jam jars. Then, with everything good to go, I radioed Sam on the walkie-talkie to bring Molly across to the terrace. As usual, my dog was overjoyed to be reunited with me and gave my face a good old lick, with a dabbing of wet nose for good measure.

"It's search time, Molls," I said, looking into her eyes and stroking her sleek black head.

With a handful of dog treats in one pocket and my handset in the other, I led Molly over to the paddock to introduce her to Chester's scent. As professional as ever, she'd already composed herself accordingly and had entered a Zen-like state of calm and concentration. As her owner and handler, I'd taught her to differentiate between her two distinct roles—her life as a pet and her life as a worker—and she was able to make the transition from Molly the cuddly cocker spaniel to Molly the cat-seeking detection dog. The moment I took her harness from my belt and presented it to her she knew full well she was in work mode.

Responding to my usual "Toma" command, she poked her nose into the glass jar and inhaled deeply. On the command of "Seek . . . seek!"—and with Margaret and Sam now by my side—I finally let her off the leash and released her into a fairly stiff spring breeze.

With a shrill yelp of excitement, Molly shot across the wide lawn like a missile and, within a few seconds, appeared to hit a scent trail. Her snout seemed to stop while the rest of her body hurtled on—like something out of a *Scooby-Doo* cartoon—and she made a sudden ninety-degree swerve to the left, toward the walled garden. Through the gate she zoomed and, once we'd gamely caught up with her, we watched as she crouched low, leaped high and gyrated around, inhaling the swirling air as she went.

However, it was when Molly zoned in on one of the largest conifers on the plot's eastern side that her behavior took a bizarre turn. Each time she took two steps forward she seemed to take one step back, all the while shooting us concerned glances. During our many searches together we had fostered a really unique understanding that often relied on eye contact and—knowing Molly as I did—I could immediately see that she had hit a scent that she'd never encountered before. As she circled the conifer, looking thoroughly dazed and disorientated, I could read her mind.

What's going on here, Dad? Why have I never smelled this before?

This erratic toing and froing continued for a few minutes and my concerns began to mount. I had rarely observed her behaving like this. My dog was becoming increasingly distressed and confused and her anxiety levels were soaring. Something was really bothering her.

"I'm going to call her off for a while," I said to Margaret and Sam, before recalling Molly with three pips of my dog whistle, the customary command that required her to pause the search and scamper back to my side.

"Don't worry, Molly," I said, comforting her with pats and hugs before letting her frolic around a field for a few minutes. Only when I sensed that her agitation had receded and I was happy that our mutual trust remained intact did I decide to restart the search.

I reintroduced Chester's scent to my dog and, as I did so, I felt the headwind noticeably dropping. Yet again, Molly darted into the walled garden and ran toward the same fir, but this time she moved with a little more confidence and self-assurance. With bated breath, we all watched her as she crawled deep beneath the tree's heavy, grass-skimming branches.

Within seconds, Molly had dramatically re-emerged and had suddenly performed the "down," lying flat, still and silent, with her front paws outstretched, her head upright and her eyes locked. Her unique success signal.

I've found what I'm looking for, she was effectively telling me. *I've done what you've asked . . .*

This most emphatic and conclusive of "downs" told me that Molly had discovered Chester's scent and had pinpointed the lost pet. But her doleful expression, together with her strangely subdued demeanor, also spoke volumes. Margaret's cat was no longer alive.

I slowly knelt down on the grass and lifted the weighty branches. Sadly, my suspicions were confirmed. Lying on his side with his eyes closed, looking like he'd fallen into a deep, peaceful sleep, was a plump tabby cat. There was definitely no pulse, and his fur was cold and wet, but neither was there any sign of injury or trauma. I could only surmise that poor Chester had succumbed to old age and had most likely passed away calmly and quietly after migrating to his little sanctuary. I knew that poorly cats often linked their sickness to their environment and would shift location to effectively "escape" the pain, in the same way that they'd flee a barking dog or a boisterous child.

"Bless you, Chester," I whispered, stroking his head before gently lowering the bough.

Then Margaret shuffled toward me, her hands clasped to her chest.

"Oh, Colin . . . has Molly found him? Is my Chester all right?"

I held her cold, fragile hands in mine as Sam looked on sadly.

"I'm afraid it's not the news you were hoping for, Margaret," I said. "I'm ever so sorry."

She promptly fell into my arms, her whole body shaking with emotion as the tears began to flow.

"Darling Chester!" she cried. "My lovely, lovely boy . . ."

After a minute or so with Margaret I discreetly caught Sam's eye, and she gently took Margaret to one side. While I understood my client's pain—I'd spent years dealing with all manner of bereavement in the police force—my focus had to be on my dog, who was both my priority and my responsibility. Out of the corner of my eye, I'd already seen Molly becoming increasingly anxious; she'd clearly picked up on Margaret's shock and my solemnity and, having never located a deceased pet before, was hugely perplexed by these negative post-search reactions. As far as she was concerned, she'd done her job as requested—at just shy of ten minutes, it had been her fastest ever cat recovery—yet, in her eyes, everyone must have seemed so unhappy. My dog, like many others, was remarkably sensitive to human emotion and it must have felt bewildering to witness such deep pain and suffering.

Compounding Molly's confusion was the absence of the usual reward experience, which—in these somber circumstances—would have been highly inappropriate and might have caused great offense to the client. I knew I had to give her the "Good girl, Molly!" treatment as soon as possible, though, since it was vital that Molly didn't associate the new scent as a negative experience but saw it as a positive. Failure to do so would mean that, next time she smelled a decaying cat, she might not indicate it for fear of upsetting me or a client.

With this in mind, I walked Molly over to the paddock, out of sight and sound of the grieving Margaret. Once inside, I rewarded her with gusto, I bombarded her with praise and laid on a quality play session.

Now this is what I call fun, she no doubt thought as she scampered after a tennis ball, deftly catching it in her mouth.

I found it a struggle to feign an upbeat cheeriness, to be honest. As an animal-lover myself, and as someone who'd mourned the loss of some beloved pets and people, Chester's death had greatly affected me, too. I felt dreadfully sorry for Margaret, but out of duty to Molly—and to preserve our regular routine—I felt obliged, as the old adage goes, to "keep calm and carry on." I remained in the paddock with Molly until I was satisfied that she'd been amply rewarded, and until I'd reinforced the fact that she hadn't been punished in any way, shape or form.

(Incidentally, this calculated decision, tough though it was, was vindicated a few weeks later when Molly found a missing cat that had sadly died after a suspected dog mauling. While the outcome was tragic, the owner was incredibly grateful to Molly and me for giving her closure to what had been a deeply upsetting experience. My dog, much to my relief, had not allowed the scent of decay to distract or distress her and so was still able to perform a successful scent match.)

While Sam led Molly to the car for some rest, I headed back to the walled garden to check on Margaret. Chester's passing had probably made her world feel a whole lot lonelier, and I got the distinct feeling that her distress was probably linked to the absence of her daughter, too. As she crouched under the conifer, stroking her cat and sobbing softly, I noticed Kathrine looming in the distance. My heart sank. I guessed she was the last person she needed to see right now.

"Don't tell me she's blubbing over a dead cat," she scoffed, once she'd lumbered over. "I bet she won't bloody cry like that when *I* die."

You're not wrong, there, I thought. *She'll probably crack open the Dom Perignon.*

"You have to appreciate that your sister is very, very upset, Kathrine," I replied. "This isn't the outcome she wanted."

"Histrionics, that's what it is," she continued. "She should be on the stage, that woman. Anyway, I'm off to find a spade. That cat needs burying before it starts to stink the place out."

She muttered something to herself before clomping toward a

nearby shed. Margaret, her cheeks streaked with tears, looked aghast.

"We can't let that happen, Colin," she wept, explaining that her sister simply hadn't the strength to dig deep into the brittle soil and would probably dump Chester in a ditch or a shallow grave, thus exposing him to marauding foxes and badgers. She paused and gazed up at me beseechingly.

"Could you possibly do it instead?" she asked. "Find a final resting place for Chester? Somewhere safe? Somewhere I can visit him?"

I thought for a moment, then nodded. While undertaking wasn't strictly part of my pet-detective remit, it was the very least I could do for this charming old lady. I radioed for Sam to distract Kathrine (an easy task, since she'd taken quite a shine to her), which allowed me to pinch the only spade in the shed and bring it back to the walled garden. Its wooden handle was rotting and its blade was corroded, but it would have to suffice.

I carefully wrapped Chester in a blanket while Margaret fetched his favorite cat bed. Then, as the springtime sun began to weaken, we wandered further into the estate to hunt for an ideal spot for him. On the way we passed a fenced-off area that contained the rusted remains of a slide, a swing (minus its seat) and a climbing frame. A warped car tire hung limply from an oak tree, to which a basketball hoop had also been nailed. I could only presume it was Elizabeth's old adventure playground, which had lain untouched for years. She went noticeably quiet as we walked by.

A few minutes later we came across a secluded little bluebell wood. With its lush carpet of violet-hued blooms and shimmering canopy of silver birches, it was picture-perfect. Margaret gave me a forlorn nod, and I set myself to my task.

I located a patch of softened earth and began to dig in earnest, hollowing out a trench large enough to accommodate Chester's cat bed. Having a pre-war spade at my disposal didn't make the job any easier and my progress was sluggish. Then, all of a sudden, I struck a rock-hard tree root. The tool handle disintegrated, causing a jagged piece of wood to ram straight up my thumbnail. The pain was so intense it brought tears to my eyes, and I had to restrain myself from bawling out a stream of expletives, biting my lip so as not to alarm my companion.

Oblivious to the blood dripping on to the bluebells, Margaret clocked my anguished expression and assumed I was overwhelmed with emotion.

"I know, it's so *desperately* sad, Colin, but please don't cry," she whispered, offering me a heartfelt hug. "My Chester's at peace now. And your Molly did a wonderful job."

I accepted the hug—how could I not?—but while my hands were patting Margaret's back I took the opportunity to surreptitiously whip out the offending splinter. "*Aaaarghhhhhhh . . . !*" yelled a voice in my head as I did the deed.

Once I'd blotted my blood-soaked hand on my trousers, I resumed digging. When the correct depth was reached, I carefully lowered Chester into the hole before replacing the subsoil and rolling back the turf. Margaret chose an unusually shaped pebble as a marker and, with our heads bowed, we both stood by his graveside for a few moments.

"I'll miss you, sweet Chester," whispered Margaret, blowing a kiss as the bluebells danced gaily in the breeze. "You filled my life with *such* joy."

On the way back from Greenlea Hall, Sam and I stopped off at a tiny rural café for a coffee. While Molly snoozed contentedly at our feet, emitting occasional snorts and snuffles, we took the opportunity to reflect upon an eventful afternoon.

"Thinking about it, Sam, I can see why Molly was so confused at the start of the search," I said, taking a frothy sip of cappuccino. "That smell of decay being blown around the garden distracted her. She'd never experienced that before."

Only when the wind had subsided, enabling the cat odor to settle and become more confined, had Molly had the conviction to isolate its location and finally find Chester.

Our conversation then moved on to the delightful Margaret, who'd clearly required our presence that day to provide her with much-needed comfort and closure.

"She needed that peace of mind, didn't she?" said Sam.

"She certainly did," I replied. "And thanks to Molly, she got it."

Upon hearing her name, my beloved dog slowly raised her head and stared into my eyes.

"You did a marvelous job, sweetheart," I said tenderly, giving her nape a little squeeze.

I'm pretty sure that Molly gave me the slightest of nods before dropping her head on to her paws and falling back to sleep.

~ 11 ~

The Dog and the Adder

Midsummer's day came and went and Molly and I reached a significant milestone. We had been together as a team for six whole months, our eventful journey having taken us from the training fields of Medical Detection Dogs to the verdant meadows of Bramble Hill Farm. Ever since that online advertisement had brought us together, Molly and I had developed an unbreakable bond and had shared some wonderful experiences. I had grown to love my little Gumtree girl with all my heart—she was my companion as much as my colleague—and I simply couldn't imagine my life without her.

"Happy half-year anniversary, sweetheart," I'd said on the morning itself, presenting her with a box of multicolored tennis balls to celebrate the fact. Sarah had watched on, highly amused.

"If memory serves, you didn't get *me* anything for putting up with you for six months," she said, with mock-displeasure. "It's a good job I'm not the jealous type, eh?"

Then Sarah smiled at my dog, a really sweet, heartfelt smile; I'd never witnessed her display affection like this toward Molly before. For me, this was a watershed moment. It had taken a while—a *very* long while—but finally my girlfriend had fallen head over heels in love with Molly.

That lunchtime the three of us visited the Horse Guards Inn, a quaint, dog-friendly pub nestled in the lovely South Downs National Park. I remember sitting at the table with my beloved partner by my side and my beautiful dog at my feet and almost pinching myself to check that I wasn't dreaming. I hadn't felt so happy in a long time. Life couldn't get much better than this, I reckoned.

I was blissfully unaware of the heartache that lay around the corner.

The following Wednesday, I awoke Molly at 5 a.m. in readiness for our latest cat search in the Wiltshire town of Amesbury. There was a valid reason for this ridiculously early start. The south of England was in the midst of a heatwave—temperatures had soared above 30°C—and I was keen to wrap up proceedings by midday in order to avoid the afternoon heat.

This particular case involved a missing cat called Cleo—a skittish, honey-colored Abyssinian—whose owner, Isobel, was an executive officer with the civil service. Her husband was a freelance cameraman, currently on an assignment in South Africa—and she'd recently returned to work following a one-year career break. She had not lived in Amesbury for long, she told me; earlier that year, the entire civil service had relocated to the town and Isobel's family had been among the first to take occupancy of one of the brand-new properties on a vast purpose-built housing estate. Before its clearance, the site—much of it woodland—had been used by the Ministry of Defense for operations and maneuvers.

In the wake of Cleo going suddenly AWOL, and with work and house-moving commitments preventing her from organizing her own search, Isobel had requested my services as a matter of urgency. She explained that she'd also been thwarted by the lack of internet connectivity in her new home—she was unable to post appeals on social media—and, with the estate barely occupied, there were few neighbors around to spread the word or display posters. Reading about one of my successful recoveries in a local newspaper had prompted her to pick up the phone.

"I'm wondering if you and Molly could possibly come tomorrow?" she'd asked in a lilting Hampshire accent. "I could try and get the day off work. I know it's short notice, but I'd be *ever* so grateful. I just feel that Molly is my last chance of finding my cat."

Despite having my reservations—primarily weather-associated—I agreed to lend my assistance. This young lady clearly had a lot to cope with; the recent house move and return to work were taking up all her spare time, and—to compound matters—had lost her pet cat. I felt dreadfully sorry for her.

There were, however, a few caveats. Mindful of the blisteringly hot conditions, I insisted on the search starting early. In addition, I'd not be expecting Molly to work past lunchtime—four hours a day was the cut-off point during the summer months, six hours when it was cooler—and she'd be doing so in twenty-minute shifts, with regular rest and refreshment breaks. And finally, if the temperature exceeded a certain level, I'd have no option but to bring the hunt for Cleo to a halt.

"I totally understand," said Isobel. "See you both tomorrow."

With the roads blissfully traffic-free, I arrived in Amesbury just after 7 a.m. I took the opportunity to have a quick drive around Isobel's estate, just so I could get a decent understanding of its layout and geography. With fewer than a quarter of the red-brick properties occupied, it looked like something out of a film set, and—with a dearth of trees and hedges—it had an eerie, soulless quality. A narrow strip of woodland—about 100 yards wide and 500 yards long—divided the estate from a busy dual carriageway, down which cars, motorbikes and HGVs hurtled at great speed.

I hope Cleo hasn't tried to cross that road, I thought to myself. *She wouldn't have lasted long if she had . . .*

Molly and I made our way to Isobel's home and were greeted in the doorway by a tall track-suited woman with a sandy-colored pixie-cut. I declined her kind offer of a coffee and a croissant—I wanted to crack on immediately—and, once Molly was exposed to a sample of Cleo's scent, the three of us began an exhaustive (and exhausting) search of the estate. We visited the occupied households first, wherein most neighbors were breakfasting or readying themselves for work; they were happy to let us explore their gardens and garages. We found no trace of the cat, unfortunately, so we switched our focus to the uninhabited properties. Molly checked front gardens and back lawns for scent trails, while Isobel and I peered through lounge windows and patio doors, just in case she'd crept in while building work was taking place. It was all to no avail, sadly.

As the mid-morning temperatures soared, the scarcity of shade became a problem. I found myself constantly stopping to give Molly a break—she was panting quite heavily—and I watched with concern as she thirstily slurped pint upon pint of fresh water. I began to get a bad feeling about the whole endeavor and started to wish I'd never agreed to pursue it in the first place.

You really shouldn't work Molly in these conditions, Colin, heckled a voice in my head. *It's not very fair on her, is it?*

However, having committed to the search, and out of duty to my careworn client, I felt obliged to continue. In hindsight, there was probably another reason for feeling this moral imperative. In the police force, whenever I'd handled a missing-persons case, I'd often been able to maintain an emotional detachment from the family, due to the involvement of specially trained liaison officers. Working as a pet detective, though, I found myself dealing directly with some very anguished clients and, for that reason, my empathy and sympathy had a habit of clouding my judgment.

My decision to persist with the search for Cleo was one that I'd come to regret deeply.

At the three-hour mark, as midday approached, I decided to investigate the wooded area nestled between the road and the estate. I hoped that its canopy of trees and the dappled sunlight would make things cooler and more comfortable for Molly.

"There's a good chance that Cleo came here to explore," I told Isobel, "so let's see if Molly can find any scent."

I gave her a totally free rein, without any guidance or direction from me ("working her nose," I called it) and observed her closely as she snuffled around shrubs and brambles at head height and grass and bracken at ground level. Within a few minutes, she appeared to detect a strong odor, whirling around and contorting her body as the scent infiltrated her nostrils. With Isobel and me following in her wake, she dashed toward a bowl-shaped dip in the ground before skidding to a sudden halt. There, much to our surprise, was a tiny fawn, no more than a few days old, trembling with fear at the sight of two perplexed humans and a puzzled dog.

"Awww, poor little mite," whispered Isobel.

"Its mother probably bolted when she heard us approaching," I replied. "She'll be back soon, I'm sure."

Other than being in panic mode, the gangly little creature seemed fit and well—I gently checked it over for injury—so we left it *in situ*, to be reunited with its parent.

The new sights, smells and sounds of the woodland had clearly heightened Molly's senses, and moments later she was charging off in pursuit of a second scent. On this occasion, however, her haphazard toings and froings reminded me of the time she had found the dearly departed Chester beneath a fir tree.

Please . . . not another dead cat, I thought, as Molly closed in on a fallen, rotten tree trunk, while Isobel peered over my shoulder. Behind it lay the source of my dog's erratic behavior: a large and lifeless badger that had most likely been hit by a vehicle on the dual carriageway before staggering to its final resting place.

"Oh, that's awful," said Isobel, averting her eyes, as a couple of hungry rooks circled above the carcass.

I felt a pang of sadness, not only for the unfortunate badger, but also for its fellow wildlife. The recent construction of the car-clogged road and the advent of the concrete-jungle estate had not only compromised their safety and seclusion but had also greatly reduced the size of their natural habitat. Years be-

fore, they'd been able to roam for miles, but now they were confined to this tiny strip of land.

It was at that point that my phone alarm beeped, reminding
me that the search for Cleo had reached the four-hour mark
and—for Molly's sake (she was becoming increasingly hot and
bothered)—it was time to wrap everything up. In a perfect
world, we'd have found the missing cat but, sadly, it wasn't to be.
Isobel looked crestfallen.

"Can we just check *one* more spot, Colin?" she begged tear-
fully. "It'll take half an hour, maximum, I promise . . ."

Against my better judgment—and undoubtedly swayed by my
client's pleading eyes—I acquiesced and allowed Isobel to lead
me to a nearby leafy glade. The ever-sensitive Molly seemed to
cotton on to this woman's despair and, as I released her from her
leash, she somehow mustered up enough energy to break cover,
galloping twenty yards ahead and zooming through a thicket of
rhododendrons.

There came a point, however, when I could hear the sound of
Molly's tail thwacking against branches but could no longer see
her in my line of vision. This was hugely remiss on my part; I'd
been taught by Rob and Mark at MDD never to lose sight of her
and never to let her stray too far ahead.

Damn, I cursed, trying desperately to catch her up, ducking
under low-hanging trees and dodging their criss-crossed roots. I
eventually spotted Molly scampering up a yard-high mound of
earth, her tail wagging, her nose snuffling, as if she'd detected
yet another scent trail. From where I stood, this small dune of
soil looked like the detritus from a fox den, which I'd encountered on many occasions in the countryside.

"She seems pretty excited about something . . ." said a hope-
ful Isobel.

"Sadly, I don't think it's Cleo," I replied. While it wasn't unusual for cats to use these snug holes as hiding places once the
foxes had departed, the absence of Molly's "down" signal suggested she hadn't found an odor match.

Then, just as I was about to recall her and bring the search to a close, Molly let out an ear-splitting, blood-curdling howl. She reared up on her back legs and fell backward, hitting the ground with an almighty thud.

"Molly . . . oh my god, *MOLLY!*" I yelled, sprinting over as fast as my legs could carry me.

I was confronted with the heart-stopping sight of my dog lying motionless on the ground, her breathing heavy and rapid, her eyes glazed and unseeing. My head was pounding but I tried to stay calm and invoke my first-aid skills, kneeling beside her to check for any blood on her body or for any sign of broken bones. All I found was a sticky, unguent substance near her throat area; it definitely wasn't blood, so I assumed it was some kind of tree sap. I also noticed a sharp, jagged stick on the ground, which led me to wonder whether she'd impaled herself in some way.

"Colin, what on *earth* has happened?" cried Isobel, rushing over to the fox earth.

"I don't know, but it's serious," I said, my voice shaking as I slowly, carefully, scooped up my dog's hot, trembling body. "I need to get her to a vet straight away."

As we hurried back to my car, Molly began to hyperventilate— she emitted a weird, low, moaning sound—and her eyes began to dilate alarmingly. Her body started to stiffen, too, as if it was going into paralysis. I quickly laid her on to a grass verge and grabbed a bottle of water from the trunk, using half of it to douse her coat and drip-feeding the rest into her lolling, drooling mouth. Isobel was already sitting in my passenger seat, telling the local veterinary surgery to expect the arrival of a very poorly cocker spaniel.

It was then that I noticed a slight swelling on Molly's chest— near where the gluey substance had oozed—and it suddenly dawned on me what might have happened.

A snakebite . . . a venomous snakebite, I thought to myself, as a chill ran down my spine. Adders were prevalent in the south of England, although, in my experience, their natural habitat tended to be open grassland and coastal areas rather than woodland.

As I lifted Molly into the car, she yowled in pain and sank her teeth into my right hand. It was a reflex response to the pain she must have been feeling and, despite being in abject agony, I let her stay clamped on until she finally relaxed her jaw and released her incisors. After gently laying my dog into her crate, I sped to the nearest surgery, using my police-driving skills to cut through the heavy traffic and parking on double-yellow lines. This was an emergency in every sense.

I left Molly in the car with Isobel—I wanted her to be assessed properly before I moved her again—and dashed into the surgery. It was a tiny place, with only one vet on site.

"My dog's extremely ill," I panted. "I'm not exactly sure what happened, but there's a chance it was a snakebite. She's in lots of pain, and she may be in paralysis. Can she be seen, please?"

The female receptionist looked up from her computer.

"Are you registered with us?"

"Er, no, I'm not local, so . . ."

She slid a two-page form over to me and handed me a pen.

"Can you fill this in first?"

I felt a sudden surge of anger.

"Can this not wait, for Christ's sake? My dog is gravely ill. She could be dying."

I didn't make a habit of berating receptionists, but this was plain ridiculous.

"It's procedure, I'm afraid," she replied, with a nonchalance that further fueled my ire.

"Sod procedure!" I yelled. "I want my dog to be seen *now*, before it's too bloody late."

The vet, who'd been loudly ordering pharmaceuticals in his office, came out to see what was causing all the commotion. Through gritted teeth, I repeated my concerns, and—after nodding knowingly at his receptionist—he agreed to check Molly over.

"In fact, let me fetch a muzzle first," he said, eyeing the angry-looking bite marks on my hand.

Outside, I thanked Isobel for waiting with Molly and gave her ten pounds for a taxi home so she could collect her daughter. My client looked mortified that the search had ended so miserably.

"I'm so sorry this has happened, Colin," she said. "Do keep me informed."

"You, too," I replied (although I later learned that Cleo was never found. I presumed she'd met the same fate as the poor badger).

As the vet and I carried a woozy and wheezy Molly from the car to the surgery, I noticed with horror that the swelling on her chest had almost tripled in size, to grapefruit-like proportions. I felt like screaming every expletive known to man. My darling dog's life was in the balance and she seemed to be slipping away before my very eyes.

"It could well be a snakebite, but I can't be sure," said the vet, moving a stethoscope around Molly's body as she lay still on the treatment table. "We're only a satellite surgery, and I think she needs specialist care at our main clinic near Stonehenge. I'll give her some painkillers for the time being, but I'd prefer it if my colleagues assessed her."

This wasn't what I wanted to hear. I'd hoped for immediate answers and treatment, and I was infuriated by the vet's apparent lack of urgency and the clinic's dearth of resources.

The receptionist called a veterinary ambulance and, within minutes, a white Range Rover arrived, sirens blaring, to whisk my poor Molly away. I planned to follow behind in my own car, once I'd filled out those precious forms.

I walked out of the surgery and virtually collapsed on to a nearby bench. I sat there for five minutes or so, my head in my hands, my stomach lurching, desperately trying to pull myself together before I made the journey. Consumed with guilt and remorse, I couldn't quite believe my own stupidity. I shouldn't have taken on the case. I shouldn't have worked Molly in that heat. I shouldn't have agreed to extend the search. And, more than anything, I shouldn't have put my client's needs before my dog's. With one hand, I'd offered a new life to the most adorable rescue puppy, and, with the other, I'd almost taken it away. I had let her down badly and I wasn't sure I could ever forgive myself.

"My poor Molly," I whispered, swallowing hard as I pictured her alone and bewildered in the ambulance. "This is all my fault, sweetheart, and I'm ever so sorry . . ."

While I'd been wrapped up in my own thoughts, a silver-haired woman with soft blue eyes had quietly taken a seat beside me.

"Pardon me for intruding," she said, leaning her tartan shopper against the bench, "and I won't be so rude as to ask what's upset you, but I just want to say that everything is going to be just fine and you don't need to worry."

"Thank you," I said to the old lady. "Thank you so much."

She patted my hand with maternal concern before going off on her way, her trolley trundling behind her.

During the drive to Stonehenge I took the opportunity to phone Sarah at home, Sam in the office and my son Sam in Manchester, as well as seeking the advice of my own Guildford-based veterinary surgeon, Graham.

"Yep, I reckon that sounds like a classic case of an adder bite," he said, having listened to a blow-by-blow account of the incident, together with a list of Molly's symptoms. He knew a lot about that species of snake, did Graham, informing me that it wasn't that uncommon for adders to slither into woodland to hunt for lizards, voles and other small animals. After making their kill, these snakes would often rest in the shade to digest their food, so lazing on a fox earth, under some trees, sounded entirely plausible.

"Molly probably detected the adder's scent and took it by surprise," he explained. "It may well have been weighed down with food so wouldn't have been able to escape as quickly as it normally would. Its only option would have been to defend itself, hence the bite and the venom release."

"Graham, I only wish you'd been my first port of call," I told my vet of choice, explaining how underwhelmed I'd been with the clinic in Amesbury and how I didn't hold out much hope for their sister practice in Wiltshire, where I was currently heading.

"Right, here's my advice, Colin," he said, with characteristic pragmatism. "My surgery's closed for the day, but I suggest you pick up Molly and take her to the animal Accident and Emergency unit here in Guildford. It'll be too late to administer anti-venom—that should have been done straight away—but she'll get the best possible care. Bring her to my surgery first thing tomorrow morning and I can examine her thoroughly and give you a much clearer diagnosis."

That sounded like a plan—I had every faith in Graham—and within the hour I'd collected Molly from Stonehenge Surgery. The good news, according to the veterinary nurse, was that her condition had remained stable during the journey and she'd maintained consciousness. As for the bad news, however, the swelling was still significant (despite the antibiotics that had been administered in the ambulance) and she was still desperately poorly. The nurse totally understood my desire to bring Molly closer to home, though, and sent us on our way with her good wishes.

After a careful drive back to Guildford I dropped Molly off at the animal A&E. There, specialist staff would monitor her around the clock and keep her as comfortable as possible. As a veterinary nurse prepared to wheel her down to the ward, I bade my beloved dog a heartfelt farewell. I kissed her shiny head, stroked her floppy ears and gazed into her glassy, rheumy eyes.

"Everything's going to be fine, Molls," I said, trying to keep my tone and gestures as cheery and upbeat as possible so as to generate positive vibes. "Everyone's going to do all they can to make you better, I promise."

My dog let out a weary little whine as the nurse gently placed her on the trolley. I didn't wait to see her being trundled off down the corridor. I didn't want her to turn around and see her owner looking so worried and upset.

Unpacking all the search kit from the car when I got back home to Cranleigh was unbearably poignant. On any normal day, Molly would have been snapping at my heels and haring around the driveway, relishing the prospect of our customary post-search play session. But it had been anything but a normal day—it had been a nightmarish day, in fact—and as I placed her UK Pet Detectives harness into my holdall I felt her absence deeply.

Sarah provided some much-needed comfort that evening, listening to my concerns and anxieties, assuring me that Molly was receiving excellent care and making me a soothing hot chocolate. It didn't have the desired soporific effect, however, and I experienced a sleepless night. I couldn't stop thinking about the day's events—particularly my own accountability—and, not only that, my hand was still throbbing in pain (mercifully, I was up to date with my tetanus jabs). Silly, I know, but I felt this was my rightful punishment for exposing Molly to danger.

Unable to get any shut-eye, I ended up paying a 2 a.m. visit to my home office, feeling a deep pang of sadness when I padded past Molly's empty bed. I spent a couple of hours surfing the internet, researching all I could about adders and how they "envenomed" their prey. The more cases I studied, the more convinced I was that Molly had been one such victim. Reassuringly, in most of these snakebite incidents, the dogs had eventually pulled through. In a few hours' time I'd find out whether Molly would do the same.

I returned to A&E at 6:30 a.m. and received the news that, while the swelling was still a major concern, Molly had slept peacefully and had responded well to medication. She was brought out by the on-call vet, looking very dazed and confused. I knelt down beside her, getting as close as I could so she could recognize my scent. My dog drowsily nuzzled into me, using what was left of her energy to give me a loving lick on the cheek.

Hey, Dad, she seemed to be saying. *What's happening to me? Who are these strangers? Where have you been all night?*

The vet helped me lift her into her crate and we headed to our fourth veterinary practice in the space of twenty-four hours. I tried not to dwell on the fact that the last time I'd been to Graham's clinic, I'd been collecting the ashes of my cherished Rottweiler, Jay. His predecessors, my dogs Tess and Max, had also been put to sleep there, and I'd never really recovered from their loss.

Please don't let this be fourth time unlucky, I thought, as we swung into the car park. *Surely life can't possibly be that cruel.*

Graham took a good look at Molly as she lay meekly on his treatment bed. She still seemed very ill, he surmised, and would need a comprehensive examination—under general anesthetic—to check the extent of the bite and the impact of her fall.

"The chest swelling is definitely a reaction to the snake venom," he said, "but I also want to arrange an X-ray. I'm rather concerned that she might have sustained an injury when she fell back on to the ground. A fracture, perhaps, where the humerus meets the scapula."

"A fracture?"

"Yep, it's entirely feasible. And I feel obliged to tell you, Colin, if it happened to be a complex break, I probably wouldn't be able to operate."

Graham saw my horrified expression and placed a soothing hand on my shoulder.

"My advice to you, my friend, is to take yourself away for a couple of hours and let me attend to Molly. Go and grab yourself some breakfast. There's no point you hanging around here; you'd only be pacing around the waiting room."

"You're probably right," I said, "but you must keep me updated."

"'Course I will, Colin." He smiled as Molly looked up at me with doleful eyes. "And please don't worry. She's in great hands."

In the Speckledy Hen Café, just around the corner from the vet's, I ate a full English breakfast, drank a gallon of coffee and answered a few texts from concerned relatives. All the café staff adored Molly and the look of shock on their faces when I explained her absence only compounded my feelings of guilt.

Just as the clock struck 10 a.m., Graham called.

"Molly's out of theater and in recovery—she's doing okay, considering—so make your way over here and I'll tell you what I've found."

Graham had plenty to impart. He hadn't discovered any broken bones, thank heavens—so no surgery would be required—and, having shaved off the fur on Molly's chest to enable closer examination, it had become apparent that she'd been bitten by the adder not once, but twice.

"Let's just say that Molly's an extremely lucky dog, Colin," said Graham. "One of the puncture wounds missed her main carotid artery by fractions of an inch, so things could have been *so* much worse. Catastrophic, in fact."

If the venom had gone straight to her heart, he explained, she could have died almost instantly. But because it hit muscle tissue instead, the toxin was dispersed much more slowly, at a rate that a young, fit, healthy dog like Molly was able to survive. I let out a huge sigh of relief.

"But we still have to proceed with caution," said the vet. "While it's true to say that Molly has withstood the initial bite, she's certainly not out of the woods, and there remains a small chance that she won't make it."

"What do you mean?" I asked, my heart racing.

"I'll be straight with you," he replied. "Snake fangs contain all sorts of nasty bacteria, and I think there's a strong possibility that Molly will contract a secondary infection, which can occasionally prove to be fatal. But your dog's a tough little cookie, Colin, and I've every faith that she'll pull through."

"My god, Graham, I hope you're right . . ."

"So here's the plan. I'm going to let you take her home, but I'll be prescribing her a course of very strong antibiotics to try and fend off any infection. She'll also need plenty of fluid, and lots of rest."

Once Molly had fully slept off the anesthetic at the surgery, I was able to drive her back home to Cranleigh. I spoon-fed her some food, gave her a bath and lowered her into her favorite bed. I then sat on the floor and talked her to sleep, just like I'd done with Sam when he was a baby. I regaled her with the story of how Molly the Clever Dog had found Rusty the Missing Cat in the summerhouse, reminding her how very, very proud she'd made me feel that day. I must have drifted off myself because, a few hours later, I felt Sarah gently shaking my shoulder.

"Come to bed, Colin," she whispered, as Molly snoozed soundly beside me. "She's nice and settled now, and you need a decent sleep, too."

Nursing Molly through those first few days was extremely tough. I kept a vigil by her bedside, attending to her every need and monitoring her every move (and mood) for signs of progress or deterioration. I totally shut myself off from work for a week— Sam and Stefan took over the reins brilliantly, ensuring the smooth running of our ongoing investigations—and, to save time, I distributed group emails instead of answering individual messages. I had received hundreds of well-wishing calls from concerned friends, family and colleagues—including the Medical Detection Dogs team—and it was so heartening to think that everybody was rooting for us.

For the first twenty-four hours, Molly seemed to rally a little—she was able to move around her room, albeit slowly and gingerly—but on day two she took a serious turn for the worse. Her temperature rocketed, her energy levels plummeted and her breathing became shallow and labored. I went into panic mode, terrified that this was the perilous secondary infection that Graham had warned me about. I rang him straight away, only for him to confirm my worst fears.

"She's clearly fighting off that infection, Colin. Keep up the antibiotics and fluids and make sure she stays cool and rested."

I did as he instructed and, for forty-eight hours, I barely left Molly's side. Gradually, she showed signs of improvement and, on the morning of day four, it was as if a magic recovery button had been pressed.

"What the heck . . . !" I gasped, as a bright-eyed Molly bounded into my bedroom early that morning, jumping on to my bed and smothering me with kisses.

I'm back!!! she seemed to be saying. *Let's play!!!*

That same afternoon, I took Molly to the vet's for a check-up. Mercifully, she was over the worst of the infection, but I was rather concerned about the pronounced limp she'd developed.

"You're right, there's a distinct lameness in her front-right paw," said Graham, examining her. "She's been over-compensating on her right-hand side, it seems, because the pain from the snake-bite was more acute on the left."

He suggested that, in order to rectify the problem, I needed to book Molly on to a course of canine aqua therapy. All being well, this non-weight-bearing exercise would reduce any feelings of pain or strain and would gradually build up her confidence.

"Eventually, she'll almost forget that she's lame," added Graham. "I wholeheartedly recommend it."

I took Graham's advice on board and reserved some sessions at a nearby specialist center. Molly looked unbearably cute in her life-jacket, and it was so funny watching from the sidelines as she doggy-paddled around. The swim therapist—who was excellent—would gently push Molly to the center of the tank before letting her swim to the steps. Then, just as she reached her destination, the therapist would nudge her back to the middle again. All the while, Molly wore a perplexed *What the heck is going on?* expression as she was cast adrift, again and again.

Much to my delight, these sessions seemed to do the trick. Soon afterward we were able to resume our country walks and begin some light exercise but, strangely enough, Molly's limp occasionally reappeared when she was at home. It was Sarah, in fact, who tactfully suggested that my darling dog might be milking things a little.

"Colin, have you noticed that Molly only limps when you're around, especially if she wants something from you?" she said, as we both watched TV one evening.

"I'm not sure that's true," I replied, thinking my girlfriend was being a tad harsh.

"But she doesn't limp at all if you're not in the room. I was looking at her through a crack in the door this morning."

"I very much doubt that, honey . . ."

Sarah was misguided, I reckoned. Granted, Molly had received oodles of attention and affection from me during her illness and recovery, but surely she couldn't be so shameless. But my partner had aroused my curiosity, so much so that, as an experiment, I rigged up one of my covert cameras in the lounge.

Sarah and I couldn't stop laughing when I played back the footage.

"Molly, you little *madam*," I grinned, watching her feign a heavy limp in return for a fuss and a cuddle, then walking completely normally once I'd left the lounge. The mischievous Molly of old was back in the room, that was for sure.

While I'd tried not to think about Molly's capacity for work during her illness—her welfare as my pet had been my prime concern—as her recovery continued apace, a few worrying questions began to swirl around my head. Would she ever be able to work alongside me again? Had the snakebite affected her scent-recognition skills? Would she ever find another missing cat? And would this harrowing experience deter her from searching woodlands?

It was time to have a frank conversation with Mark Doggett regarding her future. Concerned that the Amesbury incident might have dented both her confidence and her ability as a scent-detection dog, I needed to know what was best for her wellbeing, whether it was continuing with her work with me as normal, being re-trained from scratch at MDD, or spending the rest of her life solely as my pet. Ending our work partnership would surely break my heart—my little pal and I had made such excellent progress together—but Molly's welfare was paramount.

"The simple way to find out, Colin, is by setting up a training exercise at Bramble Hill Farm," said Mark. "No help, no promptings, no encouragement, just let her work it out for herself. You'll soon know if she's still up to the job."

So, on a cool August afternoon with a strong and steady breeze, I organized a task for Molly, like I'd done hundreds of times before. The cat-hair sample—which I'd obtained from a friend's tabby kitten—was hidden among some long grass, in the middle of a two-acre field. I also sported my GoPro camera so I could email the footage back to Mark.

"Toma," I said, my heart thumping as Molly's snout filled the jam jar and took the scent. As usual, she let out one solitary bark, which always meant *Okay, Dad, I've got the scent memorized . . . let's get going . . .*

"Molly, seek, seek!" I commanded, sending her on her way with a flourish of my hand.

The moment of truth had arrived.

She seemed a little hesitant at first—I could definitely discern a very slight limp, too—but within half a minute she had begun to bound around the field, her tail wagging vigorously behind her. I watched on nervously as she performed a series of swooping, swerving S-shapes, following the direction of the summer breeze as it dispersed an array of scent particles.

Gosh, I've missed this, Molly appeared to be saying, as if she'd suddenly remembered the freedom of the outdoors and the thrill of a search.

A smile spread across my face when, about two hundred yards ahead of me, my dog zoned in on the hidden sample and slammed her trembling body down beside it, giving me that familiar *Found it, Dad!* signal. I let out a deep sigh of relief.

Despite all that pain and trauma, Molly had clearly lost none of her incredible skills. I gave her a click on my marking device—the signal to return for her reward—and she came hurtling back across the field, sporting a wide, pink-tongued doggy-grin.

"Good *girl*, Molly," I said, clasping her close with one hand and feeding her treats with the other. "You, young lady, will never cease to amaze me . . ."

12

The Cat and the Riverboat

Although Molly and I were back in business, some serious lessons had been learned. In the wake of the snakebite incident I'd been forced to reassess my priorities and revise my procedures; from now on, no work-related matter would supersede Molly's health and wellbeing. Never again would I put her life in jeopardy by bowing down to a client's demands, however desperate the situation. My pre-search risk-assessment policy would be tightened, too, insofar as I'd simply decline to offer my assistance if Molly's safety couldn't be guaranteed. The hideous experience in Wiltshire had come as a stark reminder of my responsibilities to this precious little creature and I was determined not to lose sight of that fact.

One of our first post-illness assignments proved to be quite memorable, as it happened. I was contacted by a thirty-something couple—Edward was an art dealer and Lily was a property surveyor—who had recently rented out their first-floor flat in London and bought an old houseboat. Their reasons were twofold: firstly, their busy lifestyles meant that they hardly spent any time together, and, secondly, Lily wanted to finish her master's degree in Bristol and needed to move closer to the university to complete her studies. The couple had hatched a plan to moor their barge on the nearby canal, so that Lily could attend her lectures and Edward could set about restoring the boat and also make the occasional commute into London. They would spend a leisurely few days sailing the houseboat down the River

Thames until they reached Reading, at which point they'd lift the boat out of the water and have it transferred by a large truck to the Kennet and Avon Canal.

They wouldn't be alone on the deck, though. Traveling with them would be Sapphire, their beloved British Blue pedigree cat, who'd been part of their little family unit for years. While they were confident that their pet would love living on the houseboat once it reached its final destination, away from the hustle and bustle of London, they were also conscious that the journey might prove to be tricky. They had even considered asking Edward's father to drive Sapphire over to the Bristol marina, but not only did she suffer with car sickness, she hated being separated from her owners.

The trio began their maiden voyage along the river early one summery morning, passing Battersea Park, Kew Gardens and Hampton Court Palace before heading westward into Berkshire. Little Sapphire remained in the cozy living quarters with either Edward or Lily (the couple took turns at the controls) and spent her time curled up asleep or peeking through the port-hole windows, watching the world flow by.

As dusk set in, they moored up for the night in the village of Hurley, a few miles downriver from Henley-on-Thames. They awoke very early in the morning—the cat had spent the whole night snuggled at the foot of their bed—and after a quick bowl of cereal (and a pouch of cat food for Sapphire) they slipped the mooring ropes and continued on their journey.

Edward and Lily had been pootling toward Henley for ten minutes when they realized, much to their horror, that the cat was missing. The couple were almost certain that she'd been with them when they'd left Hurley, and Lily recalled having seen her playing with one of the boat's fenders. However, after conducting a frantic search both above and below deck, she was nowhere to be found. They made a swift about-turn and headed back to the moorings, where they spent the next few hours roaming the riverbank and beyond, repeatedly yelling, "*Sapphire* . . . ch-ch-ch . . . *Sapphire* . . . ch-ch-ch!" They were terrified that she'd fallen overboard and, in sheer desperation, searched for "pet detective" on their phone and gave me a call.

"Our cat's gone missing," Edward said, sounding utterly woe-begone. "We think she's either jumped or fallen from a houseboat and may have drowned. Please, *please*, can you help us find her? It's getting dark and we're starting to panic."

"Firstly, you need to stay calm," I replied. "Secondly, you mustn't discount the fact that she's still alive. It's not beyond the realms of possibility that she's made it ashore."

"But how?" asked Edward. "Cats can't swim."

"Ah, now that's a common misconception," I explained, re-lieved to be able to offer him a crumb of comfort. I told him that most cats could, in fact, swim—hence the evolution of their slightly webbed feet—but they invariably choose not to. Some breeds, though—like Bengals—actively loved the water and were known to jump into the bath or shower with their owners.

"That's reassuring to know," he replied, "but if it *is* the worst-case scenario and she's washed up on a riverbank, poor thing, I still need her to be found. She's like family to us, and Lily and I would want to give her a proper burial. The thought of her just drifting down the Thames, alone . . . well . . ."

And that's when his voice finally cracked.

". . . that would just break our hearts."

Keen to employ Molly's cat-detection skills, he asked if I could possibly bring my dog over to Berkshire, preferably the sooner the better. I agreed to pay him a visit the next morning—fortunately for him, my diary was free for a couple of days—but I was at pains to stress the complex nature of this case, due prin-cipally to the enormity of the search area and the ambiguity of her disappearance. I also explained to Edward that, in order to maximize the chances of finding Sapphire, he'd need to provide me with some decent cat-hair samples.

"That shouldn't be a problem," he replied. "My dad's clearing out our flat in London at the moment and Sapphire had lots of sleeping spots there so I'm sure he won't mind bringing some of her stuff over."

"Excellent. Look forward to seeing you both in the morning, Edward. And do try and get some sleep."

It was my first ever visit to the village of Hurley and, as Molly and I enjoyed a walk-about (and I performed a rigorous risk assessment), I was impressed with what I saw. Whitewashed, red-roofed houses lined the narrow roads and the charming little village comprised a quaint corner shop, an ancient priory and two lovely country pubs. There was also a typically English cricket pitch and pavilion, beyond which lay a well-maintained caravan park overlooking the River Thames.

Meeting me by the towpath, clutching a wad of MISSING CAT leaflets in one hand and a reporter's notebook in the other, was Edward's father, Godfrey. A tall gray-haired retired head-teacher, he explained that his son had decided at the last minute to continue on to Bristol with Lily; she was reluctant to sail alone—understandably so—and Edward would be joining us later that day. It seemed Godfrey had spent most of the morning scouring the streets, engaging with villagers (he'd compiled copious notes in spidery handwriting) and distributing his hastily printed handouts.

"Delighted to be joining your team for the day, Mr. Butcher," he boomed in a deep, treacly voice, startling a couple of passing ducks, who hastily waddled off in the opposite direction. "You, me and Molly will crack this case, I'm sure of it."

Suppressing a wry smile, I outlined my modus operandi to this self-appointed sleuth. I told him I was working on the optimistic theory that the cat was still alive and had either sneaked off the barge prior to setting sail the previous morning or had jumped or fallen off the deck while the barge was moving. I was holding on to the hope that she'd managed to swim ashore.

"Cats massively bond to their territory, Godfrey," I told him, "so it was probably very disorientating for Sapphire to be relocated from the flat to the houseboat. It would have been a shock to her system, and she perhaps instinctively headed back to dry land."

"Yes, that's *exactly* what I was thinking," he murmured, tapping his pencil against his crooked teeth. I couldn't quite work out whether this guy was going to be a help or a hindrance. Judging by the way she pointedly kept her distance, I don't think Molly was too sure of him either.

"First things first, Godfrey, have you brought the cat-hair samples?" I asked.

"Why, of course," he said, performing a mini-salute. "Follow me."

He led us to his bottle-green Volvo estate, where, on the back seat, lay a pile of Edward's clothing that had been collected from the flat. Nestled against it was a canvas bag full to the brim of Sapphire's toys, cushions and bedding, most of it covered in a thick layer of charcoal-gray cat hair. On the back seat was the biggest scratching post I'd ever seen.

"Took me bloody ages to get that thing in the car," said Godfrey.

I'm not surprised, I thought.

My heart sank slightly; this mix-up of items meant that I wouldn't be obtaining the purest of samples—usually, I'd extract them from the source myself, under sterile conditions—but, on this occasion, they'd just have to suffice. In any case, Molly was more than capable of isolating single odors from a mish-mash of others and there was no reason she couldn't do this again. I wielded my trusty tweezers, carefully transferred a wodge of hair into a glass jar and sealed the lid nice and tightly.

As I headed toward the river, Godfrey suddenly boomed, "Wrong way, matey!" He informed me that, during his own mini-search of the village that morning, he'd struck up a conversation with a local farmer who'd reported seeing a dark-colored cat enter one of his large barns.

"He let me have a quick look around the building," he said, nodding sagely, "and I think it could prove to be a rather promising lead. That's where I'd like to start the search, if that's okay with you."

This fellow's bumptiousness was beginning to irritate me—I had to remind myself that I was working at the behest of the distraught owners—but I took on board what he said and headed over to the farm. If it was a genuine sighting, it needed following up.

The barn in question wasn't used for farming purposes, it transpired, but rented out as a storage facility for local boat and barge owners. It housed crafts of all shapes and sizes, from single-berth speedboats to fifty-foot catamarans.

"Wow, this may take some time," I said to Godfrey, surveying this gigantic space and the plethora of potential hiding places.

I couldn't believe my eyes therefore when, within a minute of her snout snuffling the jam jar, Molly gave me a perfect "down" near the barn entrance. She flattened her body, outstretched her front paws and awaited her customary treat.

To my utter bewilderment, however, there was no trace of a cat. Godfrey and I searched high and low, corner to corner, but with zero results. There were none of the usual tell-tale signs of a feline intruder either: no smell of cat pee, no rodent remains, no makeshift bed. I even sent in Molly for a second time to double-check, and again she did the "down," even more confidently than before, perhaps, and earning herself a second batch of treats for yet another scent match.

"It's an absolute mystery," I said, scratching my head, as Molly gratefully guzzled her black-pudding goodies.

I then tried a different angle. Sometimes, when I couldn't figure out why Molly was matching a scent or I couldn't find a cat in the vicinity, I'd verbally instruct her to "show me." This command, which I'd taught her at Bramble Hill Farm, required her to be more specific and, if need be, to physically guide me to the trigger.

In this instance, her response was to spin around and home in on the barn door. She nudged a small square of sky-blue material that was affixed to its handle before giving me another "down" for good measure (I was going to run out of treats, at this rate). I gently loosened the fabric swatch from the handle and held it up to a shaft of light streaming through the window.

"Why the heck is this bothering Molly?" I wondered, feeling totally mystified.

"Ah," said Godfrey, his face reddening slightly, "maybe I should have told you about that beforehand."

I swung around to face him.

"Told me about *what*, Godfrey?"

"Well, um, I put that material there."

"*You* put it there? What on earth are you talking about?"

"Well, after I spoke to the farmer this morning, I came up with a brainwave. I thought it might be a good idea to cut up one of Edward's T-shirts and pin the pieces around this farmer's barns and stables. Sapphire might then recognize the scent and come out of hiding."

My aghast expression said it all.

"How many pieces did you put out, Godfrey?"

"Oh, I'd say about thirty. Did I do the wrong thing?"

"Er, you could say that."

It hadn't occurred to Godfrey that his "brainwave" had involved using an item of clothing from his car that had been contaminated with Sapphire's cat hair. Poor Molly had performed her duties perfectly—she'd correctly identified and isolated the cat's unique scent signature—but in this particular case it had led her straight to the T-shirt remnant.

This outcome, maddening though it was, only served to highlight Molly's fabulous knack of detecting one specific scent among a multitude of others. Canines have the remarkable ability to pinpoint and separate particular odors—much more so than any other species—something that was once explained to me with a perceptive analogy. If a human being entered a kitchen and a *boeuf bourguignon* was on the stove, he or she would generally smell the overarching aroma of the casserole. If a dog came into the kitchen, though, it would be able to scent-match each individual odor, distinguishing the beef from the bacon, the garlic from the onions, the red wine from the rose-mary. The most sensitive dog's noses (like Molly's) would even have the capacity to scent-match the metal the pan was made out of. Staggering, really.

Godfrey had been very well intentioned, but wildly mis-guided; as a result, we'd wasted valuable time and I wasn't best pleased. I didn't make a song and dance about it, though; my hyper-sensitive dog could easily detect bad vibes among hu-mans, and it was vital that she remained upbeat and positive during a search. Instead, I politely asked Godfrey to collect and discard the rest of the T-shirt remnants so that we could re-start our quest with a totally clean slate. By now I was pretty sure that the farmer's sighting was a false alarm anyway, since Molly had failed to detect any other notable scent trails. I needed to be certain that was the case, however. It took Molly a full hour to search the buildings, giving me total confidence that Sapphire was not in the area.

Edward joined us after lunch and had a few sharp words for his father when he learned of his faux pas. He struck me as a pleasant, easy-going kind of bloke—nowhere near as overbear-ing as Godfrey, mercifully—and we spent the rest of the after-noon combing the moorings area for any signs of Sapphire (we still had several miles of riverbank to search). Despite her best efforts, Molly didn't detect a thing, unfortunately, and the rest of her treats remained in my pocket.

We rounded off a fairly frustrating day with a visit to the nearby general store-cum-bakery, a mini-emporium of sweets, loaves and cakes owned by a friendly middle-aged couple. Ex-perience had shown me that it was always a good idea to forge links with the village "hub"—it was normally the easiest way to spread the word and connect with the community—and this was no exception.

"Oh, I remember seeing her on the telly with that nice Clare lady at Crufts!" cooed the wife when I introduced her to Molly, while the husband gleefully brought out an ancient Kodak camera and began snapping away, the old-fashioned flash cube rotating with each click.

"Hey, it's not often that we have a celebrity in the shop," he grinned. "Say 'cheese,' Jean!"

They listened intently as we retold the story of Sapphire and the houseboat, and how Molly, the UK's first scent-matching cat-detection dog (I liked to shoehorn that into the conversation) was endeavoring to find her in the village. The couple kindly promised to alert all their customers—we left a pile of leaflets near the till—and, as we waved goodbye, they told us we were always welcome to pop in for some homemade lemonade or some freshly baked flapjacks.

"See you soon, Molly, and good luck with finding Sapphire," they said, waving from behind the counter.

"Do people *always* go this loopy over your dog?" asked Edward, laughing.

"For the most part, yes." I smiled and explained how Molly garnered fans everywhere she went, wowing them with her talents and wooing them with her personality. During searches, she had this amazing ability to unite and rally a community: neighbors would become totally invested in our "story" and would go above and beyond to help us find the cat and solve the mystery.

"People love a happy ending, Edward," I said, "and I just hope we get one with Sapphire."

As we exited the shop, I noticed that the sunlight had begun to fade and the air had started to cool. Molly was looking tired—her head was starting to drop—and she needed some rest. She'd had a busy working day—albeit fruitless—and it was time to head back home.

I planned to return to Berkshire the following morning, however. Throughout the journey home, I kept having visions of a bedraggled little cat scrambling up a riverbank, exhausted from her tiring swim across the Thames. My gut feeling told me that Sapphire was still out there and I was determined to reunite her with her owners.

"As I've already said, Molls, cats *can* swim," I murmured as her gentle snores emanated from the back of the car.

Molly and I began day two with a house-to-house investigation along Hurley's winding country lanes, this time without Edward and Godfrey in tow. The latter was just too exhausting. On the previous day, he'd even started using some of my search commands with Molly, to which she'd responded by looking at him as if to say, *Hey, cut it out, I'm trying to work here.* I tactfully suggested that father and son were best deployed by the marina, where they could continue to engage with homeowners and holidaymakers.

"Ring me if you get any fresh leads or sightings, and I'll be straight over," I said.

"No problem," replied Edward. "We'll keep you posted."

Once I'd reintroduced Sapphire's scent to Molly, I began the usual knocking on doors, ringing on bells and pressing on buzzers. We searched half a dozen more gardens—no sign of any Sapphire scent, sadly—before reaching the corner property at the end of the lane. The door was answered by a lady in her fifties sporting a floral Laura Ashley–style dress and a floppy straw sunhat with silk dahlias around the brim. She thought we were joking at first ("A pet detective? Really? Is this *Candid Camera*?") but eventually waved us into a large back garden that—like her outfit—was ablaze with summer flowers.

I let Molly off her leash and gave her freedom to roam. A grid of gravel pathways divided the immaculate lawn into four square sections; at its center, surrounded by low rose bushes, was a two-tiered, green-tinted birdbath-cum-fountain. It was a ghastly-looking thing, to be fair—it had stone serpents and lizards wrapped around its base and a gargoyle's head as its spout—and it seemed totally incongruous among this fragrant oasis.

Molly must have built up a thirst, however, because she began to circle the fountain with intent. Before I could call her off—I wasn't sure how clean the water was—she took a short run up and, her paws gripping the second tier, took a giant slurp from the gargoyle spout. As she did so, I noticed the base starting to wobble ominously.

"Molly, *OFF!*" I shouted, sprinting toward her. But it was too late. I heard an enormous crack as the fountain keeled backward, smashing on to the York stone beneath it and breaking into two. A petrified Molly swerved out of the way just in time and promptly bolted across the lawn. Having no doubt heard all the kerfuffle, the owner came dashing out, her dress billowing behind her.

Marvelous, I thought, my heart sinking. *That's another fine mess you've gotten me into, Molly . . .*

"Oh my goodness, you've broken my fountain!" she cried, looking firstly at the smashed-up ornament and then straight at me.

"It wasn't actually me, to be fair," I replied, with an apologetic shrug. "It was my dog. It was an accident. She was trying to get some water and, well, the whole thing just toppled over."

The woman stared at me, disbelief written all over her face, and then looked at Molly, who was now sitting upright, all prim and proper, a veritable picture of innocence. My dog had done me up like a kipper, as they say.

"Listen, I'm truly sorry about your fountain," I said. "Please tell me how much it'll cost to replace and I'll pay for it."

The lady took another look at the pretty cocker spaniel in her midst, paused for thought, then gave me a resigned smile.

"No, there'll be no need for that. It was, as you say, an accident. These things happen."

"Well, that's very decent of you. Thank you."

"To be honest," she continued, "I detest that damned fountain. It was a wedding present from my mother-in-law—spitting image of that gargoyle, if truth be told—and I've been wanting to get shot of it ever since my divorce came through. You've probably done me a favor. My gardener's coming later, he'll gladly take it away for me."

"But only if you're sure . . ."

"Yes, I'm sure. Now, hang fire for a moment, and I'll bring that delightful dog of yours some proper water."

As she sashayed toward the house Molly sidled over to me and put a paw on my boot.

"Right, that's quite enough drama for one morning, young lady," I said as her big brown eyes stared up at me. It was at times like these I was reminded that, beneath that professional veneer, my dog could be as cheeky and mischievous as any other pooch.

We stopped at a lovely olde worlde village pub for something to eat and, taking advantage of the warm, sunny weather, I opted to sit on the veranda overlooking the Thames. As Molly devoured her doggy energy bar, I ate my plowman's lunch and watched the barges cruise along the river, returning friendly waves to any pleasure-boaters who offered them. I also noticed a few barges mooring up at the local caravan park, located half a mile or so downstream.

"Eat up, Molls," I said, eyeing the rows of mobile homes as the sunlight glinted off their metal roofs. "I reckon that should be our next port of call."

Fortunately for us, as it was in the midst of the summer season, most of the chalets and caravans were occupied. Some were home to permanent residents but the majority were inhabited by vacationers enjoying some Thames-side downtime. A quick recce of the site revealed plenty of potential hiding places for a sanctuary-seeking cat—a caravan door left ajar, a raised area of decking, a tarpaulin-covered trailer—although Molly's indifferent body language told me that there were no feline scent trails to excite her.

As we made our way through the park I engaged with as many caravanners as possible, showing them Sapphire's photo and asking if they'd happened to have spotted a beautiful British Blue moseying by.

"Ah, what a lovely kitty, but, no, I haven't seen anything," said a sun-tanned, bikini-clad woman languishing in a swing-seat, a stack of glossy magazines by her feet. She had a cigarette in one hand and a glass in the other, which, judging by her glazed eyes and goofy grin, most probably didn't contain water. She and her husband had taken early retirement, she told me, and they spent the summer months in the luxury mobile home they'd bought with their savings.

"We're outside all the time, either pickling ourselves in gin or poaching ourselves in our hot tub," she giggled, "so I'm pretty sure I'd have seen a cat passing."

"If you could keep an eye out, that would be great," I said, although I doubted she'd be able to focus on anything once she'd downed her bottle of Hendrick's.

"Why not stay for a quick tipple?" she slurred, patting the seat next to her. "There's ample room for two . . ."

"Thanks, but no thanks." I smiled. "Must crack on. But very nice to meet you all the same."

I gave Molly a *time for a sharp exit* look, and I couldn't have been more relieved when my dog dragged me off in a different direction.

My next encounter was with a kayak-carrying family of four who were heading for some fun on the river. Once the boy and girl had given Molly a fuss—youngsters were drawn to her like a magnet—I inquired about Sapphire.

"No, sorry, not seen a cat around here, I'm afraid," said the father, shaking his head. I handed him a leaflet and my business card and asked him to get in touch with either myself or Edward, should they happen to spot her.

"And guess what," I said to the children as they tickled Molly's chin. "If either of you find Sapphire the cat, I'll make sure Molly brings you the biggest bag of sweets in the whole wide world as a reward. Deal?"

"Deal!" yelled the boy, giving me a high-five.

"Deal!" giggled his little sister. "Can we go and look for Sapphire now, Daddy?"

As the family went on their merry way, my mobile phone rang. It was Edward.

"Colin, you need to come over to the marina, quickly," he said breathlessly. "We've found someone who thinks he might have seen Sapphire."

Within twenty minutes, Molly and I were sitting on a picnic bench with Edward, Godfrey, a gentleman called Jack and his big black Labrador, Solomon. A shaggy-haired, bushy-bearded hulk of a man—a cross between Luciano Pavarotti and Giant Haystacks—he'd worked as Hurley's resident "riverbank man" for over twenty years. Most importantly, he knew every inch of the riverbank, right up to the border with Henley. His job entailed collecting mooring fees from boat and barge owners, which he often did in the early hours, before people had the chance to skulk off without paying.

"You wouldn't believe how often that happens," he griped. "And it's often those that can afford it, too. You'd think I was asking them to shell out hundreds, not a couple of quid."

"Terrible state of affairs," said Godfrey. "Should have their licenses revoked."

Edward turned a little pink as he heard this, and I wondered whether he and Lily had attempted to evade the riverbank man themselves that fateful morning.

"Okay, Jack," I said, keen to cut to the chase. "Tell me what you know."

"Well, this morning—must have been about six o'clock—I was walking along the towpath a mile or so upriver, collecting a few fees, and Solomon suddenly started to strain on his leash."

His Labrador growled at the mention of his name, causing Molly to balk slightly.

"He then started to drag me away from the path, toward the long grass, and as we approached an old fallen oak tree I saw a cat," said Jack. "It just sat there and watched us, bold as brass. It even started licking its paws, but it didn't once take its eyes off Solomon."

On hearing his name again, the big Lab let out another grizzly growl. Molly looked at him as if to say, *Okay, buddy, that's quite enough of the growling* . . .

"How would you describe the cat, Jack?"

"Dark gray coat, bright green eyes, a bit skinny."

"And there are no other similar-looking cats in the neighborhood?"

"Nah. I know all the pets in the area. I've lived here years, walked the same route every day. Never seen it before in my life."

I showed him another photo of Sapphire. (I always liked to have a few extra images of the missing cat for this very reason; it enabled me to assess the reliability of the sighting.)

"Did it look like this?"

He produced some reading glasses from the pocket of his lumberjack shirt and studied Sapphire's photo.

"Yes, I'm pretty sure that's the cat I saw."

Edward took a sharp intake of breath.

"D'you think it's Sapphire?" he said. "D'you reckon she's still alive?"

"It's encouraging news, certainly," I replied, "but there's only one way we'll know for sure."

I took the all-important jam jar from my utility belt and crouched down next to Molly.

"We really need your help now, sweetheart," I whispered with affection. "Just do your best."

I asked Jack to take Solomon home (I feared his dog would distract Molly) but, within minutes, the riverbank man had returned to guide us along the towpath.

As we approached the fallen tree—it rested on a grassy knoll to the right of the path—I offered Molly the sample. Luckily, there'd been no rain for days, so I hoped that any lingering odor would remain strong enough for her to make a scent match.

The air was heavy with hope and expectation and the three men watched on, agog, as my smart little spaniel stuck her snout deep into the jar, her tail wagging nineteen to the dozen.

Responding to my usual "Seek, seek" command, Molly raced

into the long grass, springing high and squatting low as she traced the rise and fall of the riverside breeze. Then, suddenly, she homed in on the upended oak tree and—*bang!*—hit the deck immediately before giving me a textbook "down." She locked her brown, unblinking eyes on mine, as if to say, *FOUND IT, EVERYONE!*

"My god, that's *exactly* where I saw the cat," gasped Jack.

"Well, there you have it," I whispered to a wide-eyed, open-mouthed Edward. "Molly's signaling that Sapphire was definitely here this morning. She's telling us that your cat is still alive and well and that she clearly made it to the riverbank."

At this, Edward squealed with glee and threw his arms around his father, who somewhat stiffly returned the embrace.

"This is the best news ever!" he cried. "I need to call Lily."

Edward relayed the good news to his girlfriend, Jack headed off to the river to collect more fees and I gave Molly a run-around in a nearby clearing. Godfrey strode over to join us and watched Molly leaping into the air, trying to catch the insects that she'd disturbed. The old man seemed uncharacteristically muted, I noticed.

"Everything okay, Godfrey? You've gone all quiet."

"I'm at a loss for words, to be honest," he replied, with a slight catch in his voice. "I've seen lots of amazing things in my life, Mr. Butcher, but nothing quite like that. Your dog is truly incredible."

Witnessing Molly's unique talents for the first time could be quite an emotional experience for some people, even smart alecks like Godfrey.

"That's very kind of you to say," I said, as my dog bounded back, her snout and paws sopping wet from the long meadow grass. "She's a very special dog."

We reconvened at the riverside picnic bench, beneath which an exhausted Molly fell into a deep sleep, emitting the occasional porcine snort. Edward and Godfrey's faces fell, however, when I explained that she'd reached her working time limit and that we'd soon have to head home to Sussex. While I appreciated their desire to find Sapphire—particularly now it seemed she was alive—the snakebite incident had made me super-cautious and Molly's welfare had to take priority.

I didn't leave without giving them some advice, though, or without explaining my theory as to how the cat had gone missing. Indeed, the situation had all become very Agatha Christie because, thanks to Molly's positive scent identification, we were now dealing with a "howdunnit." How had Sapphire reached dry land? How had she managed to stay safe in the meantime? How were we going to locate her?

"I reckon she did indeed fall overboard, perhaps not long after you set sail," I told Edward. "I think she then swam ashore, perhaps navigating her way to the moorings you'd stayed at."

"And what then?"

"I suspect she just started to migrate in a random fashion, perhaps following some easy terrain, or a lit-up area."

"Like the towpath?"

"Yes, exactly. I imagine she'd have been drawn to the lights of the barges rather than the dark of the woods, put it that way. Displaced cats will always seek out human contact. They have a knack of finding other animal-lovers."

I unfurled my map of the area, using a marker pen to indicate the likely routes that Sapphire may have taken since the sighting, and slid it across the table to Edward.

"Don't give up," I said. "I'm confident you'll find her soon. Let me know how you get on this afternoon and we will see you again tomorrow morning."

"I will do," said Edward with a nod and a smile. "And thank you."

At around midnight, while I was reading *Country Life* in bed, with Sarah sleeping soundly beside me, I heard my phone buzzing in my bedside cabinet. It was Edward.

"I know it's late, and I'm sorry if I've woken you up," he said, "but I wanted you to hear this."

"Hear what?" I replied, puzzled.

"Sapphire. She's purring. She's sitting on my knee, and she's purring—"

"*You found her?*" I yelled, as poor Sarah awoke with a start.

"What's happened?" she asked, rubbing her eyes.

"Sapphire's turned up," I whispered, only for my girlfriend to roll over, muttering something about a grown man getting excited about a missing cat.

"Yep. We found her," continued Edward. "Isn't it incredible?"

It turned out that, earlier in the evening, he'd received a call from a holidaymaker at the caravan site whose young daughter had heard a cat meowing as she'd settled down to sleep. The man had searched the mobile home from top to bottom—including all cupboards, wardrobes and drawers—but had been unable to locate it. It was only when he'd gone outside, armed with a torch, that he'd spied a pretty, dark gray cat hiding in a cavity beneath the caravan. Certain it was the moggy on the leaflet given to him by the pet detective and his dog, he'd rung the owner's number straight away.

"An hour later I was standing outside the caravan with Sapphire in my arms," said Edward, his voice wavering with emotion. "Hungry and flea-ridden, but alive and kicking."

"That's fantastic news," I replied. "I'm so pleased for you all."

"I just had to ring you. I couldn't go without saying a huge thank-you to you and your fabulous dog. It was Molly who gave us that glimmer of hope, that impetus to carry on, and we'll never, ever forget that."

"Ah, thanks, Edward," I said, "and you're right, Molly is a remarkable dog. I can't wait to tell her the glad tidings in the morning."

"Oh, and one last thing," added my client. "The little girl in the caravan asked me when she'd be getting the biggest bag of sweets in the whole wide world."

"Ha, I forgot about that." I laughed. "I'll sort out some kind of treat, don't worry."

After ending the call, I switched off the bedside light, lay my head back on the pillow and smiled contentedly. While I was slightly disappointed that Molly hadn't made the actual find, hearing the relief and happiness in Edward's voice was ample compensation. My thoughts switched to my little spaniel, curled up in her bed downstairs, and I wondered how aware my little heroine was of her extraordinary ability to bring people, and their pets, together.

I'm so incredibly lucky to have her, I thought, before drifting off to sleep.

13

A Nightmare in Notting Hill

Over the years, I had worked with some wonderful clients, and a few of them had gone on to become firm friends of mine. Renu, the owner of Buffy the Coton de Tulear, was a case in point. I spent hours with her and her family in the aftermath of that terrible burglary, often acting as counselor as well as an investigator, and we kept in close contact following her dog's eventual recovery. I remember visiting their home in Willesden Green, probably a month or so after they'd been reunited, and hardly recognizing the gleaming white fluff-ball that bounded up the hallway, yapping excitedly and pawing at my ankles.

"That *can't* be Buffy, surely," I joshed, gently lifting her up for closer inspection, as Renu beamed with happiness.

Not only did the dog look a picture of health, she'd also benefited from some intense retraining courtesy of my good pal Anna. Due to the trauma of her kidnap, Buffy had acquired some deep-seated behavioral issues and, in order to iron them out, I'd happily put my client in touch with the best dog-training expert in town.

"Colin, you do realize I'm forever in your debt," said Renu, as a rejuvenated Buffy gambolled around the lounge like a spring lamb. "If I ever hear of anyone needing a pet detective, yours will be the first name on my lips."

"That's really kind of you," I replied. "Thank you so much."

Renu kept her promise, because a few weeks later I was contacted by Trine, a Danish-born woman whose five-month-old puppy—another white and tan Coton de Tulear named Newton—had gone missing near her home in west London. Having seen Trine's desperate appeal on Facebook, Renu had messaged her to express her sympathy and offer some advice.

"If you're thinking of going down the pet-detective route, I can highly recommend Colin Butcher," she'd written. "There's no way we would have recovered our beloved Buffy without him."

This had prompted Trine to contact me and, during an emotional telephone conversation, she recounted the events surrounding Newton's disappearance. She and her husband, Mark, as well as their two young children, had been attending a wedding in Denmark when they'd received a distressing phone call informing them that Newton had gone missing. He had been left in the temporary care of Trine's friend Annie, and that afternoon, she'd taken him to Holland Park for a leisurely run-about in the sunshine.

He had been playing happily off-leash with a group of small dogs when, out of the blue, a rubber ball had come flying over, hotly pursued by a snarling, slavering German shepherd. Pandemonium had ensued as it had plowed into Newton and his newfound pals, barking ferociously and biting a pug that had got in its way. All the little dogs had reared up in fright and fled in different directions and, within a matter of seconds, a terrified Newton had hightailed it out of the park. Amid all the chaos, Annie's attention had been instinctively drawn to the wounded dog, and it took her a minute or so to realize that Newton had completely vanished.

Utterly panic-stricken, she spent the rest of the afternoon combing Holland Park (a nigh-impossible task, since it comprises over fifty acres) and trying to speak to anyone who might have spotted Newton. Her search was fruitless, sadly, and she headed back to Notting Hill in floods of tears, clasping the dog's leash and dreading the phone call she knew she'd have to make.

Trine, who'd been walking to the wedding venue, almost collapsed in shock when she heard the news. Sick with worry, and eager to start hunting for Newton, she and her family flew home from Denmark the following morning, a day earlier than planned.

Upon their return to London they deluged the area with posters and flyers and bombarded Facebook, Twitter and Instagram with appeals and updates. Aside from a few upsetting crank calls, the community rallied magnificently—neighbors scoured the streets, friends shared social media posts and police officers and park wardens lent their support—but there were no concrete sightings of Newton, other than a few sketchy reports of a small white dog seen running like the wind. Following two days of constant searching, Trine soon realized that she needed additional help. Not only was the hunt for Newton threatening to consume her whole life (far from ideal, when she had a young family to look after), she also felt she was too emotionally fragile to spearhead the campaign. She needed someone who could take over the reins and mastermind the search, and employ a more strategic and objective approach.

"The lady on Facebook mentioned that you'd helped to find her puppy," said Trine, the desperation evident in her voice, "and I'm wondering if you can do the same for me."

Unfortunately, the timing of Trine's request couldn't have been worse. UKPD was absolutely swamped with work, including the bizarre case of Lulu the tabby cat—owned by a lovely retiree called Barbara—who had survived a six-story fall from a Docklands apartment in London, not far from the Thames Barrier. The poor moggy had skidded off a slippery patio during a torrential rain shower, but had seemingly disappeared into thin air. Despite Molly making a positive scent match in the tower block's basement, there'd been no trace of the cat and our search was ongoing.

With my schedule so jam-packed, I doubted I'd be able to devote the time to such a potentially complex case as Newton's. I already had three days booked that week for cat searches and I was also dealing with a messy dispute of ownership between a couple who had recently split up and both wanted to keep the family dog (the man was the registered keeper but his ex-girlfriend had possession and was refusing to reveal the dog's whereabouts). On top of that, a dog charity had asked me to investigate one of their volunteers, who had allegedly stolen one of their animals. All were potentially long-running, labor-intensive cases.

As I explained my predicament to Trine, I could sense her crushing disappointment down the phone line.

"Oh, that's such a shame," she said, her voice fading to a whisper. "I was banking on you, to be honest, and the kids would have loved to have met Molly . . ."

"I tell you what," I said, feeling my heart strings being tugged, "I'm in London tomorrow—we're searching for Lulu again—so how about I pop in for a chat around lunchtime, even if it's just to offer you some advice?"

"Oh, that would be fabulous," replied Trine.

Within an hour of meeting this delightful lady and her family (as well as a deeply traumatized Annie) and witnessing their collective anguish at first hand, I'd agreed to take on the case.

"You're such a soft touch, Colin," Sam had said, laughing, when I'd rung the office, asking her to squeeze Operation Newton into the diary.

With a dearth of witnesses and sightings of Newton (and with Annie's recollections sketchy at best), I had a distinct lack of evidence but a whole raft of questions. Was the runaway puppy the victim of dog-nappers, like Buffy? Had he become trapped or confined somewhere? Was he being harbored by a well-meaning resident? Or, more worryingly, had he come to some serious harm on the congested streets of west London? With the help of my right-hand woman and my crime-busting canine, the time had come to launch a thorough investigation of the dog's disappearance.

"Destination, Holland Park," I said, reversing out of Bramble Hill Farm's gravelly driveway with Sam sitting in the passenger seat and Molly tail-thwacking in her crate. "Time to find out exactly what's happened to Newton."

I knew Kensington and Chelsea very well—I'd lived in west London for a spell during my early days as a private investigator—so I was pretty familiar with the borough's streets, buildings and green spaces. The lush and leafy Holland Park, where I'd often taken weekend walks, comprised three distinct areas—tranquil woodland to the north, formal gardens at the center and, to the south, the opera house and recreation grounds, from where Newton had bolted.

Our first task was to pinpoint the exit route that the dog might have taken, based on the information we'd gleaned from Annie. We narrowed it down to a couple of possibilities, before quizzing a conveyor belt of passers-by in the hope that they might have witnessed Newton's great escape. We spoke to an elderly couple who recalled seeing a flustered woman on the day in question, sobbing about a lost puppy (Annie, no doubt), but they couldn't remember seeing the object of her despair.

"She was so upset, I'm afraid we couldn't understand what she was saying at first," said the husband, "but we eventually gathered that she'd lost her friend's dog."

"My heart went out to her," recalled his wife. "What an awful thing to go through."

After an hour or so—just as Molly was beginning to hanker after some Holland Park play time—we struck gold. A professional dog-walker, a red-haired Irish woman in her thirties, squinted at Newton's photo and nodded her head vigorously.

"Yeah, I'm pretty sure I saw that dog shooting through the gate toward Phillimore Gardens," she said. "It was running flat out, looking scared as hell. One of my clients has a Coton de Tulear, and I remember thinking how similar its markings were."

"How sure are you that it's the same dog?" I asked, showing her the photo again.

"Oh, ninety-nine point nine percent sure," she replied. "That's definitely the one I saw."

"Thank you *so* much for your help," said Sam as I plotted our first possible sighting on the map and made a mental note to saturate that particular street with flyers and posters.

Following a quick espresso in the Holland Park café—I
needed a caffeine injection after our early-morning start—we
headed to the recreation area for Molly's tennis-ball workout. As
we rounded a corner, however, my dog skidded to a halt and
emitted a guarded growl. Standing in the middle of the path,
fanning its glorious feathers, was a huge peacock. I'd totally
forgotten that the park was a haven for these exotic birds; over
the years, they had become something of a tourist attraction. A
flummoxed Molly didn't quite know how to react.

Should I take off, or give chase? seemed to be her sentiment,
as both animals remained firmly rooted to the spot, staring each
other out, sizing each other up. As a working cocker spaniel, the
pursuit of game birds and wild fowl was ingrained and instinc-
tive, although this colorful creature, preening itself like a panto-
mime dame, was like nothing she'd ever seen before.

A passing group of art students, clutching their folders and
sketchbooks, stopped to watch this amusing spectacle.

"Now that would be *so* great to paint," remarked one.

"'The Spaniel and the Peacock' . . . great title for it, too," replied another.

Perhaps aware of her audience, Molly took a small step forward and let out another low growl. The peacock retracted its
feathers, turned its back in disdain and strutted off in the direction of the Japanese gardens. The students went on their way,
leaving Molly to prod and sniff a bluey-green feather that the
peacock had left in its wake.

"Another scent for your repertoire, Molls." I laughed and gave
her neck a ruffle. "Not that I think we'll ever have many missing
peacocks on our books."

Lulu the Docklands cat still remained on our case list,
though—among a handful of others—and after we'd finished
our Holland Park investigation we made a quick diversion to see
her owner, Barbara. We arrived at her flat armed with a batch of
freshly printed MISSING CAT leaflets, advising her to blitz the
cluster of apartment blocks and office buildings in the area. Barbara was becoming increasingly worried that her cat had ended

up in the river, but I painstakingly reassured her that I believed Lulu to be alive and well, based on the fact that Molly had made the positive scent match in the basement.

"Lulu definitely survived the fall and, according to Molly's scent match, she should be somewhere in the underground car park," I suggested. "Why don't you speak to the security staff and see if they can remember anything about the day she went missing?"

"Yes, I'll do just that," replied Barbara.

"Take heart, and trust in Molly." I smiled, and Sam gave our client a reassuring hug.

Sam, Molly and I spent the following two days in Kensington, conducting house-to-house inquiries and canvassing local shops and businesses. Everywhere we visited—from pubs to florists, cafés to museums—we were met with kindness and congeniality. People were so helpful and generous with their time (not always the case in chaotic inner London) and went above and beyond to assist our investigation; it was as if we'd recruited an army of Newton "ambassadors," all desperate for the safe return of this cute little Coton de Tulear.

We also spent a great deal of time searching the many back-streets and side roads, deploying Molly to investigate potential hiding places. Like many working cocker spaniels—particularly those trained as sniffer dogs—Molly's agility and athleticism enabled her to explore the tightest of spots, and she'd always react by circling frantically if she ever unexpectedly encountered an animal.

Our quest received a timely boost when Kensington and Chelsea Borough Council kindly agreed to check CCTV cameras that were on the outside of the building on Kensington High Street, as did the security staff at the Design Museum, which faced the park entrance. Our high hopes were dashed, sadly, when we were told that there was no footage showing Newton.

Making up for this disappointment, however, was a slew of potential new sightings that we'd gathered from forty-eight hours' worth of exhaustive inquiries. Two separate eyewitnesses reported seeing a "white flash of a dog" sprinting past local restaurants further up Phillimore Gardens, and another pair claimed to have spotted the tiny pooch on a zebra crossing near Kensington High Street. The final reported sightings involved a puppy of Newton's description scampering down Pembroke Road before weaving in and out of vehicles on Earls Court Road. We mapped out the route Newton had taken and were staggered to discover that he was still running at full pelt over a mile away from the park.

We visited Trine in Notting Hill to give her an update, and she was both heartened and horrified by these significant developments. While she was delighted to discover that there were more possible sightings, she was terrified at the thought of Newton dodging his way through the heavy London traffic and disappearing into the heart of England's capital city.

"He's so shy and timid, and he's always been petrified of cars," she wept. "It'll be a miracle if he's come out of that unscathed. How on earth are we going to find him?"

"He's clearly a sprightly little thing," said Sam, doing her best to placate our tormented client. "You'd be surprised how resilient some dogs can be, though."

"She's right, you know. This little 'un got bitten by an adder and lived to tell the tale," I added, gently rubbing the site of Molly's snakebite.

I then explained to Trine that, having had time to assess and analyze Newton's disappearance, I was now working on the theory that this was a case of a dog lost, not a dog-nap. Sam and I had spoken to hundreds of workers and residents in an area of high density and, while some had spied a fluffy white pooch running along the road, not one person had spotted him being swiped up by a passer-by or being shoved into a car. In my opinion, it was very unlikely that he'd been stolen.

"My instinct tells me he's gone to ground, Trine," I said. "We just need to switch our attention to the location of the last sighting and speak to as many people as possible."

Before we went on our way, Trine informed us that the hunt for Newton had been given an amazing fillip by the intervention of a local celebrity. The actress, TV presenter and *Britain's Got Talent* judge Amanda Holden, a renowned dog-lover, had retweeted an appeal from the @BringNewtonHome Twitter account to her 1.9 million followers, adding a personal plea for west London residents to "Please keep an eye out."

In the wake of such fantastic support, it was desperately disappointing to see our trail going cold for the next fortnight. Our regular patrols of Kensington became largely unproductive and, while vigilance and awareness remained high within the locality, the witnesses and sightings seemed to dry up.

"Keep on trucking, Molly," I said to my diligent little dog as she trotted out from yet another back alley that bore no trace of Newton. "You're doing a marvelous job, sweetheart."

Having worked in the detection industry for over three decades, I was well accustomed to the ebb and flow of investigations, whether it involved a murder in Croydon, a missing cat in St. Albans or a lost dog in Kensington. It was par for the course to experience periods of high activity, when you'd be deluged with evidence, followed by spells of stagnation, when you'd be praying for a breakthrough. Trying to explain this unpredictability to the despairing owner of a missing pet could be tricky, however, and it was during those barren, quiet times that my counseling skills came to the fore. As the hunt for Newton appeared to stall, I realized that my heavy-hearted client needed her spirits lifted.

"Trine, I know this must be torturous for you," I said as her tears started to flow one afternoon, "but you've got to stay positive. Newton's a fit and healthy little dog, and there's every chance he's still alive."

She paused to dab her eyes with a handkerchief.

"Maybe someone has found him and decided to keep him," she said, showing me an advert that she'd seen on a puppy-sale website featuring a white dog based in Luton that was very similar to Newton in appearance. "I was wondering whether *this* could be him, Colin."

"It may look like Newton, but check out the date at the top of the ad," I said. "It's two days before he disappeared."

"You're right," she replied, looking at the floor. "It can't possibly be him, can it?"

Trine, like many pet owners in this situation, was clutching at straws, and I felt her pain.

"I honestly think he's a little closer to home," I said softly. "I truly believe that."

She lifted up her head and looked at me. "Well, if you still believe, Colin, then I still believe."

It wasn't unusual for owners of missing pets to become increasingly desperate, and it was my job to keep them focused and positive; otherwise, they'd worry themselves sick. With Newton missing for two weeks, and with Trine's anxiety levels rising, I reckoned it was time to implement a new strategy. I decided to identify the busiest thoroughfares in Kensington and, having studied traffic flow, choke points and bottlenecks, was able to pinpoint the congestion spots that would best capture commuters' attention. I then printed off some large, laminated, visually arresting posters with STILL MISSING: REWARD plastered across them in bold lettering. Underneath was an unbearably cute photograph of Newton, accompanied by Trine's mobile phone number.

Sam and I then spent a whole morning carefully affixing these eye-catching posters to a variety of lamp posts, railings, fences and bridges, in the hope that they might strike a chord with drivers stuck in traffic. I would be lying if I said that this tactic was totally legal—I fully expected our handiwork to be removed by local sticklers—but I felt our investigation needed to be ramped up a level. Besides, this strategy had often worked for me in the police when I was trying to locate a missing person, so there was no reason why it wouldn't work for Newton.

The impact was instant. Within twenty-four hours, Trine had received calls from people across the capital, all claiming to have seen dogs that matched Newton's description. I followed up every single one but, unfortunately, none proved to be genuine, bona fide leads. This included a sighting in Hyde Park which initially sounded very plausible but which was swiftly discounted upon receipt of an email attachment. The Coton de Tulear in the photograph may have been cute, white and fluffy, but it quite clearly wasn't Newton.

The following day, Molly, Sam and I found ourselves back in a cool and breezy London, this time heading to Docklands in response to a call from Lulu's owner.

"You asked me to keep you updated," said Barbara, barely able to contain her excitement, "and I've just had a call from a woman on the second floor who says she might have found Lulu. I'm off to see her now."

"We'll be right with you," I'd replied.

By the time we arrived, a beaming Barbara was already cradling a miraculously unscathed Lulu in her arms. She told us how the woman, who happened to work as a cleaner in the apartment block, had apparently gone into the basement storage room on the night that Lulu went missing and had found the puss cowering in a cupboard. Believing her to be a stray, she'd taken her home and cared for her; it was only when a leaflet was dropped on to her doormat bearing Lulu's picture that she realized the tabby belonged to a neighbor.

"I think she was a bit reluctant to hand her over, to be honest," admitted Barbara.

"Who could blame her?" said Sam as she gently stroked the purring cat. "She's absolutely gorgeous."

Molly's scent match in the basement had been spot-on, therefore, and—since it suggested the cat was still alive—had given my client the impetus and confidence to carry on searching. While it wasn't a direct "find" on our part, our involvement had helped to reunite a very hardy cat with a very happy owner.

"Put that down to a team effort . . . high-fives all round," I said, smiling, as we walked back to the car park.

As I drove off toward Greenwich, having bid a fond farewell to Barbara and Lulu, my phone trilled. It was Trine.

"I've just taken a call from a guy who's noticed one of our giant posters," she said. "He's the manager of a recycling depot on Pembroke Road. Reckons he saw a white Persian cat in his yard a few days ago but, now that he's seen Newton's photo, he thinks it could have been a dog."

This sounded very intriguing and hugely promising—the location was in close proximity to the final eyewitness sighting of Newton—but I was careful to keep my response measured. My client's illusions had been shattered by a succession of red herrings and false alarms and there was every likelihood that this was another.

"My satnav says I can be at Pembroke Road in half an hour, Trine. Give me this fella's number and I'll arrange to meet him there."

"Oh, that's wonderful, Colin. And keep me in the picture, obviously."

The depot manager, an affable chap called Adam, met us at the front entrance. He listened with interest when I explained who UK Pet Detectives were and when I detailed what role Molly played.

"I flippin' love cocker spaniels," he grinned, gently patting Molly's back. "I've got one of my own at home, actually, but I'm not sure my Bella is as clever as *this* little one."

Adam pointed out the place where he'd seen the "cat"—he'd spotted it scavenging food from a Dumpster—and gave us carte blanche to search wherever we wanted. Before heading back to his office, however, he informed us that the depot had to be locked up at five o'clock and that we'd have to vacate the premises before the gates shut for the night.

"That gives us just over three hours," I said to Sam, while looking nervously at my watch and scanning the concrete jungle that lay before us. "Looks like we might need every second of every minute."

Facing us was an enormous yard that contained a variety of bins, boxes and Dumpsters. Adjacent to it was an imposing warehouse with a huge roller shutter door which housed all manner of refuse vehicles and recycling machines. Linking the two were a number of narrow, moss-lined alleyways, flanked by tall, red-brick walls.

"Let's use our time wisely," I said to Sam, "and let's get Molly's nose on the case."

In this scenario, she may not have had a specific scent to work off, but I knew that Molly's gun-dog instinct often sought out other living creatures. Indeed, back home at Bramble Hill Farm, she'd quite easily detect the odor of rabbits, deer and pheasants and would enjoy lolloping after them as they tried to make a quick getaway.

When I finally let Molly off her leash she scurried around the yard for a good twenty minutes, allowing her ultra-sensitive nose to lead the way as she circled the Dumpsters and bins and explored the nooks and crannies. She then began to zig-zag across the network of alleyways, her snout nudging the left-hand brick wall, and then the right-hand one—and it was while running down a particularly murky passageway that she suddenly screeched to a halt. She immediately looked up at me, with unblinking eyes, and her tail began to wag furiously. I had seen this self-assured behavior many times during training searches at Bramble Hill Farm.

"Molly's telling us she's got a whiff of something interesting," I said, beckoning Sam to follow me as I crept toward the alleyway.

"It's dog poop," I whispered as I inched closer, my nostrils twitching. "It's dollops and dollops of dog poop."

"The question is, though," said Sam, screwing up her nose against the smell, "does the poop belong to Newton?"

I took a few steps forward and shone my torch down the dark, dank passageway. At its foot, no more than five yards away, was a brick wall sheathed in intertwining, vine-like plants. Creating a significant obstacle to any further exploration, however, was a tier of thick steel piping originating from a large air-conditioning unit. With Molly following closely behind me, I managed to squeeze under the metalwork ("I didn't know you could limbo, Colin," grinned Sam) and, once upright, I tiptoed toward the back wall.

It was only when Molly pawed impatiently at the matted vines, causing them to peel away and fall to the ground, that I noticed a slender crevice between the brickwork. The gap was certainly large enough to be accessed by a puppy—it measured the width of two outstretched hands—but there didn't appear to be any movement inside. I idly picked up a few twigs and aimed them into the hole, just to check for any signs of life.

And that's when I heard a low, lugubrious growl.

At first, I presumed it was Molly—"What's bothering you, missus?" I asked—but, when I heard the noise again, accompanied by a faint rustling, I realized it was emanating from the chasm in the brickwork. Then, as the beam from my torch flicked from side to side and from top to bottom, I caught sight of a pair of tiny, glinting eyes and, beneath them, the glimmer of a heart-shaped name disc. The animal before me was shaking in fear and keeping his distance, but it was quite obvious who I was looking at. He was a little white dog with a patch of tan. He was a lost and lonesome dog called Newton.

I slowly reached for the phone in my jeans pocket and pressed "T" for Trine.

As my shell-shocked client made a mad dash from Notting Hill, armed with Newton's favorite toys and treats, I asked Sam to take Molly back to the car. I don't think my dog was very impressed to be hauled off the job (she loved being in work mode, she craved the thrill of a search and she'd done a great job tracking Newton to his hidey-hole) but, if I was going to successfully recover Trine's dog, I needed to operate in a totally serene environment. The situation remained extremely precarious—the little pup was holed up deep inside the crevice—and any barks, whines or grunts from Molly might just cause him to retreat.

I'd already primed Trine not to expect a joyful *Lassie*-style reunion. Not only was Newton frightened to death, he didn't appear to be in the best of health either. His frame was scrawny, his fur was matted and his eyes looked badly swollen, perhaps due to a tick infestation. Despite the advance warning, though, nothing could have prepared Trine for the pitiful sight that confronted her when she arrived.

"My little baby," she whispered, gulping down tears as her dog peeped out from the darkness.

I suggested to my client that, in order to coax Newton out of his hidey-hole, and in order to gain his confidence, we needed to adopt a softly-softly approach.

"The mere sound of your voice should be a comfort to him," I said, "so I suggest we stand here and chat quietly and calmly until he feels ready to move."

I had always loved my work, and I'd often found myself searching in some beautiful locations, but I'd never expected to be chatting casually with a client in the smelly alleyway of a refuse-truck depot. Trine and I tackled every conversation topic known to man. Current affairs, TV programs, family matters . . . you name it, we covered it. Frustratingly, Newton remained firmly rooted to the spot.

"We're probably boring him senseless, poor thing," said Trine.

"Maybe it was a bad idea to bring up Brexit," I replied, which prompted a half-smile.

Following a fruitless attempt to lure Newton out using his squashy toys—we'd hoped he might respond positively to the scent of home—we decided to introduce his doggy treats. We sprinkled some near the den's entrance and some on the alleyway floor, and—thank goodness—he slowly and steadily snaffled them up, inching ever closer to us as he did so. At one point a loud bang from the warehouse spooked him and, much to our horror, he swiftly retreated into the darkness. For two long minutes our hearts were in our mouths—we hadn't blown it, *surely*—but he promptly reappeared, no doubt governed by his hunger pangs.

After a fraught thirty minutes, Newton finally summoned the strength and courage to crawl out of the hole. As he hobbled toward us, however, the full extent of his visibility problem became clear. His eyes were so infected he could hardly see and it was clear he was being directed purely by his sense of smell.

"Remember, Trine, no sudden movements," I whispered as he edged to within a yard of her feet. "Don't be tempted to grab him. You must let him come to you."

Much to our delight, Newton recognized Trine's scent, joyfully wagged his stubby tail and leaped into his tearful owner's arms. Seeing the look of relief on Trine's face as she held Newton tight was one of those "gold dust" moments, beyond overwhelming.

I dropped off Trine and Newton at the vet's, and Sam and I took Molly back to Holland Park for a run-around and handful of beef jerky in recognition of the vital role she'd played in the recovery.

"Had you not found that poop, Molly, and had you not clawed the vines, I honestly don't think we'd have found Newton," I said, shaking my head. "Another successful investigation, thanks to you."

During our homeward journey, Sam and I reflected on a day of charged emotions. We both agreed that, had we not discovered him in the depot that afternoon, Newton wouldn't have survived for much longer. For eighteen days, the resourceful little pup had managed to locate himself a shelter, scavenge food from bins and lap water from puddles, but he'd have invariably succumbed to the untreated infection, had it spread to his bloodstream.

"It just doesn't bear thinking about, does it?" said Sam, shaking her head.

"No, it doesn't." I shuddered. "Imagine Trine having to live the rest of her life never knowing what had happened to him."

We also surmised that, as I'd suspected, Newton hadn't been dog-napped (his intact collar and nametag corroborated this) and that, in all likelihood, he'd probably bolted into the depot the very day he went missing, seeking sanctuary from the busy London streets.

I arrived back at Bramble Hill Farm just before dusk. Molly dashed straight into the garden and dived into one of the herbaceous borders, no doubt scaring the living daylights out of some unsuspecting wildlife, while I lay down upon a warm patch of grass and gazed up at the farmhouse, its sash windows reflecting the pinky-gray sky. I was so tired—both mentally and physically—that I could hardly keep my eyes open. A few minutes later I found myself beginning to doze off when Molly bounded up and snuffled my face, her snout encased in dried grass and straw, looking like she'd just emerged head first out of a haystack. I grinned and rubbed my eyes.

"What on earth would I do without you, Molly?" I said, as an image of Newton and Trine's soul-stirring reunion flashed through my mind. I could hardly bear the thought of being separated from my beautiful dog.

A *few days* later, once everything had settled down, I gave Trine a call. She told me that Newton had been dosed up with antibiotics—the vet had never seen such a severe eye infection—but that he was now recovering well and was being fussed over and cared for by his family. The "Bring Newton Home" social media accounts had evidently gone into meltdown when the news of his recovery had filtered through—well-wishers from all around the world had posted photos of themselves jumping for joy and holding NEWTON IS HOME!!! posters—and it seemed the little dog had become something of a celebrity, both at home and abroad.

"This whole experience has been so traumatic, Colin, and I wouldn't wish it on my worst enemy," said Trine, "but it's given me the biggest life lesson, too."

"And what's that?" I asked.

"Don't give up," she said. "And never, ever lose hope."

14

A Missing Cat and a Grumpy Neighbor

Life as a cat-detection dog could get quite exhausting, and it was vitally important that Molly received plenty of downtime. After most searches I gave her a rest day, allowing her a long, undisturbed lie-in, a lazy potter around the house (often with her soft toy rabbit in tow) and, just before dinner, a leisurely walk in the woods. If it was a summer's day, Molly would invariably find the warmest place in the house for a spot of sunbathing; like many cats and dogs, she loved basking slap-bang in the middle of the brightest shaft of sunlight.

Molly would usually spend her days off with me but, if I ever had any private-investigation duties to attend to, Sarah would step in. This was indeed the case in late September 2017, when a Belgravia-based client of mine asked Stefan and me to conduct a surveillance operation. I finally returned to Cranleigh at nine o'clock that evening—the job had been a long-drawn-out affair—but any stresses and strains evaporated as soon as I opened the front door.

There before me, in the living room, lay a vision of domestic bliss. Sarah was curled up on the sofa with Marian Keyes's latest novel and a glass of wine and wrapped around her feet was a snoozing, snoring Molly. I couldn't help but smile. Once upon a time, Sarah—an avowed cat-lover—could hardly bear to be within a yard of this hair-shedding, handbag-snuffling rescue mutt, but now here they were, snuggling together like a pair of old friends.

"Well, well, well . . . just look at you two," I grinned, feeling all aglow. "Who'd have thought it, eh?"

"We've had the *best* girly day out *ever*," beamed Sarah, gazing fondly at Molly as she slept beside her. "Shopping in Guildford, lunch in Cranleigh and a work-out on the common. We've not missed you one jot, Colin."

"Well, that's just *charming*," I said, rolling my eyes in mock-indignation.

In reality, I was beyond thrilled to see my two favorite girls getting along so famously and appearing so calm and comfortable in each other's company. I had become Sarah's biggest fan ever since the day we'd first met, but to see her bonding so beautifully with Molly only strengthened my feelings of respect and gratitude. Giving my dog a loving and caring home was so important to me, on both a personal and a professional level and—that evening—it felt like the final piece of the jigsaw was in place.

I hung up my coat, lit the open fire, made us a coffee and sat down on the rug in front of Molly. She soon sensed my presence, awoke from her slumbers and, after giving me a sleepy lick, jumped up and climbed into my lap.

"Okay, missy, you can have a ten-minute cuddle, but then it's definitely time for bed," I said, kissing her snout. "We've got an early start tomorrow morning—we're traveling south—and I need you to be bright-eyed and bushy-tailed."

A ginger tomcat, Simba, had gone missing in Devon (I'd received the SOS call earlier that day) and the owners were desperate to draft in our help. As with so many of our cases, marvelous Molly was their only remaining hope.

Our drive from south Surrey to south Devon, via Hampshire, Wiltshire and Dorset, was as scenic as expected. The autumn sun hung low in the sky, its slanting rays adding a lustrous glow to the auburn-leaved oaks that lined the roadside. From east to west, honey-colored wheat fields stretched out toward the horizon, blanketed by a layer of early-morning mist.

"Isn't it glorious?" I said, smiling at Sam in the passenger seat.

"Let's just say I've had worse commutes to work," replied my colleague.

We arrived in the village of Lower Chillington a little earlier than planned—the roads had been nice and quiet—so we stopped off for a quick coffee and scone at a local café and, within minutes, Molly had all the staff doting on her.

Then, as always, we undertook a pre-search walkabout, observing the layout of the roads and the location of buildings, as well as any hazards or obstacles that might put Molly at risk. As we ambled around the country lanes, it was clear that we were in picture-postcard territory. Olde worlde thatched cottages lined the maze of cobbled streets and at the heart of the village lay a church, a cenotaph and a duck pond, complete with floating lily pads. Lower Chillington would have been a perfect setting for one of Enid Blyton's Famous Five novels, I reckoned.

As we began to make our way back to the car, we heard a clippety-clop of hooves. Emerging around the corner, riding a dark-brown show hunter, was a horsewoman wearing the regulation boots, jacket and jodhpurs combo. This striking-looking lady was flanked by two stocky Irish wolfhounds, running fast and loose, their pink tongues lolling. Molly sat down and watched the trio and their owner shoot past.

Wow, what was that, Dad? she seemed to be saying.

"Good morning to you," said the woman, smiling and slowing down slightly and doffing her riding cap to reveal a tightly wound blonde chignon. "Have a super day!"

With a dig of the heels and a tug of the reins, she galloped along the lane, her doggy duo cavorting behind her.

Chugging in the opposite direction, past the old schoolhouse, came an old tractor towing a trailer packed with apple crates. The flat-capped farmer at the wheel honked his horn and raised his palm in acknowledgment, as if he'd known us all his life.

"Remind me again, Colin, which year have we traveled back to?" joked Sam.

"Nineteen fifty-eight, I reckon," I winked, half expecting Dixon of Dock Green to come cycling around the corner.

Half an hour later I was knocking on the door of a stone-built semi-detached cottage, where Lindsey, Simba's owner, was staying. Molly and Sam remained in the car, as they often did while I interviewed the family and obtained the cat-hair sample.

A slightly built, young girl in her early teens, Lindsey had been lodging with her family friend while her mother and father were holidaying in Majorca. I gathered she'd been recovering from a serious illness—I didn't pry any further—and that her parents had preferred not to leave her alone during their Balearic break. As a result, their daughter had temporarily decamped from Yeovil to Lower Chillington, arriving holding her suitcase in one hand and her cat carrier in the other.

To say that Lindsey adored her chubby, cheeky ginger tom was an understatement. They were simply inseparable. Rescued ten years previously from a cat shelter, Simba had been a constant presence during Lindsey's childhood and had been a source of comfort and affection as she'd battled through some tough times. Other than a long-held love of literature, spending quality time with her noisy and mischievous furball was one of her favorite hobbies, and she'd spend hours testing his dexterity with ping-pong balls or teasing him with a medley of fluffy cat toys.

During the warmer months Lindsey would sit with Simba in the garden, reading one of her favorite historical novels as he lazed in the sunshine. Occasionally, the cat would spring into action if a robin or song thrush dared to hop on to his patch—despite his advancing years (and burgeoning weight), his hunting instinct remained strong—but Lindsey's shrill cry of *"Simba!"* would usually distract both parties and avert a skirmish. She was also mindful of the fact that her father was a keen birdwatcher who never appreciated lifeless, feathery "gifts" being delivered through the cat flap.

With his owner by his side, Simba initially seemed to have

settled into his new environment in Lower Chillington. Lindsey had kept him indoors at first, but after the first week had caved in to his constant back-door scratching and had let him outdoors to explore. Within a few days, however, her cherished pet had gone missing and her world had fallen apart.

Upon hearing the news—and conscious of Lindsey's emotional state—her mother and father, Chris and Wendy, had flown home from their sunshine break to join the search for Simba. Having combed the village's cobbled streets and back gardens, they'd hit a metaphorical brick wall and, having read about Molly in a newspaper, her dad had decided to give UK Pet Detectives a call.

"My daughter is fragile enough at the best of times," he'd explained, "but Simba going AWOL has got her teetering on the brink. She's devoted to him, Mr. Butcher, and we desperately need your help to find him."

Deepest Devon was way beyond my usual catchment area, of course—I tried not to stray too far from the Home Counties—but due to the delicate nature of the case I agreed to lend a hand. Other factors swayed my decision, too. Firstly, I hoped the compact nature of the village would work in our favor, since there'd only be a relatively small number of buildings to search. Secondly, since Simba had gone missing from a single-pet household, I was confident that we'd be able to extract a high-quality hair sample, which would benefit Molly's scent-matching process.

Unsurprisingly, the atmosphere around the breakfast table that morning was fraught. A teary Lindsey was inconsolable—"How can I carry on without Simba?" she kept repeating—and both parents, sitting either side of their daughter, tried their utmost to reassure her.

"Colin and Molly are going to do their very best," said her mother, clasping Lindsey's hand in hers. "Everything will be all right in the end, darling, I promise."

If only her family friend had been as sensitive.

"The thing is, though, can Molly still find a cat if it's dead?"

she asked, prompting a loud wail from Lindsey and a chastening glare from Wendy.

"There's *every* reason to believe that Simba is alive and well, so my glass will remain half full," I replied, doing my damnedest to smother the impact of the friend's clanger. "I've dealt with many cases like this over the years and, more often than not, these moggies are holed up in hiding places, almost waiting to be found."

I felt it was important, however, that I added some context to Simba's disappearance. Without blinding Lindsey with science, I explained that there were generally two causes of pet migration—intrinsic and extrinsic—both of which I'd observed during my "Cat-Cam" experiment in Shamley Green, which had given me a real insight into feline behavior. Extrinsic migration related to external, outdoor forces that were often beyond the control of the owner: an aggressive dog moving in next door, perhaps; fireworks being set off in a local park; or builders digging up a nearby road. Intrinsic migration, on the other hand—which applied to Simba, I believed—was generally connected to the owner in some way and was related to the cat's indoor environment. This could be the arrival of a new pet or baby, maybe, an unwanted change in diet or, as in this case, a disorientating house move.

In order to escape from its feelings of anxiety, therefore, the cat would often physically extract itself from the root cause in order to migrate elsewhere. In this case, I surmised that Simba had been unsettled by the move to the family friend's house and had absconded at the first opportunity.

"What's interesting, though," I added, "is that with intrinsic migration—more so than extrinsic—the cat's stress levels soon reduce, which sometimes means it will return home of its own volition."

"Oh, please let that be the case," said Lindsey, managing a weak smile, as she blotted her damp cheeks with a handkerchief.

With my client feeling a little more optimistic, I went upstairs to the spare room to collect the required cat hair from

Simba's fleecy blanket. As I did so, I contemplated the task that lay ahead. It felt like I was in the middle of a *Midsomer Murders* case in many respects, since our village location was similarly quaint and rustic and teeming with a cast of colorful characters. The central theme of this particular episode was abundantly clear, of course: where on earth was Simba? Had he wandered off and got lost? Was he trapped in an outbuilding? Had he been kidnapped by a local? Was he still alive, even? Fortunately, I had my problem-solving pooch waiting in the wings, who'd no doubt help me to get to the bottom of it.

Let's pray this story's got a happy ending, I remember thinking to myself as I dropped a clump of ginger fluff into my jam jar. *For Lindsey's sake.*

Chris asked if he could join us on the search for Simba—he was keen to help, and I knew his local knowledge would prove invaluable—while Wendy remained at the house with her daughter. As soon as he unlatched the front door, however, it was abundantly clear that we had a huge problem. Plumes of smoke billowed from a nearby field and the air was heavy with the acrid smell of burning wood. It seemed a local farmer had lit an early-morning bonfire.

"I don't want to alarm you, Chris, but Molly won't be able to work today if that fire continues to rage," I said. "It'll badly affect her sense of smell and it'll mask the cat scent."

"Leave this to me," hissed Chris. "I know that farmer. I'm going to give him a piece of my mind. He shouldn't be lighting fires at this time of day, anyway."

He stomped over to confront him, and I watched as their finger-wagging contest threatened to descend into a full-blown fist-fight. The farmer reluctantly agreed to quell the fire, thank goodness, and Chris marched back, shaking his head.

"He's lucky I didn't put him on top of that bloomin' bonfire," he said, brushing flecks of ash from his shoulders.

We had to wait an hour for the smoke to disperse before we

could commence the search—it was incredibly frustrating, to be honest—so we made good use of the time by walking around the village and introducing ourselves to more passers-by. Once the bonfire fumes had finally dissipated, I gave Molly the green light to inhale Simba's scent and we began the search in earnest. As we scoured the main street, a succession of back doors and French windows seemed to open automatically, out of which friendly Devonians poked their smiley faces.

"Would you like a glass of apple juice?"

"Hello there, can I help in any way?"

"Can I give your lovely dog a biscuit?"

Everyone was so amenable and, had it not been for the fact that we had a cat to find, I'd have gladly accepted each kind invitation. We had to stick around at one particular cottage, though, because in its front garden was a wheelbarrow groaning with fruit, vegetables, jams and chutneys for passers-by to purchase. I was a sucker for local produce, so I took a couple of minutes out of the search to load up my car trunk with a variety of Lower Chillington goodies, while Sam fed coins into the honesty box.

The three of us continued along the country lane, laughing at Molly as she snapped at the falling leaves pirouetting in the wind. We soon approached a beautiful stone-built property, its grounds aflame with tawny beeches and scarlet maples, and were greeted in the driveway by the owner. Dressed in a lilac paisley shirt and khaki cargo shorts and sporting a peroxide quiff, he looked a tad incongruous in this ultra-traditional village. The way he kept his distance from Molly suggested that—unlike his neighbors—he wasn't one of life's dog-lovers.

"Search away, by all means," he said, after we'd introduced ourselves and explained our circumstances, "but please don't let your dog anywhere near my pond. I keep koi carp, you see; they're very sensitive fish and I don't want them being startled."

He was about to head back to his house when he stopped in his tracks, as if he'd just remembered something.

"Oh, I forgot . . . you need to keep an eye out for our three-foot hedgehog, too."

"Excuse me?" I replied. Either this fella had got his woodland animals mixed up or he'd dropped some LSD into his tea that morning.

"Yeah, there's a three-foot hedgehog that often visits at this time of year." He nodded earnestly. "Mrs. Bumble, I call her. Hunts around the logs and tree stumps for slugs and snails, and I leave out bowls of water for her. I wouldn't like her to get spooked by your dog, so please do be careful."

"We will, don't worry," I said, as Sam rolled her eyes and stifled a giggle.

"Beware of gentle fish and giant hedgehogs . . . *is he for real?*" she whispered.

I let Molly off her leash and, with Simba's scent still pervading her nostrils, she charged around the garden, snuffling beneath shrubs, sniffing around tree trunks and scattering leaves in her wake like confetti. At one point she raced over to the koi-carp pond, impishly dipping in her paw before my cry of "Molly, *OFF!*" diverted her from the fluorescent fish gliding beneath. They seemed completely unfazed by the intrusion, however, and several of them surfaced to see if there was any food on offer.

Then, about ten minutes into the search, my dog's body language and behavior pattern completely changed. She became quite hyperactive, bouncing on her front paws, scampering back and forth in a state of mild confusion and making weird snorting noises. She had certainly detected some kind of scent trail, but her lack of certainty—and the absence of a meaningful "down"—suggested that it didn't belong to Simba the cat.

She then began to circle a large mound of soggy oak leaves. Chris, Sam and I edged closer, nudging each other as we saw something moving sideways beneath it. Suddenly, a large, upturned plastic bowl emerged and began to shimmy toward the back wall, as if it were being remotely controlled. Molly went totally haywire, whinnying loudly, spinning around in circles and rearing up on her hind legs like a fretful foal. For her own safety—and conscious of the house-owner's twitching curtains—I recalled my dog immediately and re-attached her leash, handing her over to Sam while I investigated further. I crept over to the bowl, carefully lifted it up and, lo and behold, there sat a quaking little hedgehog. It contracted into a tight ball—the normal defense mechanism—but by then I'd already noticed its physical impediment. Its back foot was missing. It only had three legs. Mrs. Bumble, it appeared, was a *three-footed* hedgehog, not a three-foot hedgehog. I chuckled to myself—had I really expected to discover a hedgehog bigger than Molly?—and gave the spiny creature the gentlest of prods, so that it lopsidedly scuttled under a nearby holly bush, out of my dog's eye-line. I refilled Mrs. B's feeding bowl with the water bottle in my utility belt and ambled back up the garden.

"Well, you've unearthed one cute little animal," I said to Molly. "Let's just hope the next one's Simba."

While we'd managed to comb much of the village, aided and abetted by some very helpful neighbors, by lunchtime Molly hadn't got a sniff of Simba, quite literally. When we resumed the search, however—down the quaintly named Honeysuckle Lane—she became very interested in an obsolete Victorian drainage system that ran beneath some of the back gardens and was exposed in others (among them the garden from which Simba had escaped). While it wasn't safe enough for me to allow Molly to run through this cracked, crumbling pipeline, her tail wagged nineteen to the dozen whenever she got near. I couldn't help but wonder whether any local cats—more specifically Simba—had used it as a convenient little tunnel between gardens.

Much to my chagrin, this culvert opened out into a garden that we'd been unable to access. My numerous raps on the front door of Wren Cottage had remained unanswered, yet I'd noticed a shadowy presence hovering behind the cream-colored net curtains and seen the flicker of a television screen. Someone was definitely inside but, for whatever reason, they hadn't fancied coming out. In normal circumstances, I'd have just shrugged my shoulders and moved on to the next house, but Molly was champing at the bit to explore this particular property.

"Oh, you mean Old Mr. Grumpy?" two teenage boys had sniggered when I'd inquired about Wren Cottage's owner. "He's a total misery-guts. He only ever comes out to tell us to stop playing football or to clear off home."

The local postman painted a similar picture, albeit with a little more compassion.

"When his wife died, Alf became a bit of a hermit, I suppose, and since then he's tended to keep himself to himself," he explained. "He likes the occasional moan on his doorstep, mind. Too many young families moving into the village, he told me the other day. Ruining his bloomin' peace, apparently . . ."

I wasn't going to be deterred, regardless of Old Mr. Grumpy's reputation, and in spite of the two locked and bolted wrought-iron gates that blocked entry to his garden. Lower Chillington must have one of the lowest crime rates in the county—if not the country—and these high-security measures seemed both incongruous and unnecessary.

With Molly leading the way, and with Chris and Sam by my side, I followed the narrow passageway that separated the back gardens from the village cemetery and peeked over this gentleman's fence. If I was expecting a dull space to match his dour character, I was sorely mistaken. Parked on his driveway was an orange Volkswagen camper van—vintage, but pristine—and in his garden lay three immaculate sheds, their pastel colors giving them the appearance of seaside beach huts. Wooden bird feeders were dotted around the rectangular lawn, a third of which was devoted to a neat fruit and vegetable patch.

"Ooh, purple sprouting broccoli, my favorite," sniggered Sam, who was in a particularly sassy mood that afternoon. She had found the "three-foot hedgehog" incident highly amusing and had been teasing me about it ever since.

The adjoining patio was jet-washed and moss-free and featured some impressive makeshift planters that had been fashioned from old car tires and hobnail boots. Bamboo trellises had been attached to the back wall and were interwoven with blazing-red Boston ivy.

"Looks like somebody's got *Gardeners' World* on series link." Chris smiled.

As we admired Mr. Grumpy's garden, Molly was becoming increasingly uptight—she was continuously pawing at the back fence—and I realized it was time for action.

"Right, we need to find a way to gain access," I said. "This guy's not answering his front door, so we're going to have to bend the rules a little."

Sam and I gave Chris a leg-up over the fence and into the garden—not difficult, since he was a very slim and wiry guy—and I asked him to go and rap on Mr. Grumpy's back door. (I reckoned he'd respond more favorably to a fellow Devonian.)

After five minutes of constant knocking, Chris finally got a response.

"All right, all right, I can bloody hear you," a gruff voice shouted from behind the door, as we heard a key turning in the lock and a succession of bolts being undone. Standing there, with a face like thunder, was a burly fellow in his early eighties, with thinning salt-and-pepper hair and wearing high-waisted slacks, thick braces and a checked shirt with rolled-up sleeves.

"What d'you think you're playing at, climbing over my fence?" he snapped.

"Well, er . . ." stammered Chris, slightly taken aback by this imposing figure of a man.

"Are you police or something?" continued Old Mr. Grumpy, gesturing at me and Sam as we lurked behind his gate. "Here to find those vandals who kick footballs into my garden, are you? Brought your sniffer dog to help, eh?"

"Well, not exactly," replied Chris falteringly, "but I'm wondering if you could kindly unlock the gate so my colleagues can have a quick word."

"It had better be quick," he scowled, producing a huge set of keys from his pocket and pacing toward the gate. "I'm a busy man. Got stuff to do."

So far, so good—Chris had managed a tricky situation well—but it was now time for me to launch a full-on charm offensive. I had dealt with many bolshie characters in my time and, in order to get them onside, I often had to wrongfoot them a little. I handed Molly's leash to Sam, flashed a big smile in this chap's direction and offered him my firmest handshake.

"What an *amazing* garden you have here, sir," I gushed. "My grandfather's vegetable patch in Gloucestershire looks a bit like this, but maybe not as well stocked. In fact, you even look like my grandpa, just a younger version. And I must say, Alf—can I call you Alf?—your purple flowering broccoli looks *magnificent*."

Ignoring Sam's muffled snort, I continued to shower Mr. Grumpy with compliments, the plan being to prevent him getting a word in edgeways until I discerned a thaw in his attitude.

". . . and as for your boot and tire planters, the great Monty Don would be proud to have those on his own patio, I'm sure of it."

That's when he smiled. Bull's-eye.

"So you watch *Gardeners' World*, then?" he asked, nodding in approval.

"Never miss an episode," I fibbed. "My TV highlight of the week."

"Well, you'll know how much hard work it takes to get a garden looking like this," said Alf, holding up his sandpaper-rough hands. "And that's why I get so cross when those bloody footballs turn my soft fruit into smoothies."

"I can appreciate that, Alf," I said. "But listen. I need a little favor from you, if that's okay."

I then proceeded to tell him all about Molly—who was being valiantly reined in by Sam—and described our painstaking search for poor Simba.

"We're looking for a ginger tomcat," I said. "He's a bit old, and a bit plump—like Bagpuss, but orange—but he's still quite a lively chap. We think he might have been using the old drainage pipe to travel between gardens and might well have ended up in yours."

"My daughter's missing him *so* much," added Chris, showing him a photograph, "so if you'd let us have a look around, we'd be most grateful."

"Well I never!" he exclaimed, squinting at the picture. "I've definitely seen that moggy."

"Really?" Chris gasped.

"Oh, yes I thought it was a stray. He's been here every morning for the last few days. Bit of a pest, to be honest. Keeps bothering the sparrows and blue tits. Tried to jump on my bird feeder yesterday, but he was so fat it toppled over."

"That sounds *just* like our Simba," said Chris excitedly. "Can we start looking now?"

"Feel free." Alf hesitated for a couple of seconds and then answered. "Not that you'll find him here now, though. He usually pops over before breakfast. I never see him in the afternoon."

I released Molly from her leash and, like a grayhound chasing a hare, she shot off toward the middle shed. She skidded to a halt in front of the dark-green door, whirled around a few times and—*bang!*—performed the mother of all "downs."

"What on earth is she doing?" said Alf, as Molly adopted her sphinx pose, shuddering with excitement.

"Molly's telling me that she has scent-matched Simba's smell," I explained, reaching into my utility belt for Molly's black-pudding treats. "And that means the cat is either inside that shed right now or was in there earlier."

"But that's where I keep my lawnmowers," said Alf, delving for his keys once again. "I can't imagine a cat would want to go in there. And I certainly didn't notice anything when I went in this morning."

Alf opened the shed door and I kept a close eye on Molly as she crossed the threshold. Inside was a shiny orange sit-in mower, a couple of old wooden benches and various hessian bags and containers. I was confident that my dog's nose would be able to discern Simba's scent through the damp, tangy smell of cut grass mixed with the aroma of engine oil, and she didn't disappoint. In the far corner of the shed, beneath a gaping window,

Molly gave us yet another positive, definitive signal. There was no trace of the cat himself, unfortunately—although judging from Molly's animated body language I reckoned that we'd only just missed him.

I dropped another handful of treats in front of Molly and as I did so, I noticed a half-eaten can of tuna under one of the benches. I looked at Alf and he turned away furtively. Not wanting to embarrass him in front of Chris, I said, "Okay, Sam, if you and Chris search the front of the property, Molly and I will search behind these sheds."

After completing the search of the rear garden, Alf kindly let me give Molly a run-around on his patio—play was always part of the reward process—but only if I kept her away from his veg patch. I devised a game that involved bouncing a tennis ball against each one of the three shed doors, in random order, which she tackled with gusto.

"Bravo, Molly!" clapped Alf every time she leaped horizontally, like a Premier League goalie, before trapping the ball between her jaws. The old boy seemed to take a real shine to my dog and it was nice to see him smiling so broadly.

Once I had tired Molly out and given her some water, I joined Alf on his patio bench. We chatted about his life in the village—he was Lower Chillington born and bred—and he talked about its history and how much the area had changed in recent times. ("Not all for the better, mind," he stressed. "Too many cars, too many kids . . .")

Then, after pouring us both a glass of homemade elderflower cordial—the finest I'd ever tasted—he loosened up a little, giving me the distinct impression that he'd not chatted like this for a long while. I listened to him as he freely admitted that, following his wife's death, his confidence and *joie de vivre* had ebbed away and he'd become quite solitary in nature.

"Edith was the life and soul, you see, and had so much get-up-and-go," he said. "It was her idea to get the camper van—

she loved an adventure—and now and again we'd escape to the Yorkshire Dales or the Lake District. But when she passed away I just felt so empty, so alone."

A tired-out Molly pushed herself between the two of us, prompting Alf to give her an affectionate pat.

"I turned my back on everything—and everyone—I suppose," he continued, "and just withdrew into a life of *Gardeners' World* and the *Telegraph* crossword. And that's where I'm still at, to be honest."

"But that's totally understandable, Alf," I replied, casting my mind back to my brother David's untimely death and remembering how lost and devastated I'd felt at the time. "Grief affects people in different ways. It can take months—years—to get your old self back."

"That's true enough," he said, gazing into the distance, "but I don't think some of my neighbors quite grasp that concept. I know they call me Old Mr. Grumpy—those bloomin' kids do, anyway—but if anything, it's more a case of Old Mr. L—"

He paused, as if he couldn't quite summon up the word.

"Lonely?"

"Yes," he said, nodding his head. "And that little cat has been good company over the last few days, which is why I've been feeding him."

We sipped our drinks in silence for a few moments, until my walkie-talkie spluttered into action.

"Colin, are you there?" yelled a frantic-sounding Sam.

"Yes, I'm right here," I said, lifting up the handset. "Whatever's the matter?"

"Oh my god, you're never going to believe this, but I can see Simba."

"*What?*"

"Seriously. He's at the gate in front of Alf's house as I speak. What should we do?"

"Sam, it's really important that you both remain calm and maintain your distance. We don't want the cat getting spooked and hurtling off. Stay right there and leave this to me."

I put Molly on a short leash and gave her the hand-down signal, which meant *stay calm*. I then crept around the side of the house, as stealthily as I could, and there—coolly padding along the front garden wall, with his head held high and his tail pointing north—was the unmistakable sight of Simba. He saw me advancing toward the wall, made a funny little *brrrrrrp* sound and swaggered over, like an old cowboy. This was no knock-kneed scaredy-cat.

With Chris and Sam looking on nervously, I gently inched toward Simba and lifted up my hand to stroke him. He brushed his head under my palm a couple of times, giving me a snuffle and a lick for good measure. He then looked down at Molly, who was standing there quietly, and meowed. I nodded to Sam, who slowly stepped forward and lifted Simba off the wall. Nobody said a word but, as the cat rested his front paws on my colleague's shoulders and nuzzled into her neck, the air fizzed with emotion. The cat had been found, and Lindsey's nightmare was over.

Sam handed Simba to Chris, then took Molly back to the car and, after bidding Alf a fond farewell, Chris and I made the short walk through Lower Chillington to the family friend's cottage. Simba was happily ensconced in Chris's arms, although lugging this podgy moggy up a steep cobbled hill was no mean feat.

As news of his recovery swept through the village, a string of locals emerged from doorways.

"The lost pussycat's been found, Ben!" cooed a pregnant lady to her toddler.

"Excellent work, chaps," added her sergeant major–type neighbor.

But the biggest fanfare of all took place back at the house, where a beaming Lindsey finally clapped eyes on her precious Simba.

"I thought you'd gone forever!" she squealed, flinging her arms around him and smothering him in kisses. "You'll never know how much I missed you."

With the objective met, it was time for me to say my good-byes and head back to Molly. Before I did so, however, I asked a favor of the family.

"This is just a suggestion, and please don't feel obliged, but I think it might be nice if you popped in to see Alf at some point," I said.

"Old Mr. Grumpy?" said Chris. "Are you serious?"

"His bark's much worse than his bite, I can assure you," I said, smiling, "and we have a lot to thank him for. Had he not allowed Molly in his garden, we might have been forced to look elsewhere, and we might never have found Simba."

"We'll pay him a visit, for sure," said Lindsey. "It's the least we can do."

"Stick around for a chat and a glass of elderflower cordial, if you can," I added. "Something tells me that he'd really appreciate that."

After dropping off Sam in Cranleigh, I stopped by at Bramble Hill Farm. The journey from Devon had ended up being a fair old slog—I'd hit some heavy traffic near Salisbury—and Molly badly needed to stretch her legs. As soon as we swung into the driveway, she realized that fresh-air play was incoming and her tail began its Ringo Starr drumroll.

"Out you pop, Molls," I said, before leading her through the jasmine-entwined gate that opened out into the orchard. Of all the farm's many beauty spots, it was here that autumn truly exploded into life. Boughs groaned with plump pears and rosy apples, starlings nibbled at mauve-colored damsons and the ground was swathed in a crisp-leaved carpet of copper, bronze and amber.

Molly slalomed through the orchard toward her favorite barley field. The long grass attracted all manner of small rodents— voles, shrews and field mice—and she loved nothing more than snuffling them out and watching them scampering and scurrying around. Occasionally, these whiskery creatures would be at the receiving end of a gentle prod from a fluffy paw, but Molly never hurt them or caught them; she just liked to observe Mr. and Mrs. Dormouse going about their daily business.

I leaned against an oak tree and gazed across at my lovely little dog. I thought about that day's Devonshire adventure and reflected upon Molly's amazing ability to charm everyone whose path she crossed and to attract so much love and attention along the way (why, even the koi carp had popped up to say hello). I allowed my crazy little dog a few more minutes to chase the field mice she'd never catch before calling her back to my side.

"Time for your beauty sleep, missus," I said. "Let's head back home."

15

Molly and the Ex-pat Cats

Countless studies have shown that pet ownership can be hugely therapeutic. Our furry friends cheer us up when we're down, and comfort us when we're sick. They offer calm when we're stressed and provide companionship when we're lonely. Stroking a cat or walking a dog can often help life's worries melt away, and there's nothing like arriving home, following a hard day's work, to be greeted by a bouncing Beagle or a purring Persian. When I worked as a detective inspector for Surrey Police I regularly completed grueling fourteen-hour shifts and often had to deal with some extremely grisly crime scenes. Seeing my Rottweilers Max and Jay bounding up to my car when it finally swung into my driveway was always a welcome relief from a traumatic day. Once I was in their company, all my toils and troubles seemed to melt away.

Pets could indeed be the best medicine, something that a client of mine, Debbie, knew only too well. Born in Wales to Italian immigrant parents, Debbie had spent much of her adult life in Western Australia, working in the local marina office and living in a downtown Fremantle bungalow. In the summer of 2017, though, her life had changed forever. Having felt lethargic and light-headed for weeks, a doctor had delivered the bombshell news that Debbie was suffering with a rare and aggressive form of cancer. After she'd overcome the initial shock—she'd cried for days—she made it her mission to locate the best possible course of treatment and, in doing so, pinpointed a specialist consultant in the East Midlands area of England. With most of her family still residing in the county of Suffolk—including her beloved sister, to whom she'd remained close—it seemed entirely logical to move back home to the UK. It would be a wrench to leave Australia—she adored her adoptive country—but her instinct told her it was the right thing to do.

But there was someone else in the equation to consider. For the previous year, Debbie had been the proud owner of Cuddles, a honey-colored, short-haired cat with white socks, a white bib and perky, tortilla-chip-shaped ears. She just happened to be a rescue cat, too. One sweltering afternoon a female stray had given birth to a litter of kittens in one of the boathouses and, believing they wouldn't survive in such a hot and hazardous environment, Debbie and her colleagues had arranged for the mother and her litter to be taken to a local animal shelter, with a view to the fur-babies being rehomed once they'd been weaned, vaccinated and socialized. It was decided that at least one puss would remain with its mum.

Debbie was enchanted by the smallest kitten in the litter—"She's just so *adorable*," she'd said when she'd first clapped eyes on the peachy little fluff-ball—and, three months later, she'd welcomed Cuddles into her life. The cat was pretty high-maintenance—she was a live wire and demanded food, play and attention—but in return she lavished her new owner with oodles of love, affection and companionship. Indeed, after a demanding day's work, Debbie liked nothing more than flopping on to the sofa to watch a movie, a box of popcorn by her side and her darling pet on her lap. Sometimes, when she was being stroked, Cuddles would purr so loudly and deeply that Debbie would have to turn up the volume.

"Jeez, can you turn down the bass? I can't hear a word Tom Cruise is saying," she'd giggle, reaching for the remote control.

Within a few months, sadly, Debbie's health had deteriorated and she became so fatigued that she was forced to give up the job she loved. Back in the bungalow, though, Cuddles continued to live up to her name. Whenever her owner was feeling sad or sick, the cat was always on hand to offer comfort, either nestling into her lap during the day or nuzzling against her legs during the night. Their bond grew from strength to strength and, as Debbie made plans to move to Britain for her health's sake, she knew for sure that Cuddles would be coming with her.

"We're going on a big adventure, you and me," she told Cuddles one morning. "A whole new chapter awaits us, honeybun . . ."

Debbie and Cuddles jetted off to London in the autumn of 2017—the cat traveled in a specially designed travel crate—and, after the eight-hour flight, both were thrilled to be reunited at Heathrow Airport. They were met in the arrivals lounge by Debbie's sister, Mandy, who drove them down to their new home in the town of Mildenhall. The house—a modern red-brick semi-detached property—had been chosen carefully, with Cuddles very much in mind. It was situated on a private road, solely accessible to residents, so there was minimal traffic. The garden was a good size with a variety of trees, shrubs and hedges so the cat had plenty of space for play and exploration.

Mildenhall was also the perfect environment for Debbie. Quiet and peaceful, with an abundance of fresh air and open spaces, it would no doubt benefit her emotional wellbeing and physical recovery, post-treatment. She also felt somewhat comforted by the fact that her home lay within a stone's throw of a magnificent medieval church, the tower of which frequently cast a shadow across her back garden.

There was, coincidentally enough, a significant Australian presence in the area. An international school was located nearby, so it wasn't unusual to hear a smattering of stateside accents around the town and it wasn't difficult to find a cinnamon bagel on a café's breakfast menu.

"Hey, Cuddles, maybe we won't feel so homesick after all." Debbie smiled as she scooped her Australian moggy out of its carrier before introducing her to all the sights, sounds and smells of her new home.

A few weeks later Debbie underwent her surgery at a specialist hospital—Mandy babysat Cuddles at home—before commencing a punishing course of chemotherapy. Her amazingly perceptive pussycat was the perfect tonic, however, lifting her spirit whenever it flagged and providing comfort when times got tough.

"It's like she's got a sixth sense," Debbie remarked to her sister. "She just seems to know when I'm in the doldrums, and when I need some extra TLC."

When the weather was warm ("warm" constituting 20-plus degrees in Suffolk, as opposed to 30-plus degrees in Fremantle) Debbie liked to make herself a fruit juice, wheel out a sun-lounger from the garage, turn on Classic FM and idly watch Cuddles as she skulked around the garden, seeking new hidey-holes and lookout posts. On one such afternoon in early September, a sudden movement in a laurel bush seemed to spook the little thing—a predatory tomcat, Debbie presumed, or the pet rabbit that kept escaping from next door. As a consequence, Cuddles scrambled up the garden fence, scampered along the top and disappeared clean out of sight.

Ah, she'll be back soon . . . it's dinner time in half an hour, thought her owner, taking a sip of her mango smoothie and trying to quell her gnawing sense of panic.

But Cuddles didn't come back soon. She didn't even come back that night. In fact, she still hadn't returned home a week later.

Too emotionally and physically weak to handle this crisis alone, Debbie drafted in the help of her sister and her neighbors. They mounted a concerted search for Cuddles, spending their free time door-stepping residents, pounding the pavements and posting appeals on social media. Conscious that the clock was ticking and keen to adopt a more tactical approach, Debbie did her own online research. She saw an article about "Molly the

Cat-detection Dog" and watched the footage from *This Morning*, and couldn't get on the phone quick enough.

As I sat in my home office, with Molly snoozing in a nearby bed, a tearful Debbie told me her backstory and outlined her fears. She was very concerned that, being a newbie to the area, Cuddles had lost her bearings, become disorientated and been unable to find her way home. Also, having been told some nightmarish stories by some insensitive neighbors, Debbie was petrified that her cat had been attacked by a fox.

"That really is quite rare," I explained, attempting to put her mind at ease. "In my experience, cats and foxes are much more likely to live in harmony. They tend not to compete with each other and they rarely seek out fights, so please try not to worry."

"You seem to know your stuff, Colin," she said, speaking with a hint of an Australian accent. "D'you reckon there's any way you could help me find Cuddles?"

Although Suffolk wasn't exactly on my doorstep—and my right-hand woman Sam was on annual leave—I felt duty bound to make the trip to Mildenhall. This poor woman had been through hell and I wanted to give her hope and ease her heartache. After all, a case similar to this—involving Oscar the British shorthair and his owner, Suzie—had prompted me to train up a cat-detection dog in the first place. Now Molly had yet another opportunity to find a pet in peril and to help an owner in crisis and I felt compelled to help.

"I've got another search to attend tomorrow, Debbie, but I can pencil you in for Wednesday, if that's okay?" I said.

"Oh, wow, that's more than okay, that's *wonderful*," she replied. "Thank you *so* much."

The Suffolk skies were laden with grayish-white clouds when Molly and I arrived in Mildenhall but, fortunately, none of them threatened rain. We parked up outside a bustling town-center café, which, judging by the multitude of Australian voices (and the cinnamon toast and eggs over-easy on the menu board), was the eaterie of choice for the local air-base staff. I grabbed myself a latté and a bowl of cool water for Molly and sat at one of the chrome tables.

Once my dog had quenched her thirst, she jumped up on to my lap, and I took the opportunity to give her a little pep talk. I often did this prior to a search, as it helped me to collect my thoughts as well as focus on the task in hand. All our cases were important—I wanted every single client to benefit from our combined expertise—but I was particularly determined to solve this mystery. Debbie's cancer ordeal had reminded me of my brother's failing health, all those years ago, and her predicament had really struck a chord.

"Molly, it's vitally important we find Cuddles today," I said, as she stared up at me with her big chestnut eyes. "She was a rescue, just like you, and she needs to be back at home with Debbie. Today's all about teamwork, sweetheart, so let's get a good result, and *let's do this!*"

I gave her a high-five, but she just stared blankly at me.

You all right? she seemed to be saying. *You losing your marbles?*

Molly licked my chin—she'd probably spotted some milk foam—and it was then that I noticed the entire café was staring at us. Like many pet-lovers, I chatted to my cocker spaniel like she was a human being and—I admit—it probably looked a little bizarre. Evidently, Molly wasn't the only one who thought I was going slightly barmy.

"C'mon, Molly," I whispered, feeling my cheeks reddening. "I think it's time to hook up with Debbie."

Meeting us on her doorstep was a very tall, blackhaired woman with hazel-brown eyes and an engaging smile. Debbie looked very pale and a little fragile, but she told me she'd had a good night's sleep—without any fox-related nightmares—and that she felt ready and able to help us with the search.

"But only if you feel up to it," I said. "Just give me the nod if you're struggling in any way."

Unsurprisingly, Debbie was very taken with Molly—she reminded her of the fantastic search-and-rescue dogs in the Australian outback—and, judging by the amount of hugging and nuzzling going on, I think the feeling was mutual.

"Ah, I've missed these snuggles *so much*," sighed Debbie, as Molly wallowed in all the attention.

My client gave us a whistle-stop tour of Mildenhall's handsome town center and, as we stopped for a rest on a park bench, I grilled Debbie about her cat's behavior and probed the circumstances of her disappearance. Evidently, Cuddles had become anxious and had gone AWOL, but I needed to establish whether it had been extrinsic (triggered by the tomcat in a bush, perhaps) or whether it had been a more intrinsic response to the general upheaval of the house move. After listening to Debbie, I suspected it was a mixture of the two. Cuddles the cat had been displaced from a large bungalow in a big city to a tiny property in a small town and could have been forgiven for feeling a little bewildered. In any case, experience told me that Cuddles would not have gone too far and was probably tucked away in a temporary bolt-hole.

Conspiring against us, however, was the fact that we had to work with a fairly weak cat-hair sample. Debbie had only shipped over the bare necessities from Australia, so all the lived-in cat beds and well-used scratching posts had been given away. She still possessed Cuddles's harness, though—it wasn't just dogs who liked their "walkies"—and this accessory had snagged strands of the cat's caramel-colored hair.

In order to check that the scent was strong enough I decided to give Molly a little test. I detached the collar from the harness and hid it under a plant pot on Debbie's patio, allowing the aroma to settle for thirty minutes or so. I then prepped Molly, gave her the source scent from the harness and unleashed her into the back garden. She ferreted about the lawn and the patio and, after five minutes, found the collar and gave me a perfect "down," just as I'd hoped.

"*Good girl*, Molly," I said, as an impressed Debbie shook her head in awe. "I think that means we can make a start."

We began a systematic search of the nearby gardens, many of which Debbie had already searched with her friends. Most of the neighbors were pleasant and helpful, with the exception of a sour-faced, bald-headed bloke who had a serious attitude problem. He complained about the number of "those bloody leaflets" that had been shoved through his door and demanded to know when the MISSING CAT posters would be coming down. He sneered at me when I told him that Molly recovered lost cats ("What's the point of that? It's probably dead anyway . . .") and refused us entry to his garden, citing his wife's severe dog allergy. I could see that Debbie was on the cusp of tears—and that was the very last thing I wanted—so I thanked him for his time and neighborly spirit, walking away before I ended up telling him what an insensitive prat he was.

"What a dipstick," I said, shaking my head as he continued to chunter from his doorstep.

"Or what a drongo, as they'd say in Australia," added Debbie.

The next household—a young father—was far more accommodating, thank goodness. He ushered the three of us through his back gate and, five minutes later, appeared on the patio with his toddler, who was clad in an all-in-one playsuit.

"You don't mind if we watch, do you?" he asked. "Ethan and I have had enough of *Tom and Jerry* for one morning. Molly the detection dog seems far more exciting."

"No, not at all," I replied, "but try to keep the noise down, if you can. We wouldn't want to scare the cat if she was in your garden."

"A pussycat? In *gargen*?" gasped the little boy. "Me like pussycats! Dey go *meeooow* . . ."

Molly—ever the performer—seemed very aware that she was being watched and duly played up to her audience on the patio, completing a couple of very agile leaps on to a brick wall and air-sniffing some plant pots.

Then, right in the middle of the garden, she stopped suddenly, as if she'd been caught in the center-stage spotlight. She sniffed the ground, looked back at me knowingly, then adopted a very familiar crouching stance.

Oh god, no, Molly, not here, I thought.

"Molly!" I hissed. But it was too late.

"What's dat doggy doing, Daddy?" said little Ethan, as my dog, her eyes watering, deposited a steaming brown dollop on the sparkling snow-white gravel. "She doing a *poo-poo*, Daddy! Molly doing a poo-poo!"

If I'd had a spade, I'd have gladly dug myself a hole to crawl into.

"Oh my goodness, I'm *so* sorry," I said, breaking the world record for the ten-yard poop-bag sprint before scooping up the offending matter. "Molly's never done this during a search before. It's totally out of character, and . . ."

I looked across to the patio and realized that my apologies were falling on deaf ears. Father and son were hooting with laughter, and Debbie was steadying herself against a wall because she was guffawing so much.

"Who needs *Tom and Jerry* when you've got entertainment like that in your back garden?" said the dad, grinning at me. "Funniest thing ever. The look on your face . . . absolutely priceless."

"Well, thank you for being so understanding," I said, as a puzzled Molly cocked her head to one side, confused by all this brouhaha.

I was still smarting with embarrassment as we walked back up the driveway. Molly trotted nonchalantly beside me—a few pounds lighter, probably—and Debbie continued to wipe the tears from her eyes.

"Oh my, I haven't laughed so much in weeks," she said.

"Well, at least *you* found it funny," I said, my eyebrows raised. "Rather unbecoming behavior from the UK's top cat-detection dog, though, I must say."

And then I began laughing, too.

Our next port of call was a rather tatty bungalow which, with its peeling paint and grimy windows, stuck out like a sore thumb among its smarter counterparts. Answering the door was a wiry, wrinkly guy with long, straggly dyed-black hair and a roll-up dangling from his mouth. The guy was a dead ringer, I reckoned, for Rolling Stones guitarist Ronnie Wood.

"Course you caaaan, maaaan," he said, when I asked for a quick peek at his garden. "It's a bit of a mess, though, mate. I'm an indoorsy dude, not an outdoorsy dude."

Molly stared intently at this chap, poked her nose into his hallway and looked back at me.

What's that strange aroma, Dad? she seemed to be saying. *I've never smelled that before . . .*

I smiled to myself as I caught a distinctive whiff of cannabis.

In another lifetime, Molly, you and I would have been searching this guy's house for his stash, I thought. *How times change, eh . . . ?*

The Ronnie Wood lookalike wasn't wrong about his garden. It was more like an Amazonian jungle and I had to keep a close eye on Molly as she struggled to negotiate her way through the knotted grass and the tangled shrubs. She seemed drawn to an old, overgrown yew hedge at the rear of the lawn, and when she eventually reached it she locked her eyes with mine, thudded her body to the ground and gave me a "down."

"Well, then, Debbie. Looks like Cuddles has been here at some point."

"You're kidding me?"

"Nope," I said, advancing toward Molly and peering into the twisted yew. "The bad news, though, is that this hedge is full of brambles so I can't let her search any further."

"Oh no, that's a shame," she said sadly.

As Molly munched down some Cheddar-cheese treats, I tried to wrench apart the gnarled branches to check for any traces of Cuddles. I was fighting a losing battle, unfortunately. As I'd feared, the hedge was virtually impenetrable, demonstrated by the razor-sharp thorns that shredded my forearms.

"Okay, let's try next door instead," I said, leading Molly back down the garden. However, as we tramped past our Ronnie lookalike's ramshackle shed—*kapow!*—my dog gave us another definitive "down." The rickety door was already ajar and Molly shot in like a bullet, heading straight to a pile of stripy seat pads. The uppermost cushion clearly matched the scent in her nostrils and, not only that, it just happened to be swathed in silken, honey-hued cat hair.

"Oh, my goodness," murmured Debbie as I showed her the evidence. "That looks like Cuddles's fur, all right. What a clever little dog you have."

In her inimitable way, Molly had now helped me to build up a picture of the cat's likely movements. It certainly appeared that she was using this unkempt garden as her base, sensibly gravitating toward the comfort of the garden shed after initially taking shelter under the yew hedge. The intensity of Molly's "downs" also suggested that Cuddles had been in the vicinity very recently, probably within the last few hours, judging by her level of excitement. I had a sinking feeling that we might have even disturbed her from the shed ourselves and, if we all stuck around, there was a risk that we'd drive her further away.

With this in mind, I hatched a plan.

"Debbie, I'm going to withdraw Molly from the scene and you're going to sit in the garden, alone, and then you're just going to talk to your cat very, very softly."

"Really? That sounds a little crazy . . ."

"Cuddles is probably feeling a bit lost out there and your voice may act as a source of comfort to her, a link to something familiar."

"Okay—I'll give anything a try. And to be honest, Colin, I'm getting tired and I could do with a sit down."

So, with the owner's consent—"Sure thing, maaaaan," he'd drawled—Debbie pulled up a chair and positioned it beneath the canopy of a knobbly old pear tree. As Molly and I departed the garden, I could just make out her voice.

"Cuddles, honey, it's your mommy here. I miss you so, so much. Hey, why don't you come out and say hello?"

Half an hour later, while Molly was enjoying a run-around on a football pitch, my phone vibrated. It was Debbie. I took a deep breath and answered the call.

"You were right!" she yelled jubilantly as I whooped and punched the air. "It worked! She came! She's here!"

Both cat and owner were now firmly ensconced at home and, according to Debbie, would be curling up in front of a movie with some popcorn later that evening, just like they used to do in Fremantle.

"Now *that's* what it's all about, Molls," I said, lobbing her tennis ball over a goal post. "*That's* why we do what we do."

Yet again, my decision to find myself a cat-detection dog—and to adopt my gorgeous Molly—had been totally and utterly vindicated. Being able to reunite lost pets with their "parents" had been my motivation from day one, yet to actually put this into practice was more fulfilling than I could have ever imagined. Thanks to Team Molly, Debbie and Cuddles's loving bond had been restored, and it was the best feeling ever.

As it happened, a week or so later we found ourselves searching for another ex-pat cat. A streetwise tiger-striped tomcat with a yowl that could keep the whole street awake, Tom had been born a stray in the German city of Frankfurt but had subsequently been rescued by an ex-pat Brazilian, Marcella, who worked in the city as a media executive. Tom became the apple of her eye and lived the life of a pampered puss. She fed him only the finest cat food—he enjoyed lightly poached haddock every evening, served in a porcelain dish—and before his bedtime she would brush his coat until it shone like satin. She adored her *menino*, her little boy.

In late 2017, however, Marcella was transferred to an office in the UK town of Worthing. She was quite excited about this new challenge and was looking forward to a change of scenery, but she wasn't prepared to be parted from Tom during the long journey to England. She decided against a cross-channel ferry or a flight to Gatwick. Instead, she hired a "pet taxi," operated by a firm that specialized in transporting cats and dogs with their owners. By doing this, she was able to sit beside Tom as they traveled through Germany, Belgium and France, and whizzed through the Eurotunnel. Tom settled into his new home nicely, Marcella transitioned seamlessly into her new job, and life was good.

One autumn evening Marcella returned home from work to find a handwritten note on her doormat.

Please come to number 78, it said. *I think your cat has been involved in an accident. Neil.*

Neil was Marcella's next-door-but-one neighbor, and it was left to him to break the awful news that, just after lunchtime, he'd seen Tom running across the road, straight into the path of a blue estate car.

"Oh meu deus, meu pobre bébé!" cried Marcella, clasping her hands to her face. "Was he badly hurt?"

"I'm not sure, but he was hit really hard and he legged it up the driveway over there," said Neil, gesturing to a house across the road. "I went over to have a look but couldn't see a thing. I'm really sorry."

Marcella took the following day off work to search for Tom, but she had no joy whatsoever.

The following morning I was taking delivery of six new hens on the farm—with Molly watching intently—when I received a call from this deeply traumatized Brazilian lady, who was fearing the worst about her injured cat. This was an emergency—Tom's life was perhaps in danger—and that afternoon's scheduled training exercise at Bramble Hill was duly abandoned.

"Right, Molls, change of plan. Seems like we're off to Worthing," I said, ushering the last of the birds into the henhouse.

Before our journey south we stopped off at my house in Cranleigh to collect some maps and search equipment. Sarah was working from home that day and greeted us at the front door.

"I'm glad you've popped by," she said, her eyes glinting with a smile. "I've got a rather large bone to pick with you, Molly, my dear . . ."

"Oops, what's she done now?" I asked. While our dog's indoor behavior had improved markedly, she was still quite capable of making mischief.

Sporting a doleful *I'm in trouble, aren't I?* expression, Molly glanced at Sarah, then at me, then back at Sarah.

"Well, as you know, Colin, I'd been wondering where all my day socks had disappeared to, and I think I've found the answer," she said, delving into the pocket of her cardigan and fishing out a handful of woolly pastel-colored socks with rubber grips. Some sported big gaping holes and others looked like they'd been wrung through a mangle.

"Go on . . ." I said, as our canine culprit let out a guilty little whine and shuffled on her paws.

"It seems that this little monkey has devised a game called Steal Sarah's Socks," she said, trying valiantly to suppress a giggle.

Sarah's theory was that, while her back had been turned, Molly had been sneakily pilfering her sock supply from the laundry basket and the chest of drawers (or from the sofa, if they'd been casually left there). Clamping them in her jaws, she'd then wandered around the house, hiding them in the weirdest of places.

"You see, I had one of my little tidy-ups this morning, Colin, and I found one sock wedged under the sofa seat-pad, one stuck behind the cooker, one stuffed underneath the spare-room mattress and another behind a plant pot."

"I think Molly needs a trip to Marks and Spencer to get some replacements, don't you?" I smiled.

"I think she does," she replied, her face breaking into a wide grin. Molly, as intuitive as ever, sensed my girlfriend's bonhomie. She wagged her tail, trotted over to Sarah, gave her an *Am I forgiven?* look and was given a good-humored hug in return.

I then explained to Sarah that Molly and I were off to Worthing for the afternoon, in order to mount a search for Tom.

"I suggest you take your gloves, then," she said. "It could be really chilly on the coast."

"Good idea," I replied, and went to fetch them from the cloakroom. I took one look at my black leather gloves, however, and burst out laughing. Every single finger had been chewed right off.

"*MOLLY!*" cried Sarah and I in unison.

During the forty-five-minute journey to Worthing, with Molly, the sock-stealing, glove-gnawing minx asleep in her crate, I pondered the task ahead. The likelihood that Tom had been hit by a car made this an incredibly time-critical case. In normal circumstances, a cat wouldn't survive a traumatic injury beyond a week; open wounds or broken bones could get infected, for instance, and dehydration could set in if the cat was bleeding internally, or didn't have enough mobility to access water.

Working in our favor was the fact that the animal probably wouldn't have strayed too far, so the search catchment area was unlikely to be wide. Years of experience had shown me that, when a cat was involved in an accident and was injured and traumatized, it would instinctively take flight in order to escape the source of the pain. Triggered by a shock reflex and powered by adrenaline, it would often hotfoot it to the first place of safety: the sanctuary of a nearby shed, perhaps, or an open garage. The sickly cat wouldn't have the compulsion to bolt back home and would effectively take itself hostage, well away from the site of the accident.

I could only hope that my knowledge of cat behavior, allied with Molly's consummate scent-detection skills, would help us to locate the cat. We would be racing against the clock, that was for sure. But Molly and I had trained day in, day out to handle exactly this kind of scenario and I was confident that, by working as a team, we would find Tom.

It took me about half an hour to calm Marcella down—"I cannot *cope* if he is dead!" she cried, running her hands through her black, spiraly curls—but once I did, she was able to tell me about Tom's traits and habits, enabling me to build up a good general picture of her pet. Marcella provided me with a sizeable cat-hair sample (a thick clump from his deluxe velvet bed), which, as usual, I popped into a sterile jar and took outside to Molly, who'd been waiting patiently in the car with a few squeaky toys for company.

Marcella had already hinted to me that she wasn't massively fond of dogs—cats had always rocked her world—but I saw her visibly melt when Molly sprang out of her crate, looking as pretty and as perky as ever.

"Marcella, meet Molly," I said.

"Wow, what a beautiful little lady," she said, smiling.

Molly's ability to break down the barriers between cat and dog owners and to bring both "camps" together was quite remarkable. She could charm and disarm the most avowed felinophile—I think her friendly and placid manner helped in that respect—and the fact that she'd been trained to find their missing cats only added to her charisma. Not only that, she had a wonderful calming effect upon clients like Marcella, who, when they first clapped eyes on this sparky little spaniel in her UKPD harness, were suddenly instilled with a real sense of faith, hope and optimism.

I gave Tom's scent to Molly—her increased tail wags per minute suggested it was a good-quality sample—and we immediately set ourselves to our task. In these fraught circumstances, however, there was simply no space for chit-chat. Time was of the essence and, if we were going to find Tom alive, we had to gain access to as many properties as we could, and as quickly as possible. Molly and I swiftly worked our way down the Victorian villas lining Marcella's avenue, sweet-talking a host of friendly locals so they'd kindly open their garden gates and garage doors. From the south-facing lawns, I could see the gray-blue glimmer of the English Channel, upon which distant white yachts dipped and bobbed. The gentle sea breeze brought with it a salty tang, too, which I hoped wouldn't distract Molly from the target scent.

Neil from number 78 made a timely appearance—along with a handful of curious neighbors—and directed us to the driveway down which Tom had bolted. Molly eagerly sprinted to the end of the tarmac, pawed at a red-brick wall, spun around to face the group of onlookers, slammed her body down and gave me her resolute "FOUND IT!" signal. She also gave out a little tell-tale snort; she often did this when she hit the scent profile, as it was a way of drawing in more odor for better analysis.

Hey, I've matched the smell in the jam jar, she seemed to be saying. *Now can I have my black pudding, please?*

"*Qué? Qué?* What's happening?" squealed Marcella.

"Now, it's important that we remain calm," I told my client, "but it seems that Molly has picked up a strong scent signature near the wall area, and perhaps beyond. We need to access the house behind it."

We made our way around to the property and politely asked its somewhat doddery owners if we could search the large double garage that backed on to the red-brick wall.

"There's no point," croaked the husband. "I've not been in the garage for weeks. It's padlocked to the hilt. There's no way a cat could've got in."

His wife nodded in agreement.

"He's right," she bleated. "You'd only be wasting your time."

"I'd really like to have a quick peek, in any case," I said, trying not to appear too rankled. "It'll take two minutes, I promise."

"Didn't you hear me? I'm afraid the answer's no," sniffed the old bloke, and the front door was shut in our faces.

"Damn," I said, under my breath.

"*Idiota,*" hissed Marcella.

One of us wasn't taking no for an answer, though. I unclipped Molly's leash and she zoomed along the garden, vaulting over an old Belfast sink, hurdling over a metal wheelbarrow and flinging herself against the garage door. I wasn't exactly surprised when she gave me an impeccable, indisputable "down."

"Right, this is ridiculous," I said, stomping back toward the house to have another word with Darby and Joan. As I did so, I noticed a car pulling up on the driveway, out of which climbed a forty-something man wearing a tracksuit. I assumed he was the couple's son, judging by the striking resemblance to his father.

"Er, can I help you?" he asked suspiciously, probably wondering what this official-looking chap and his black dog were doing on his parents' property.

I told him who I was and what I was up to.

"I'm not here to cause any problems, honestly," I explained, "but my dog's indicating that there may be a cat trapped in your parents' garage. They tell me they've not been in there for weeks, so they're not letting me in."

"Well, *they* haven't been in the garage for weeks, that's true," he said, rolling his eyes, "but *I* have. I was giving it a good clear-out the day before yesterday. Back-breaking. Took me hours."

"Could you possibly get hold of the key?"

"Of course . . . I'll go and find out where it is," he said, and—sure enough—he returned a couple of minutes later clutching it in his hand.

As soon as the son turned the key in the lock, we heard a cat's plaintive mewing.

"Tom! Tom! *Mi pequeño bébé!*" sobbed Marcella as her beloved pet slowly emerged from the dark recesses of the garage. The poor thing was limping terribly—he'd badly injured his hind leg—so I told my client to sit by his side and comfort him while a neighbor fetched a cat carrier. I gave Tom a quick examination, noting that the limb appeared broken and, equally worryingly, that his eyes looked dull and unresponsive.

"You need to get him to a vet straight away," I said, hoping and praying that Tom had enough strength and resilience to pull through.

*A **fortnight later*** I was sitting in the office at Bramble Hill Farm, with Molly on my knee, preparing to make a couple of catch-up phone calls. The first was to Debbie; I wanted to check on her health, above all, but I was also keen to get a progress report on her cat.

"Hey, Colin, good to hear from you," she said. "Cuddles is doing brilliantly, thanks. Very happy, really settled, and no more walkabouts to Ronnie Wood's house, thank goodness."

"And how are *you* feeling, Debbie?"

"I'm getting there. Slowly but surely, but I think I'm over the worst, touch wood."

"That's marvelous news."

"Cat therapy has definitely helped my recovery, you know," she chortled. "Cuddles has got me through this, I swear. My sister says they should put her on the NHS . . ."

Then, adopting a more somber tone, she thanked us both for our help.

"You guys were incredible," she said. "Give Molly another big hug from me, won't you?"

"Of course I will, Debbie," I replied. "And give Cuddles a cuddle from me, too."

My next conversation was with Marcella. Tom had arrived at the vet's in a very bad state—it had been touch and go for the first twenty-four hours—but he'd undergone successful surgery on his rear left leg, which had indeed been broken in the collision.

"So how's the little fella getting on?" I asked.

"Well, his leg has to be in a splint for the next few months, which he's not very happy about, but apart from that, he's doing okay."

"I'm so pleased that's the case, Marcella."

"But without you and Molly he wouldn't be here at all, Colin," she added, her voice wavering, "and I'll never, *ever* forget what you did for us."

Molly gazed up at me and I gave her chin a little tickle. "The pleasure was all ours, Marcella." I smiled. "All ours."

I replaced the phone in its cradle and reclined in my office chair. As I did so, the old leather creaked, causing Molly to look up, raise her left eyebrow and tilt her head slightly to the side.

Are we going out, Dad?

I leaned back and contemplated the call that I'd taken from my client Suzie all those years ago, agonizing about her lost cat Oscar, and I remembered the pledge I'd made to myself that day about getting a cat-detection dog. Out of curiosity, I reached into my drawer for my old desk diary and flicked through its yellowing pages.

"Well I never, Molly!" I exclaimed, when I finally pinpointed the corresponding date, with "Suzie and Oscar, East Meon" scrawled in the margin. "Five whole years ago. Half a decade. I can't quite believe it."

Molly gave my hand a big, sloppy lick—something she always did when she wanted a walk—and fixed her eyes upon me.

Well, are we going out, Dad?

"Yes, we *are* going out." I smiled, closed the diary and replaced it in the drawer. "We're going to hop into the car, drive down to West Wittering and have a nice long play on the beach. Is that okay with you?"

Clever little Molly observed my body language, watched me nod my head and heard me utter the words "beach" and "play." She bounced out of her bed, leaped into my lap and started to plant kisses all over my face.

"I'll take that as a yes, then," I said, and grinned.

16

The Runaway Brixton Tomcat

Many of our missing-pet searches took place in London, and whenever Molly and I visited the capital she always created a bit of a stir. Everywhere we went—whether it was St. James's Park for a run-around or dog-friendly shops to buy some pet toys—people would always stop to fuss her. At first I used to think they were gravitating to her because she was so sweet-looking, but then I realized that my super-clever, attention-craving dog was almost mesmerizing them. She would often use eye contact with passers-by to encourage interaction, and few could resist stopping and petting her once she locked her big brown eyes with theirs. Tourists from overseas, especially, seemed to adore her.

"Oh my, what a pretty dog," they'd say, crouching down to take selfies with Molly, often with Big Ben or Tower Bridge in the background.

We have traveled all over the city to hunt for lost pets, from an overly curious tabby we found locked in an empty house in Greenwich to a timid ragdoll recovered from the engine of an abandoned van in Camden. And then there was the elderly tortoiseshell we discovered in a bin cupboard in Battersea and the Russian Blue kitten we found in a boiler room in Westminster.

One particular search, based in northwest London, resulted in a truly unexpected outcome. A middle-aged couple had contacted me about their dog, a Patterdale terrier called Cola, who, one afternoon, had gone missing from their Hampstead home. It transpired that a removal company had been in and out of the house all day (the owners, Trevor and Pamela, were temporarily vacating their property while some major renovation work was carried out) and their dog had scarpered out of the front door toward nearby Hampstead Heath.

"We reckon he's gone off chasing foxes," said Trevor. "It's hard-wired into his DNA, apparently."

It all sounded quite plausible; I'd come across Patterdale terriers before and was aware of their traits and tendencies. More of a "type" than a breed, they were originally reared by hunt masters to flush out foxes in the wild terrain of the Lake District. However, after fox hunting was outlawed in 2004, the Patterdale became obsolete as a working dog and, due to its rather challenging behavior, was not the most popular choice of pet. Those owners that did take them on—like Trevor and Pamela—would soon discover that chasing foxes still remained second nature, albeit in local parks and woodland. On this particular occasion, Cola had gone missing for over a day and it was feared that a fox earth had collapsed on him, or he'd become trapped in it. I had dealt with a fair few cases of terriers getting stuck in fox dens and badger setts, so for me it was not an uncommon case.

"If you gave your dog Cola's scent, do you think she'd be able to sniff him out?" asked Trevor during our initial phone conversation. I explained that Molly had been trained primarily as a cat-detection dog but that she had, in fact, been involved in successful searches for other missing dogs, notably Buffy and Newton.

"While I can't offer you any guarantees, we can certainly give it a go," I said, agreeing to drive over to his house the next day.

Trevor and his wife lived in a swish private estate flanked by opulent mansions, some of which, he told me, were home to a variety of A-list celebrities and overseas dignitaries. As the two of us walked with Molly along the leafy Hampstead avenues, I could see exactly why it had become one of the capital's most sought-after postcodes. At one point we stopped to admire a particularly grand property—a huge, red-brick detached house—only to find ourselves being challenged by a security guard who'd spotted us on CCTV and asked to see our ID. It seemed that we'd chosen to loiter outside the Malaysian ambassador's residence, which had not long since suffered a break-in, hence this guy's hypervigilance. He eventually allowed us to go on our way, but not before he'd given Molly a massive fuss.

"I used to work with cocker spaniel sniffer dogs many moons ago." He smiled as Molly placed a front paw on his foot. "Fantastic animals. Love them to bits. Fancy a job swap?"

"Not likely," I said, laughing.

As we neared Hampstead Heath, Trevor explained that he'd spent the morning pinpointing many of the area's fox earths. There were dozens, I discovered, ranging from dens built underneath woodpiles to bolt-holes hollowed out from the soil. It was quite commonplace for a vixen to build numerous earths, flitting between them with her cubs to seek warmth and avoid predators. Trevor reckoned there were about four or five females on the Heath at that time of year, which meant that, potentially, there could be anything up to forty hideaways.

"You've got your work cut out here, missus," I said to Molly as she excitedly inhaled Cola's scent sample from the jam jar. I then allowed her to "run with her nose" (essentially giving her a free rein, with minimal direction) and we moved from one den to the next, as stealthily as possible so as not to disturb any occupants. Molly had been trained to be inconspicuous—she was incredibly discreet during searches—so she was able to do this brilliantly.

Three hours later, with the skies getting darker and the air becoming damper, we'd still not found any sign of Cola. As time marched on, and as Molly continued to hunt in vain, I began to suspect that Trevor's dog had ventured further afield.

"Perhaps a vixen has drawn Cola further away from the Heath, maybe to ward him off her newborns," I suggested, aware that this was a relatively frequent occurrence. "Let's give it another twenty minutes, and then I'm afraid we'll have to call it a day."

"I totally understand, Colin," replied Trevor, somewhat despondently.

We approached a small glade that was carpeted with leaves, branches and fungi and shaded by an old horse-chestnut tree. Molly charged on ahead of us, kicking up twigs and flicking up toadstools, but as soon as she reached the tree she stopped in her tracks, wheeled herself around and locked her eyes with mine. Over the past year I'd learned to read Molly's body language and behavior, just as she had mine, and quite often there was no need for words because I could instinctively understand what she was telling me. From what I could gather here, she was indicating that she'd hit a strange, confusing odor, something that she wasn't altogether sure about.

I've detected something, but it's not the target scent . . . what d'you want me to do, Dad? seemed to be the nub of it.

"What have you found, girl? Show me," I said, walking over to investigate at closer quarters.

All I could see was leaf matter—there were no objects or creatures of interest—so I decided to call Molly off. However, just as I was about to give her the command, she began to dig furiously, raking up the soil around her and thrusting her nose into the ever-deepening hole. All of a sudden, I saw her tugging something out with her teeth; it appeared to be a blue velvet bag, about the size of a hot-water bottle and encrusted in a thick layer of grime. Having managed to drag it out, Molly released her jaw and flung the bag across the ground and, as she did so, a variety of shiny, jangly items cascaded out and landed by my feet.

"Oh my goodness." Trevor laughed and surveyed the glinting pile of necklaces, rings and bracelets. "Your dog's sniffed out the Crown Jewels."

I gave Molly a small kibble treat (she was staring up at me beseechingly, clearly expecting a reward for her efforts) then told her to lie down while I explored further. I knelt on the ground, peered into the hole and scraped away at the soil with my fingers. Two minutes later I'd unearthed the remnants of two wooden jewelry boxes, both covered in soggy blue silk, which almost disintegrated when I gently lifted them to the surface. Molly's snout appeared under my arm—as always, curiosity had got the better of her—and she watched earnestly as I opened the boxes and, one by one, lifted out a selection of gold chains and pearl necklaces, as well as a handful of earrings, brooches and cufflinks. Particularly eye-catching was a beautiful antique ring studded with tiny diamonds and rubies.

"Wow, just look at that, Molls!" I said, as the ring's gemstones glimmered in the watery sunlight. "Someone out there is missing some lovely jewelry."

I carefully transferred our little haul into a carrier bag (I always kept one in my utility-belt pocket) and knotted it securely.

It was at that juncture, when I felt Molly could do no more, that we had to bid a reluctant farewell to Trevor.

"I'm so sorry you didn't have the outcome you wanted," I said, shaking his hand, "but please keep me informed. I'm confident that Cola will come back at some point. And if you find any more fox earths in the area, don't hesitate to call me. I'd be more than happy to return with Molly."

"Ah, that's very kind," he replied, "and I sincerely appreciate everything you've both done today, even though the little blighter's still on the run."

My perceptive little dog then stepped in close, leaned against his leg and let out a soft whine, as if she somehow understood the pain he was suffering.

While I was dreadfully disappointed that we hadn't located the dog, I was satisfied—as was Trevor, I think—that we'd done all we could in the circumstances. Molly had searched every single fox earth, which meant that our client had at least been able to go home knowing that the immediate area had been combed extensively and could still cling on to the hope that his dog was still alive, albeit further afield.

The following morning, in the Bramble Hill Farm kitchen, Sam gave the jewelry a thorough clean and polish before laying it across the draining board to dry. Upon closer inspection, half of Molly's haul appeared to consist of decent-quality vintage pieces in gold and silver (some adorned with diamonds, rubies and semi-precious stones), with the rest comprising fairly chunky and garish costume jewelry.

"How much do you reckon it's worth?" asked Sam, trying on a pearl choker for size, as Molly nosed around the kitchen.

"It's hard to say," I shrugged. "Hopefully, I can find out who it belongs to. Maybe they'll have an idea. But if the gemstones are diamonds and rubies, then it's bound to have a value over ten grand."

Over the next few days I contacted a host of different people and places in an attempt to locate the jewelry's rightful owner. First and foremost, I reached out to the Malaysian ambassador's office, mindful of what the Hampstead security guard had told me about the burglary. Was Molly's surprise discovery part of a robber's swag-bag? Had they buried the treasure in the woods, with a view to one day reclaiming it? Was the ambassador's wife pining for her favorite jewels? Disappointingly, however, the staff chose not to return my numerous calls and emails, so I could only assume that I was wide of the mark.

I then contacted the Metropolitan Police, only to be told by a civilian operative that there was little point bringing it into the police station. There was no way of knowing how long the jewelry had lain hidden underground—and I didn't know for certain that it was stolen—so it would simply take too long to check through all the old crime reports.

"The best thing to do is hang on to them for the time being and try to find the owner," she said breezily. "If no one comes forward, then you can keep it."

I fully appreciated their stretched resources—I'd been a police officer myself, of course—but in my day I'm pretty sure that, at the very least, we'd have asked the finder to bring their hoard into the station for inspection.

My search continued regardless, and I circulated photos of some of the jewelry to the local newspapers and to community websites. I received a handful of inquiries in response, but they were largely opportunistic and nobody was able to verify ownership.

Back in the office, Sam and I made arrangements to send the gems to a local secondhand jewelry shop; the owner agreed to hang on to them until an owner came forward.

"So, as it stands, Molly, all this bling belongs to you," I grinned, balancing a dainty tiara between her floppy ears. "Finders, keepers, eh?"

As Sam took a photograph of a regal-looking Molly striking a pose, my phone rang. It was Trevor, passing on the marvelous news that Cola had returned home. His Hampstead Heath escapade had left him utterly exhausted and he had sandy soil wedged in every orifice, but he was safe and well.

"That's made my day, Trevor," I said, hearing the terrier yapping excitedly in the background.

In December 2017 I found myself back in the capital with my trusty sidekick, having agreed to take on a case in the south London district of Brixton. The missing cat, a marmalade-colored British Shorthair called Columbus, belonged to a teenager, Harriet, who lived with her parents and four other cats. The story went that, one morning, the father—Kenneth—had been due to take Columbus to the local vet for a routine check-up (Harriet had a mock-examination at college that morning, so was unable to oblige herself). However, since it was a lovely crisp, cold and sunny winter's day, Kenneth had decided to go on foot instead of using the car. He had ushered a rather belligerent Columbus into a well-worn canvas pet carrier and had taken a short cut through the local park, dodging the frozen puddles and brushing past the frosted conifers that overhung the footpath. He had then walked out of the exit gate toward the high street and switched the cat carrier to his right hand—Columbus was a hefty puss—before crossing over to the veterinary surgery.

Just as Kenneth had approached the sliding door, a young

man had rushed out, clinging desperately to a lead attached to a big, barking English setter. Anxious and agitated, the dog had taken one look at the cat carrier and, with a slavering snarl, had forcefully shoved its snout into the mesh frontage. Poor Columbus must have been petrified.

"Control your damned dog, will you?" Kenneth had yelled, hurrying toward the entrance. As he did so, though, Columbus's right paw suddenly clawed out of the netting. In the blink of an eye, the cat had ripped away a huge hole, muscled its way through and scarpered off. Kenneth had thrown down the cat carrier and given chase, only to see Columbus disappearing over a ten-foot wall. Despite the efforts of some helpful passers-by, the cat couldn't be found anywhere.

Breaking the bad news to Harriet that afternoon had been traumatic. The young girl was beyond distressed, fearing that she'd never see her darling Columbus again.

"I told you that carrier was falling apart, Dad, and that we needed a new one," she'd shouted, clutching her cat's favorite blanket. "You didn't listen to me, did you, and *now* look what's happened. It's all *your* fault, and Columbus is probably *dead*, and Christmas will be *ruined* . . ."

As a tearful Harriet stormed upstairs to her bedroom, Kenneth's wife, Sally, tried to console him.

"She doesn't mean it, love. She's just in shock. Give her time, and she'll soon come around."

Harriet did eventually calm down—she sheepishly apologized to her dad, too—and for the next forty-eight hours they both combed the busy streets of Brixton, calling out Columbus's name until they were hoarse and handing out hastily printed CAT: MISSING leaflets. There were no confirmed sightings, sadly— he'd most likely gone to ground—and it was a very exhausted and demoralized owner who called me the following morning. She had posted a Columbus-related appeal on social media, and one of the replies had suggested contacting "that pet-detective bloke with the dog who was on *This Morning*." She took their advice and got in touch.

Harriet was in luck. Molly and I had just completed a two-hour training search—I'd been catching up with some admin with Sam when the call had come through—and I felt that this case of a south London feline escapologist was something we could definitely get our teeth into. There were, however, two areas of concern. Firstly, our search area was built up and populous, which—with all the noise and smells, and all the hustle and bustle—could possibly hamper Molly's finely tuned detection skills. Urban searches tended to be trickier and more time-consuming than their rural counterparts, too; put it this way, it would have been far easier to find a missing cat in Brixham, Devon, than in Brixton, London. My second reservation related to the fact that Columbus resided in a multi-cat household—he had four feline "siblings"—and if I couldn't locate a unique sample of his scent, then the search would simply not go ahead.

"I won't be long, sweetheart," I said to Molly as I pulled up outside Kenneth and Harriet's red-brick Victorian terrace house. Our journey had taken us an hour and a half, and Molly was champing at the bit to get started, but—as always—it was important that I spent some time with the owners. I needed to glean as much information about their cat as possible, as well as obtaining a nice wad of Columbus's fur.

Harriet—a tall, sturdy girl with a chunky auburn plait—told me that she'd had him since he was a kitten and, since he was always off exploring somewhere, had named him Columbus. Her cat was anything but timid ("He's a proper tough cookie," she said) and was, by all accounts, a very confident and capable creature.

"Oh, no one messes with Columbus," said Harriet. "My other cats often bear the brunt of his temper. He goes *mad* when they pinch his food . . . he's got an appetite the size of this house."

She also told me that he hated attending his regular checkups at the vet's, which made it fairly easy to identify the cause and trigger of his dash for freedom. The bumpy journey in a flimsy cat carrier along the bustling streets of Brixton would have sent Columbus's stress levels rocketing. Then, when he was confronted with the sight and scent of the dreaded surgery, he'd been ready to make a break for it. The unwanted hairy dog snout had been the final straw and had triggered his frantic escape.

Twenty minutes later our four-strong search party—father, daughter, Molly and me—commenced the hunt for Columbus, all of us sporting thick, warm jackets to combat the wintry chill. As I'd suspected, the sheer density of the area was going to make this a rather onerous task. This part of Brixton was a jam-packed mix of retail and residential, with most shops and houses boasting courtyards, outbuildings or both. There were a couple of bustling parks in the vicinity that would probably need checking out, too, and looming in the background was a huge railway bridge, under which a dozen or so arches were occupied by a clutch of businesses and lock-ups.

We headed to the veterinary surgery to survey Columbus's escape route ("Wow, that's one agile cat," I said, when I spied the imposing wall) and decided to visit the properties that backed on to it. I had some concerns about gaining access; compared with country-folk, streetwise city dwellers tended to be cagier and more suspicious when they answered their door to a guy dressed in an official-looking "uniform" with a sniffer dog at the end of a leash. I needn't have worried, though, since the vast majority of the shopkeepers and householders I encountered that day were extremely helpful and obliging.

This included the staff of a senior citizens' care home located in a handsome red-brick building which we visited about two hours into our search. With the sample scent still coursing through her nostrils, Molly had become rather animated as we'd walked up the driveway—up until that moment, she'd not had a sniff, as it were—so I was very keen to access its grounds. I managed to waylay a senior nurse who was clocking on to her shift and, as luck would have it, she just happened to be a committed cat-lover. Her face fell when Harriet and I told her about Columbus's disappearance.

"Oh, that's so, so sad," she said in a soft southern Irish accent. "Meet me around the back of the building and I'll let you through the gate. I'm not *really* supposed to do this, but in the circumstances . . ."

Kenneth and Harriet remained outside—I didn't want to enter mob-handed—while Molly and I began to search the care-home garden. Green space could be scarce in inner-city areas like Brixton, but this place was like a little oasis. Three quarters of it was taken up with a large, square lawn, with various ornaments, planters and birdbaths. At the rear was a large allotment, its furrows bearing a harvest of winter vegetables: broccoli, cabbages, onions and parsnips.

"The residents like to sit out here, especially when the sun's out," said the nurse, gesturing toward the wrought-iron chairs that were dotted around the perimeter. "They like watching the garden grow . . ."

". . . and we love to see what's going in our vegetable soup, too," piped up a voice behind us. I swung around to see a tiny, gray-haired woman wearing a woolly purple coat and a matching beret. A pair of black-rimmed, thick-lensed spectacles dominated her face, giving her an almost cartoonish appearance.

"I'm Gracie," she said, smiling, and offered me a trembling handshake. "I saw your delightful little dog from the conservatory and I just had to come out and say hello."

The lady asked if she could give Molly a pat and a stroke and took the opportunity to tell me about the various cats, dogs, parrots and budgies that she'd owned in her lifetime. Pets weren't allowed in the care home—much to her disappointment—but she told me how she tried to stay close to nature by filling up the birdbaths with fresh water, especially during this cold snap, and by creeping into the garden every evening to feed cat food or dog food to the local hedgehogs, foxes and, occasionally, stray moggies.

Cat food? I thought to myself. *The sooner we get this garden searched, the better . . .*

While Molly was as patient as ever, bless her, after a few

minutes of fussing and petting from the old lady I could sense that, like me, she was itching to continue with our mission.

"It's been lovely talking to you, Gracie," I said, "but I'm afraid we need to crack on."

"Of course," she said. "Wishing you the best of British. I do hope you find Columbus the cat."

Clinging on to the nurse's arm for extra support, she proceeded to hobble back toward the house.

I reintroduced the sample scent to Molly, just for a quick turbo boost. She promptly skyrocketed to the far end of the garden and, after feverishly snuffling around a hole in a fence panel, gave me the most beautiful "down." As I edged closer, I could even spot stray wisps of ginger hair on the gap's jagged edges. I think we could safely say that Columbus Woz 'Ere.

"Brilliant work, Molly," I said as she hoovered up some black-pudding titbits from the palm of my hand.

Kenneth and Harriet were thrilled at this positive development, and we popped back to their house for a debrief. I reckoned that Columbus had probably visited the care-home garden to drink the fresh water from the birdbaths and—in order to satisfy his hearty appetite—may well have pilfered the cat food that Gracie had left for the hedgehogs. I believed that he'd made his foray late at night—perhaps waiting for "lights out" time at the care home—before heading back to a place of shelter, perhaps deep within a nearby railway arch.

A night-time stake-out at the care home wouldn't be possible, sadly; Molly had almost exceeded her maximum six hours a day limit—any longer was too physically demanding—and I'd soon have to take her back to Cranleigh. As an alternative, I decided to rig up a network of high-tech night-vision cameras in the grounds. These would be linked up to my laptop so that, when I got home, I could monitor the footage and alert my clients to any significant activity (they only lived 200 yards away from the care home, so could hurry over if necessary). One camera would be trained on a strategically placed dish of dried whitebait, which I believed would be a sure-fire way to lure out a ravenous Columbus. I always carried a sachet of this snack with me—I called it cat caviar—because it was irresistible to felines, who could often smell its fishy odor for hundreds of yards.

With all this in mind, I popped back to the care home to consult with the cat-loving nurse, who kindly gave us the green light to deploy our cameras. I happened to spot Gracie sitting in the communal TV lounge watching *Mary Berry's Christmas Party*, and—since I had a big favor to ask—I went over for a quick chat. Her eyes widened when she saw me approaching.

"Have you found the cat?"

"Not yet," I said, smiling, "but I have good reason to believe that he's been in your garden, maybe even pinching your cat food."

"Really?"

"It's looking that way, yes."

I then told her how Operation Columbus was going to work, explaining that, in addition to the cameras, I really needed an extra set of eyes to watch from indoors.

"D'you think that's something you could assist me with, Gracie?" I asked. "All you'd have to do is keep a watchful eye on the garden, like you usually do, and get on the phone to Columbus's owners if you happen to see him. You'd be *such* a great help."

"You're asking *me* to help *you*?"

"Yes, I am. Consider yourself part of Team Molly tonight."

I was somewhat taken aback to see her eyes filling with tears.

"How very kind of you to ask," she said, patting my hand. "It's nice to feel wanted, for a change. I'm afraid you tend to feel a bit invisible when you get past ninety."

What a delightful lady, I thought as I headed out of the care home and back to the car.

At *about* 9:45 that evening, a tired and hungry marmalade cat crept through the hole in the fence, padded over to the plate of whitebait and began to gobble up the fishy morsels. At the same time, an elderly lady, sitting by her bedroom window, squinted through her black-rimmed spectacles at the shadowy four-legged figure. She let out a little coo of delight and swiftly telephoned the number on the Post-it note she'd been clasping since dinner.

Within two minutes, Columbus was back in the arms of his owner, and our happy ending was complete.

I felt thrilled for Harriet—all she'd wanted for Christmas was Columbus, after all—but I felt as equally pleased for Gracie, as all she'd really wanted was to feel needed.

The following day, Molly and I returned to south London. Our first port of call was Kenneth's house in Brixton, where, beside a huge, twinkling Christmas tree, we found Harriet and Columbus curled up together on the sofa. The teenager's dreamy expression said it all.

"I don't think it's just the cat who's purring," grinned Kenneth. "She's hardly left his side. No need to cancel Christmas, thanks to you guys."

Then it was time for a pit stop at the care home to pick up my assorted field cameras. Molly and I were ushered through the garden gate by the friendly Irish nurse, who expressed her delight and relief that Columbus had been found and informed us that Gracie—who was having her afternoon nap—had been similarly thrilled to bits.

"I'm so glad I've seen you today, Mr. Butcher, because I wanted to thank you personally for being so kind to Gracie," she said. "She's a very bright lady, and I think she sometimes gets a little bored in here. But she was so happy at the breakfast table this morning. She couldn't stop smiling. She had to tell all the residents that she'd helped to solve Operation Columbus."

"Ah, that's lovely to hear." I smiled. "In fact, could you ensure she gets this?"

I fished a photo of Molly from my wallet and whipped out a Biro from my pocket.

"To Gracie," I wrote. "We couldn't have done it without you. Best wishes, Team Molly."

By the time I'd packed all my cameras away, dusk had begun to set in. The clouded sky had taken on a sepia tint—was snow on the way? I wondered—and a chilly breeze had gathered impetus. I didn't fancy the prospect of spending hours battling through the rush-hour traffic, so I decided to make the five-minute drive to Clapham Common. I could while away some time in my favorite south London park—I hadn't visited for a while, as it happened—and Molly could enjoy a leg-stretching run-around prior to our homeward-bound journey. It was only when I parked up near my usual spot—near the lovely Holy Trinity Church, with its distinctive white tower—that I realized the common had gone Christmas-crazy.

"*WELCOME TO WINTERVILLE!*" shouted the posters affixed to the tree trunks and lamp posts that we ambled past. It seemed that, every December, the place was transformed into a festive theme park: the lido became an ice rink, a marquee housed a circus and the rest of the park teemed with food stalls and fairground rides. It was so nice to see happy families mingling with loved-up couples and lively schoolkids, all of them abuzz with festive spirit.

"Well, this is a turn-up, Molls," I said, attaching her bright red training harness with its small blue light. "C'mon, let's find some space to play."

We walked a little further afield, away from the crowds, passing through a rather dense, muddy wooded area. We finally arrived at a clearing, where we spent a good forty minutes playing tug-of-war with a pair of knotted football socks. Every now and then I'd let Molly win our tussle, and she'd run a few victory laps around me, the socks clenched between her teeth like a trophy. She would then bound back to my side for another round.

When my dog began to flag, and when I felt a hunger pang, I reattached her leash and walked back toward the bustling Winterville. I headed over to a German-style food chalet, manned by jolly staff in elf costumes, and ordered myself a hot chocolate and a bratwurst, as well as some water for Molly to accompany her treats. I noticed Chief Elf suppressing a grin when he handed over our fare, no doubt amused by the sight of a mud-spattered man and his dirt-encrusted dog, both plastered with soggy twigs and leaves.

I flopped, exhausted, on to a nearby bench. Moments later Molly jumped up, too, shuffling in close and staring at me wistfully with those big, brown eyes as I took a bite of my hot dog.

"No chance, missus, you've had your treat," I said, which elicited a whine, followed by an enormous yawn.

She crawled on to my lap, licked my cheek and gently placed her paw on my wrist. For a few minutes I sat there, watching the Ferris wheel slowly turning in the darkening sky, listening to the cheery chatter between families and friends and breathing in the aroma of mulled wine and mince pies. All the while, a cavalcade of brightly lit London buses glided around the park's perimeter, stopping to offload more festive revellers. As Molly snuggled in closer, I could feel her heartbeat next to mine—*thumpity-thump, thumpity-thump*—and, as I so often did when we were together like this, I began chatting to her.

"Do you realize, Molly," I said, tenderly stroking her head, "that we've been together for nearly one whole year?"

She looked up at me and blinked those long eyelashes of hers, as if to say, *Really? Wow!*

"What an adventure we've had, eh?" I smiled. "All those lovely people we've met, and all those fabulous places we've visited."

Oblivious to the people walking along the footpath, I began to scroll through my memory bank, reeling off the names of some of the pets and clients whose lives had been touched by my amazing rescue dog. Tim and Rusty. Margaret and Chester. Renu and Buffy. Edward and Sapphire. Trine and Newton. Debbie and Cuddles. And, of course, Harriet and Columbus. Then I ran through a cast list of people who'd supported us along this wonderful journey: Claire, Rob, Astrid and Mark at Medical Detection Dogs; my lovely friend Anna; my parents, my son, my girlfriend . . .

I glanced down at Molly and noticed that her eyelids were becoming droopy and her breathing was getting heavy.

"Sorry, am I talking you to sleep, Molls?" I smiled.

Quite suddenly, I noticed something white and fluffy landing on her snout. And another. And then another. Molly shook herself awake and deftly sprang off my lap, and—much to the amusement of passers-by—began to snap at the snowflakes that had started to spiral down from the sky.

Now this is what I call FUN, Dad! she seemed to say. *I haven't played in this white stuff for AGES!*

I let her prance and pirouette for a good fifteen minutes— she was like an excited toddler—before calling her back to me and gently stroking the back of her head. She sat on the bench with her tongue lolling out of the side of her mouth, panting out clouds of vapor.

"Right, I think it's home time, young lady," I said, brushing the snowflakes from her coat and attaching her leash. "Looks like the traffic's finally calmed down."

As we passed Holy Trinity Church again, I felt compelled to stop for a moment and savor the view. The building looked magnificent, artfully illuminated against the wintry backdrop and, as I gazed up at it, Molly at my heel, I felt truly blessed. Here I was, in my favorite city, on a magical evening, spending quality time with my beautiful cocker spaniel.

You need to capture this moment, Colin, I said to myself.

So I did. I angled my phone, held my dog close, flashed a big grin and took a quick selfie. The resulting photo made me smile—two scruff-bags, albeit two happy scruff-bags—and I promptly forwarded it to Sarah, along with a caption.

"Molly and Me," it said.

Epilogue

My story began on the edges of the rainforests of Malaysia and Singapore, where my brother and I, accompanied by our faithful canine friends, scampered around like characters from a Rudyard Kipling novel. They were good years, full of incredible experiences, and most certainly influenced all my decisions on the pets I have owned.

In mid-December 2018 Molly reached her century of searches and has now helped in the recovery of seventy-four missing cats, six dogs—and one Hermann's tortoise—many of which would have perished without her assistance. The other twenty-six cats have still not been found, although we did our utmost to locate them. Some will have fallen foul of the internal combustion engine or slipped off to a quiet corner and yielded to old age. Others will have become victims of their insatiable curiosity, accidentally transported to a new neighborhood, but some cats just don't want to be found and will have adopted new owners or returned to the wild.

Molly is a truly remarkable dog and she never ceases to amaze me, constantly testing every rule I put in place, never fully accepting my right to impose my will upon her, though, why should she? We are, after all, a team and she deserves to be treated equally. She is an excellent problem-solver and remembers every location where she has found a missing cat. Her quickest recovery has been under five minutes and she recently started to nose-touch the hiding places of missing cats, something she could only have picked up while watching the bio-detection dogs working at the MDD training academy.

Although she is prepared to share all that she knows about her world, the same cannot be said of cats. They have a reputation for being secretive and indifferent, often behaving in the most unpredictable way, happy one day and gone the next. However, I am an experienced detective and have learned the value of being patient. With every passing investigation, I discover just a little bit more about these supposedly furtive creatures and I am starting to identify patterns in their behavior, which is helping me to develop my understanding of why they go missing and, most importantly, where to start searching when they do. It seems to me that cats are not that secretive after all. An unhappy cat will often go to considerable lengths to let their owner know about their displeasure long before abandoning the family home. If you notice your cat behaving in an unusual way, then it's because your cat wants you to, so pay attention, because you could save yourself an awful lot of heartache.

On a final note, I would have loved to have included every case that we have investigated and to mention all the wonderful people that we have worked with, but there are simply too many for one book. In addition, there will be many more cases to investigate throughout 2019, and I also have plans to find a new apprentice . . . but that is a whole new story.

Acknowledgments

I have dedicated my book to my brother David, who died just short of his twenty-first birthday, in the arms of his young wife, Katrina. In all the years that he struggled so ardently to defeat that awful disease, I never once heard him complain, he just soaked up everything life threw at him and soldiered on, always hoping that the doctors would make him better. To this day, I feel that my brother is watching over me, inspiring me to do the very best I can. He never gave up, so neither will I, and it's only with his guidance that I have managed to complete my journey with Molly. We proved the doubters wrong, David, and achieved what so many said could not be done. I only wish you were around to see it.

To my parents, I want to say thank you for allowing me the freedom to explore the natural world of Malaysia, Singapore and England, for the many animals you brought into my life and for press-ganging me into the Royal Navy. By the way, I'm sorry about the mice. I know you always thought it was the cats that were bringing them home.

My journey from police officer to private sleuth and, finally, pet detective has been an incredibly rewarding experience and throughout my book I have given recognition to those who inspired or supported me along the way. There are, however, a few who I think are worthy of additional praise.

Both Sam and Stefan have left the company to follow different paths, but they remain good friends and always will be.

The three of us had some amazing adventures together, both as private sleuths and as pet detectives, and I could not have built UKPD without their loyalty and support. I am forever indebted to them.

Thank you to my good friend and canine guru Anna Webb. But for her, I would never have met the amazing team at Medical Detection Dogs. To Dr. Claire Guest, Dr. Astrid Concha, Rob Harris and Mark Doggett, to all the volunteers and Molly's foster family. You did a great job. Molly is a star.

To my agents, Rowan Lawton and Eugenie Furniss, thank you for putting your trust in me and for allowing me to tell my story my way, and to the Furniss and Lawton team, Rory, Rachel, Liane and Lucy, thank you for all your hard work in bringing my book to a global audience. My heartfelt thanks go to Joanne Lake, who has brought so much depth and color to my story and whose patience, expert advice and skill has helped to create such a wonderful tale. Thank you, Zennor Compton, whose enthusiasm and energy ensured I selected the right publisher and to my editor, Charlotte Hardman, for her insight and professionalism and her ability to enhance the story.

To my darling Sarah, who has been so incredibly supportive and understanding over the last few years, for her intuition and wise counsel and, most of all, for accepting my troublesome and mischievous spaniel into her life.

Then there is my amazing, enchanting and adorable sidekick Molly. Without her, none of this would have been possible. She tests me relentlessly, always surprises me and never lets me down. She really is one in a million.

Finally, to all the pet owners who have put their faith and trust in Molly and me. Thank you for allowing us into your lives. We enjoyed meeting every single one of you.